WHAT THE ACADEMY TAUGHT US

Improving Schools from the Bottom Up in a Top-Down Transformation Era

— Eric Kalenze —

First Published 2019

by John Catt Educational Ltd,
15 Riduna Park, Station Road,
Melton, Woodbridge IP12 1QT

Tel: +44 (0) 1394 389850
Email: enquiries@johncatt.com
Website: www.johncatt.com

ISBN: 978 1 912906 26 0

Set and designed by John Catt Educational Limited

Contents

Part Three

Part One

Pre-2004: Foundation

In the clump of teenagers, there's a girl who looks like she's being pulled apart—like she'd move herself backward if she could, but she can't because the rest of her is bent forward, trunk twisting. Her long brown hair is being stretched, wound into the left hand of a girl facing her. Her face is fully open to the hair-puller, whose fist fiercely connects—bap! bap! bap!—just below the helpless girl's eye. Unable to move much in any direction, the victim points her face straight down and hopes to avoid contact. Save for the locks still clenched in her assailant's hand, the target's full hair now flies fully over her face. The puncher coolly changes her jabs to quick uppercuts. Somehow, a third girl moves among this activity to scrawl something onto the victim's cheek with a permanent Sharpie marker.

It happens so suddenly that I need a few seconds to process what I'm seeing: a coordinated assault, just a few feet away from me and my classroom. As the image sharpens, I notice that the puncher, the scrawler, and others in proximity are all my kids. Academy kids. They're supposed to be on the other end of the building at this hour, though. What's going *on*?!

Other students, all making their way to their next classes, have noticed the scene and are now swarming to get a look. Their voices rise in excitement, jolting me out of my seconds-long delay. I let out a loud yell to cut through the adolescent cheering, and I move the few steps it takes to get between the helpless girl and her attackers. The melee breaks at once, and the assailants smoothly slip away—weaving through the crowd of hooting, laughing students and *gone*.

I guide the victim into my classroom and help her clear the hair veiling her face. I know her: she's an outgoing and popular senior, and I'd had her in my class two years ago. Her left cheek is reddening, and I can see that it's beginning to swell. I ask her if she's going to be okay, and I tell her she's safe. She can't even get a word out in response. I think to myself that her shock makes sense—before what'd just happened to her, she'd probably never even imagined being punched in the face.

A neighboring teacher has joined me beside the stunned and swelling student. I ask her to please stay here and to call the office so I can get after finding the girls that did this. I know who it was, and they all know me well. And though I don't have any idea if they're heading to their next class, I know exactly where they're supposed to be. (Incidentally, I have no idea what I will say to them when I find them, either. I just want to be the first adult they talk to after what I saw them do.) The teacher nods, and I tear out of my room down the hallway in the direction the four sprinted off in.

Halfway down the hall, I take the available stairway down to the first floor. I practically fly down them—two, three at a time. And when I reach the bottom, what I see quickly stops my flight: the puncher, the scrawler, and a few others I spotted blocking off the fray—my kids, Academy kids—are standing, waiting. Not running, scattering, or making any sound. They're stilled, and it's clear they'd been waiting for me to reach them. Like I'd kept them waiting long enough. Passing time's up, so it's pretty well just me and them in the entire vast hallway.

I know I have to stay calm with them, so I hold down my first reaction. I can't, however, hold back cursing. 'What the hell was that, you guys? What's going on?'

They all let their story fly at once.

Chapter 1

A Simple, Sincere Beginning

'It's the action, not the fruit of the action, that's important. You have to do the right thing. It may not be in your power, may not be in your time, that there'll be any fruit. But that doesn't mean you stop doing the right thing. You may never know what results come from your action. But if you do nothing, there will be no result.'

– Mahatma Ghandi

When my principal, Dr. Robert Perdaems, poked his head into my classroom one afternoon in early 2004, he didn't intend to change my life forever. He just wanted to chat about our school's dropouts.

Our school was Osseo Senior High, a three-year,[1] 1800-student school parked in Osseo, Minnesota, about 20 minutes northwest from the Twin Cities of Minneapolis and St. Paul, and the dropouts on his mind hadn't dropped out—yet, anyway. Perdaems, a soft-spoken, salt-and-pepper-mustachioed education doctorate-holder we all called 'Dr. Bob', had been studying our graduation statistics and he couldn't stop thinking about what he found. Namely, he'd recognized that the kids who'd dropped out or needed extra time to graduate didn't fail all at once. Rather, they held in common that they'd ended their sophomore years below a certain minimum credit threshold. As such, Dr. Bob believed you could predict who was likely to drop out by checking their sophomore year credits. And that meant we had an opportunity to help them before it was too late.

'I guess I've learned that we've been trying to address dropouts all wrong,' he said, standing as he always did when he came by to chat about school things—a few steps inside my door as I got my activities ready for the next hour. 'I'm thinking we could do things a bit differently, but it won't be an easy fix.'

Interesting, sure, I thought. I was always interested with Dr. Bob's takes on how we could do things better. At that point of the year (mid-winter, which is brutal on schools everywhere but even more so on cooped-up Minnesotans), though, and with another few classes on the way in under 30 minutes, I won't pretend that I was excited or even intrigued by it. I had enough to worry about.

The main point Dr. Bob wanted to get across, though, was that in essence, every incoming sophomore class contained a group of invisible dropouts. Kids who were on the way to dropping out but didn't know it yet. Kids school professionals didn't recognize until it was too late.

Helping them after this critical sophomore year didn't typically do much good, basically, as the damage was done. The hole they had already started to dig would be too deep to escape.

'I want to break this pattern,' Dr. Bob said.

What he was planning to do was change when and how we helped these kids. Typically we approached them like trauma patients rushed into a senior-year 'emergency room'. Dr. Bob wanted to take a more preventive approach. He wanted to diagnose them sooner and start treatment earlier to keep at-risk sophomores from falling below the crucial credit threshold. He had a particular treatment in mind: a school-within-a-school where a select group of teachers would work intensively with dropouts-in-progress for their core subjects of social studies, science, math, and English. This model was growing in popularity in the U.S. at the time as a dropout-prevention strategy, and Dr. Bob thought it might work at Osseo too.

The details were not mapped out, but the basic principles were in place. The school-within-a-school would function according to the same school structures, such as bell schedules and behavior policies. But the teachers would have license to diverge from programmatic/curricular scripts and to tweak operations in whatever ways they believed would support their students most effectively. Academic demands, however, would remain at school-standard levels. This was non-negotiable. The idea was not to give credits away so kids could earn empty diplomas. The whole point was to give challenged kids more support and guidance during what we suspected was an absolutely crucial year.

As Dr. Bob saw it, these conceptual basics were all he needed to get things rolling. He could have been more prescriptive about what the school-within-a-school would look like, but—crucially—he wasn't. He felt it was more appropriate to hand those decisions over to the teachers who were going to be living it each day. In his mind, the teachers he was choosing were the key to making it all work.

That's when he popped the question.

'So,' he said, and paused. 'Do you think you'd want to join us? I think it could do a lot of good for kids who need it, and I believe you'd be a good fit.'

Everything I was thinking at that moment told me to say no.

What I heard in Dr. Bob's proposal was:

'Do you want to teach entire classes of the challenging kids you usually only encounter one or two at a time?' That made me think of kids like Mike, a student I had at the time who regularly blurted insults at fellow classmates, and who'd even once jumped on a baggie full of ketchup in my classroom—splattering mess over everything. Could I handle a room full of Mikes?

'Do you want to teach these kids without backing off on current curricular and performance standards?' I thought of trying to get a classroom of Mikes, not a couple of him at a time, to dig into reading Shakespeare without cutting any corners or researching in the media center for a persuasive essay. My eyeballs throbbed.

'Do you want to have a lot more meetings, working in close collaboration with teachers from other departments?' Hard pass.

'Do you want all the pressure of success or failure placed squarely on you?' I wasn't a rookie any more. I had become much more efficient when it came to sizing up my time, energy, and angst commitments. But this idea seemed awfully risky on all fronts.

In other words, Dr. Bob was politely asking if he could put me through the wringer. I thought of my family. My oldest daughter was on the cusp of kindergarten and my youngest wasn't even walking yet. I was already feeling fried a lot of the time. The job was tough enough without all of this extra effort.

And yet I was intrigued. I couldn't help it.

Like Dr. Bob, I couldn't get past the data and what they said about the predictive power of sophomore credit deficiencies and our collective failures to address them. This was right in my wheelhouse. I had done part-time teaching at nights to help adults—some who were new to the country but many others who were high school dropouts—earn their diplomas. The experience taught me a lot about the importance of a high school education done well. I had also been doing more independent study of educational research and history to sharpen my instructional philosophies, practices, and policies, and I could see my classroom practice really taking off as a result. Permission to go off script would give me a chance to try out even more of these ideas. And teaming up with other teachers to improve a group of *kids*—as opposed to our shared content, like we usually did—was especially attractive.

Additionally, I didn't disagree with Dr. Bob that I seemed like a good fit for his school-within-a-school's English teacher. I had taught at least two sections of sophomore English for all of my six years at Osseo. I had been part of the cross-district writing team that aligned the curriculum to revised state standards a few years prior, giving me pretty deep awareness of our feeder schools' sequences and rationales. And I had built a reputation for working well with our more challenging students. (Like Mike. Hell, I actually loved having Mike in my class, ketchup aside.)

And on top of all that, the opportunity was attractive because it was *different*. Typical asks in our district involved serving on some committee for new elective courses to be offered or attending a workshop on using more projects in class or taking part in one of dozens of similarly superficial demonstrations of teacher-leadership. The school-within-a-school sounded like a chance to lead in a meaningful way. I mean, actually lead. In a way that could benefit kids who desperately needed it and our entire school. And Dr. Bob was offering it because of what he observed in me and my teaching. Requests like these didn't come along very often, and so I couldn't help but be flattered.[2]

Flattered at the offer to do really hard work? Yes. Being selected to do meaningful work based on one's merits doesn't happen real frequently in education. What does get offered doesn't include decision-making responsibilities or additional pay, so it's quite common for teachers to steer clear of them. (And really, can you blame them?) As a result, much 'leadership' in education falls to whoever is willing to volunteer, not teachers who are hand-picked by administrators based on their demonstrated talents. (It probably won't surprise you to learn that conferring special duties on classroom-level staff is politically tricky for administrators. Dr. Bob took a lot of heat from other teachers in the building who hadn't been chosen for the school-within-a-school and believed the selection process should have been voluntary.)

Dr. Bob grinned. He could see me talking myself into it.

There were too many positives to ignore. As I realized this, my initial wariness disappeared. Heck, I decided in that moment that I didn't even need to know what the whole thing would look like or who the other teachers would be. As for how it would play at home, I knew my wife would be in once she heard how it matched to so much I found important. I thanked Dr. Bob for thinking of me and told him to count me in.

* * *

I'm not exaggerating when I say my decision to participate in this school-within-a-school, which eventually became known as the Sophomore Academy, changed my life forever.

The Academy ran for four years, from 2004 to 2008, and that period taught me more about young people, effective instructional practice, and comprehensive school improvement than any personal or professional experience before or since. My time in the Academy propelled me to study harder about education and to dedicate myself to impacting the field at large more intensely than I had ever imagined possible in the first years of my teaching career. Teaching in the Academy made me want to be a better educator.

To this day, I can confidently trace my deepest educational beliefs—about organizational improvement, about 'right-side-up' classroom instruction and policies,[3] about the importance of school culture (and what that actually means)—back to lightbulbs that popped on for me when I was meeting with my Academy colleagues to figure out how to reach a kid who'd gone suddenly, disquietingly distant or how to give the entire group a jolt of motivation.

Today, my work in education is more administrative and consultative. But I still find myself telling the educators I work with about what the Academy taught us. How our team planned and carried out actions. How the school administration challenged and supported the Academy without ever over-managing it. How the Academy teachers made tough decisions together—and how we stuck together when the students pushed back. How we relied on systems and consistency and relationships over anything faddish or canned or expensive or WiFi-enabled. How the Academy kids held one another up. And on and on. As you can probably tell, when I start talking about what the Academy taught us, it's kind of hard to stop.

As the experience has gotten further behind me, I often ask myself some tough questions about the entire Sophomore Academy experiment and other improvement actions going on at Osseo Senior High School back then. (You'll see: as continuous school improvement goes, we had some pretty special things going.)

Was it a great professional-growth opportunity for all the Academy's teachers, or just for me? It had a profound and transformative impact on me, but did my colleagues feel the same way? Did their time in the Academy transform their ideals and practices and collaborative capacities? Did their careers change paths? Were they full of fond memories or regrets?

What impressions—if any—did the Academy leave on Osseo Senior High? Did anything we learned translate into building-wide improvements? Did we affect ongoing attitudes, policies, and practices across the school? If we did, were those policies and practices durable enough to withstand the last decade's Accountability Era and its attendant emphases? (Remember, Big Data hadn't yet reached top speed at this time.) What has the last decade looked like at Osseo? Is the school better off?

And, naturally, I've wondered—a *lot*, you can be sure—about whether or not the Academy fulfilled its mission. Did we do for the invisible dropouts what Dr. Bob had in mind when he first came up with the idea? Beyond keeping our Academy students on track for high-school graduation, did we prepare them for the rest of high school and beyond? Ten years later, how are they doing? From being labeled 'at-risk' after junior high to spending a year in our Academy, did they believe school was valuable enough—and their teachers in their corner enough—to invest in their own academic success? Put another way, were the guesses we made about them and what they needed right? Did the environment we created actually prepare them for the world beyond school?

In short, I often wonder about how our Academy alumni look back on the experience, and whether or not they think it was worth it. These kids are all in their mid- to late-20s right now. Knowing how it would all turn out, would they advise us to do anything differently? For after all, if the kids we taught don't consider their lives much better as a result, then it really doesn't matter how personally and professionally fulfilling it may have been for me, my colleagues, Osseo Senior, and the field of education.

* * *

To answer all of these questions, I had to write this book. In it, I will revisit my Sophomore Academy years with the intent to:

- Share effective practical models through details about how the Academy initiative came together, what it looked like in practice, and what it did to continually improve itself;
- Examine ongoing educational debates and phenomena through the lenses of the Academy, Osseo Senior High's other school-improvement actions at the time, and the district's later attempts at transformational system change, and to consider all critically with the aid of educational research literature;
- Encourage educators to consider future actions relating to individual students' growth, teachers' professional-development and teaming routines in light of methods used or inspired by those we employed in the Academy, as well as other concurrent efforts by the school to create comprehensive, continuing school improvements;
- Explore questions about various impacts—on the Academy staff, on the school at large, and on the Academy's students;
- Inspire conversations about what effective education and continuous school improvement look like and how it can be achieved, all without having to sacrifice its beautiful humanity and humor.

To do all of this, I spoke at length with Academy (and Academy-adjacent) students, teachers, and administrators. The result is a blend of big-picture and in-the-weeds history, stories of what happened and how it affected us at the time, and reflections on what we learned. While educational researchers and commentators will play a part, their role in this book will be a bit different than they were in my first book, *Education is Upside-Down*. In that book, education research—of field-wide performance/results, of education history and philosophy, and of cognitive science—provided support for my positions. Here my task is different. Research will most often appear to set the Academy's practices within wider, more carefully controlled views.

This is a book about what the Academy (and other concurrent school improvements) taught all of us: the educators and young people directly involved in it and the larger school community the Academy lived within. I'm sharing this story because I believe it can teach all of us across education a great deal about effective classroom practices, meaningful teacher-leadership, essentials schools need to continuously improve, and full-school belief systems, operations, and cultures that improve kids' preparation. And not just in theory or sweeping thought experiments, but directly from the ground of one school that decided to try some new things and worked their tails off to see it through. I know Osseo Senior High's story isn't the only one of its kind. There are likely hundreds of similar schools operating successfully and changing lives all over America at this moment. Simple innovations like the ones this school deployed, though, are usually not shared widely across our field—at least not in much depth or with anywhere near the frequency of much-ballyhooed (and generally evidence-weak) 'cool practices' everyone knows, like personalized learning, restorative practices, differentiated instruction, and so many others.

You're likely going to get sick of hearing me say the Academy and other improvements we built ourselves had profound, lasting effects on my education career. But it's undeniably true. I lean on parts of the experience every single day, and I always will. My hope is that you'll understand why their impacts have been so strong and find some practical, worthwhile lessons for your own school's benefit.

So, I said yes to Dr. Bob. But before jumping into everything that happened after that—including how we got kids to buy heartily into something they initially hated—we need to set the scene. Specifically, we need to take a closer look at how the early 2000s was treating Osseo Senior High School, the surrounding communities, and U.S. education policy, as each placed unique pressure on the Academy from day one.

Endnotes

1. The school served grades 10-12 at the time. It is now a grade 9-12 school.

2. I mean, I'd been the school's journalism teacher/newspaper adviser for five years, but teaching electives like journalism is hardly a distinction for most teachers. More so, electives like journalism and newspaper are like 'hot-potato' charges: no one in the department wants them, so they 'hot-potato' out of everyone's hands into the least-senior members'. To wit, the journalism assignment was given to me as part of my *first-year* teaching duties.

3. For more on this idea, see my 2014 book *Education is Upside-Down: Reframing Reform to Focus on the Right Problems* (Rowman & Littlefield Publishers).

Chapter 2

Negotiating the Grid

'Swing is extreme coordination. It's a maintaining balance, equilibrium. It's about executing very difficult rhythms with panache and a feeling in the context of very strict time. So everything about the swing is about some guideline and some grid and the elegant way that you negotiate your way through that grid.'

– Wynton Marsalis

In the opening chapter I offered that my experience teaching in the Sophomore Academy was a transformative one—a time that ultimately had a larger impact on my overall professional arc than any period before or after it.

With regard to my teaching practice and philosophies, it was an experience that moved me to repeatedly reconsider my educational beliefs and practices, regularly leave my practical comfort zones, and independently sharpen my educational research-literacy. Additionally, my four years in the Academy (and other improvement initiatives happening at the same time at Osseo Senior High, ones I'll visit later in the course of this book) gave me a view of education-professional matters like teacher-leadership, collaborative solutions-design, and comprehensive school improvement that few teachers get to experience.

And to this day, I view my Sophomore Academy experience as the engine pushing pretty well everything else in my career. Whether I'm writing about how schooling builds crucial institutional virtues through academic study, working with schools about how to best implement their own improvements, organizing conferences so more teachers can learn about evidence-informed practices, or whatever else, close to everything I know and everything I am passionate about improving in education connects back to when I was teaching tough tenth-graders in Osseo Senior High's Sophomore Academy.

With all that in mind, none of these effects would have been recorded if not for the convergence of contextual factors that brought the Sophomore Academy into existence in the first place. In fact, the factors are so unique and 'perfect storm'-like—and they allowed me to eventually learn and experience so much—that I've often thought of myself as having been in exactly the right place at the right time. After all, if I'd been teaching a few years sooner or after that period or a few miles north/south of that location (the early 2000s at Minnesota's Osseo Senior High School, that is), it's very likely that I never would have had such a multiply instructive opportunity.

Speaking more specifically and locally, the decade or so leading up to the Academy initiative were very important within the histories of Osseo Senior High, the Osseo Public School District, and the communities that fed into them:[1] populations were exploding overall, new schools were being built to accommodate the swelling numbers of students, and a wider range of social realities—and hence wider range of educational needs, challenges, and complexities (replete with all manners of political entanglements)—were coming into play for district educators.

From a higher level, our school/district/communities were at the time, just like everyone in education, subject to considerable shifts in U.S. educational policy, procedures, and accountabilities. 2001's federal No Child Left Behind (NCLB) Act ramped standardized testing—as well as ranking and visibility of schools' performances—up to new heights, kicking off whole new ways of thinking about school improvement, teacher evaluation, professional development, and, by extension, pretty well everything else. These developments weighed especially on the minds of Minnesota teachers, who'd spent the decade prior (not to mention considerable amounts of money and angst) prepping for, launching, and implementing the Profile of Learning, an ambitious attempt at results-oriented graduation requirements.

Taken together, the population and education-procedural shifts that converged around the time of the Sophomore Academy created a particularly fertile ground for me, my Academy teammates, our school's leadership, and the school as a whole. And as there was so much complexity, both for us to understand and to figure out best ways of managing, we learned *loads*—both about our own practice and about how to maintain focus on prioritized school-improvement actions as the interlocking 'grid' of nascent education reforms and emerging community realities fell into place around us.

Before diving fully into the Sophomore Academy's players, design, operations, and lessons, then, this chapter will do a brief flyover of the context the Academy took place within: what was happening around the turn of the 21st century at Osseo Senior High School and its surrounding communities, as well as what was being mandated from federal and state education circles. It's a unique and complex context, and one that pushed on every part of the Sophomore Academy's story.

Community matters: A metro region in wild flux

While the Osseo Public School District draws from seven communities, three—Osseo, Maple Grove, and Brooklyn Park—are critical to understand when considering how the Sophomore Academy came into being and operated as it did. One (Osseo) is a historic centerpiece of the district, while the other two are major Twin Cities suburbs that underwent dramatic transformations in very little time leading up to and during the Sophomore Academy's operation.

Osseo: 'That small town northwest of the city'

Despite the Osseo Public School District's metro-area location and sizable footprint (it's Minnesota's fifth-largest, serving around 20,000 students), many long-time residents of the Twin Cities metro view the town of Osseo itself as 'that small town 20 minutes northwest of the city'. Thinking of Osseo as a small town was new to me when I moved to the Twin Cities after college, though, as I'd grown up picturing something much different thanks to Osseo Senior High School's *sports programs*.

Yes, really.

I'd grown up an avid athlete in northern Minnesota in the 1980s and, knowing Osseo Senior High as a perennial state power in pretty well *everything*, my naïve and small-town-raised younger version just kind of conjured up the rest around that basic nucleus.

For instance, I knew about Osseo's basic, big-shouldered approach to football—my main sport—first because it was the very type of approach my own high-school team aspired to run, and second because

I admired how their sound, efficient philosophy could drive them deep into the big-school playoffs each year. Also, their hockey program was of a caliber that could occasionally produce a big-time player like Trent Klatt (who graduated from high school the same year I did, was awarded a full scholarship by the University of Minnesota, and ultimately went on to play 14 years in the NHL), their girls basketball team was the best in the state (they won the state championship my senior year of high school), they sent multiple wrestlers to the state tournament each year throughout the 1980s, and so on.

As my smaller hometown was couple athletic classes down from Osseo in the state high school league's organization, in fact, the place even gave me a little bit of a little-brother complex. To wit, I actually got sheepish in my collegiate sophomore year when I learned our football team had landed a recruit from Osseo Senior High to play in my position group. I'd never seen him play, but my awe of Osseo Senior's reputation made me concerned he would summarily take my spot on the varsity depth chart.

Strange, perhaps, but it was just my young-athlete-from-a-small-town's frame of mind: I was a highly competitive kid and, out of my sheer, long-running respect for Osseo's athletic program, my younger mind had formed a picture of Osseo as the kind of elite athletic environment I'd only seen in movies. When I pictured the place, I could only see lots of beautiful and athletic people, a generally competitive and fast-paced way of life, flashy sporting facilities all throughout the town, and such like.

With these kinds of pictures in mind, it never really squared for me that Osseo could be like so many in the Twin Cities metro described it—again, as that 'small town 20 minutes northwest of here'—when I made the Twin Cities my home in the early 1990s.

When I took my first drive through the town, though, in the spring of 1998 (for my job interview at Osseo Senior, actually), I saw it to be much more like my blue-collar hometown in northwestern Minnesota than like the gleaming, big-city athletics factory I'd been expecting. With its typical American Main Street (Central Avenue, that is) and its typical American Main Street businesses (two bars, a bakery, a bank, and so on, with no large chains outside of a Holiday gas station/convenience store), Osseo was—and, indeed, is to this day—much more 'small-town America' than 'suburban America'. Spend an hour or two on Osseo's Central Avenue today, in fact, and you'll likely find it a little hard to believe you're in the heart of a U.S. metropolitan area.

Statistically speaking, too, the town of Osseo itself—nucleus to the large Osseo Public School District and Osseo Senior High—has remained fairly stable for decades. U.S. Census data collected over the last half-century or so, for example, show that Osseo's total population hasn't fluctuated far in any direction over that span. While there have been slight dips and recoveries, things have remained remarkably steady overall: where the 1970 census's total population figure came in at 2908, for example, 2016's estimated population (the most-recent available data) was reported as 2752.[2]

And consistent with many smaller U.S. communities, the town of Osseo's demographic profile also hasn't shifted much over time. According to U.S. Census data leading up to and just beyond the Sophomore Academy years of 2004-2008, Osseo showed as very predominantly—over 90%—white and, with percentages below poverty level consistently in single digits, financially solid. Also, while data from the years observed rarely showed median household income levels to be sliding, their slow climb in comparison to the surrounding metro region would indicate a relative lack of dynamism in the Osseo economy over that particular time period.[3]

Taken together, then, it's actually quite true: in many ways, Osseo is indeed still, even today, 'that small town 20 minutes outside the city'. The same certainly cannot be said, however, for Osseo's suburban neighbors. While Osseo has maintained its small-town essence for decades, the communities that surround Osseo and that feed students into the Osseo-based school district have transformed dramatically.

In the late 1990s into present day—and especially actively in the years framing Osseo Senior's Sophomore Academy initiative—these communities saw drastic and rapid changes in their sizes and demographics. Also—and importantly with regard to the overall Sophomore Academy story—these communities' transformations followed patterns that are, according to compass directions of west and east, close to being diametrically opposed. And at Osseo Senior High, the Osseo district's geographically central high school, this meant getting caught in a demographic and political tug-of-war that presented a unique diversity of issues and concerns.

While the Osseo Public School District serves seven area communities in total, the district's two largest feeder communities—Maple Grove on the district's west side and Brooklyn Park to the east—will be briefly spotlighted here to illustrate the types of opposing forces that were pulling on Osseo Senior High and the Osseo district at large in the late 1990s and early 2000s.

Maple Grove: Explosive, impactful growth to the west

If my mistaken preconceptions of the Osseo community's characteristics had been formed by following newspapers' sports sections in my youth, my perceptions about the suburb of Maple Grove were acquired a bit more first-hand—thanks, of all things, to how Maple Grove is positioned along U.S. Interstate 94, a highway my parents and I drove dozens of times in the late 1980s and early 1990s when I was in college a bit south of the Twin Cities.

From the car window on those trips, I was able to watch Maple Grove sprout—almost as if in time-lapse photography—from a landscape of fields, a massive beige water tower that seemed rather out of place, and an off-interstate rest area (yes, a *rest area*) into one of the Twin Cities metro area's most populous and commercially active suburbs. Chain restaurants, movie theaters, and retailers grew up from the one-time fields, even hopping over onto the freeway's west side—and yes, fairly encircling the once-solitary rest area—by the early 2000s. I didn't need to be a demographist, in other words, to first get introduced to the idea that things were absolutely booming in Maple Grove in the late 20th century.

The explosion of commerce I was able to see from the family station-wagon was happening to accommodate Maple Grove's meteorically rising residency and average income levels. Maple Grove's population skyrocketed 53% in the years from 1990 to 2005 (from 38,854 to 59,465) and, in the same rough span, its median household and per-capita personal incomes jumped 83.4% and 133.7%, respectively. Contrast these increases to those of Osseo's in the same period (median household income increase 33.3%, per-capita personal income increase 98.5%), and it should be fairly clear to see that Maple Grove evolved into a whole different kind of neighbor in that decade and a half.[4]

On that note, Maple Grove's growing populace distinguished itself as a not particularly welcoming or inclusive neighbor in these years. In the 1990s, for instance, as the Osseo School District was erecting new schools for the growing numbers of Maple Grove children (Maple Grove Junior High went up in 1990 and Maple Grove Senior High in 1996), the very predominantly white Maple Grove community[5] attracted a fair amount of negative attention when citizen groups pressured the city to reject lower-income housing developments. Though Maple Grove's all-white City Council attempted in this period to assuage rising concerns that the town was deliberately putting walls up around the town and schools to keep non-white, non-affluent people out, their actions generally sent very different messages—and thus attracted a fair amount of controversy—over the course of Maple Grove's dramatic transformation.[6]

Relatedly, while vocal sections of the new Maple Grove citizenry were getting protective about the public services and resources they clearly saw as theirs alone, some also began using their swelling influence to press on the whole of the Osseo school district and the education it made available. By the early 2000s, for example, a citizens group led by Maple Grove's Jeri Gort (a devout Christian who claimed to be led by divine intervention) ultimately pushed the district to offer both abstinence-only and traditional sexual education content—a dual offering that, according to a 2001 story in *The American Prospect*, landed the district 'a page in sex-ed history'.[7] Reflecting on how the Gort-spurred group of parents came to push the policy into effect, the Osseo district's then-curriculum-and-instruction specialist B. J. Anderson said, 'What I quickly learned in this particular case was that when we work with... people who live with absolute belief systems, they cannot compromise.'[8]

I was able to get some unique views of these situations even before I was a full-time employee of the Osseo district, courtesy of a year-long practicum I was assigned while a teacher-in-training at the University of Minnesota—at, of all places, the then-one-year-old Maple Grove Senior High School over the course of 1997-98. (Recall how I said I'd been in the exact right places at the right times?) Better yet, my program paired me with a cooperating teacher who was a seasoned Osseo-district veteran. He had seen every piece and every phase of Maple Grove Senior's establishment. While I may have been too early in my career at that point to fully appreciate how all his perspectives intersected, as well as how the intersections came to bear on instructional and administrative decisions within the school, I can well remember how items he shared helped many future confusing and/or frustrating realities check out—if not, of course, make much better sense.

In the year I worked alongside him, he helped me understand more 'insider' details about district shifts and politics—and how they manifested in in-school policies and structures—than I could ever have assembled on my own. He always took time to draw clear lines for me between school operations/students' expectations and what had emerged in recent years as community demands, as well as to fill me in on how these demands weren't anywhere near uniform across the larger Osseo district, and why that could, in his view, present some real issues for the district in the years ahead.

Brooklyn Park: 'The new face of suburbia' emerging in the east

While the Osseo school district was negotiating the grid being placed upon it by its growing western end's privilege, religious fundamentalism, and protectionism in the late 1990s-early 2000s, completely different factors were pressing in from the district's east side. In particular, the large Osseo-district feeder city of Brooklyn Park was both growing in size (from 56,450 in 1990 to 67,551 in 2000—and it's near 80,000 at the time of this writing[9]) and demographic complexity. Where 1990 U.S. Census figures showed Brooklyn Park as once having a very Osseo- and Maple Grove-like demographic profile (i.e. just 10% of its citizens were non-white), the city showed 30% of its population as non-white in the census just ten years later.[10]

For Brooklyn Park, this steadily escalating trend continued over the Sophomore Academy years of 2004-2008 and into the present day. Today, Brooklyn Park is a 'majority-minority' suburb of 78,000 with significant communities of Africans (from Kenya, Somalia, Liberia, and other countries), African Americans, Hmong, Vietnamese, and Latinos. This shift over time was captured well by Brooklyn Park resident Joy Marsh Stephens in a 2016 story for CityLab, an online news outlet that covers issues facing the world's metro areas and neighborhoods: 'It's a very different city than it was when I moved there in 1998. We were the only family of color on our block, with the exception of one other family. [...] Now, a solid half of the families on the block are people of color, who represent a lot of different racial and ethnic groups.[...] I often tell people it's the best block in the city.'[11]

Not everything about Brooklyn Park's diversification in this period was positive, however. The same CityLab story, for instance, pointed out how the city's period of explosive growth and demographic change also saw concurrent rises in poverty and declines in median home values in the period described by Stephens. In fact, Brooklyn Park's deteriorating conditions and growing inequities were enough in the early 2000s to get the attention of fair-housing advocates like the University of Minnesota's Myron Orfield. Orfield and other advocates saw Brooklyn Park as a textbook case of what can result from the Twin Cities metro area's tendency toward deliberate economic and racial segregation. (And in light of Maple Grove citizens' aforementioned efforts to block affordable housing units in their burgeoning burg, he certainly seemed to be onto something. By 2014, Orfield even went so far as to help Brooklyn Park and two other racially diverse Twin Cities suburbs file a discrimination complaint with the U.S. Department of Housing and Urban Development.)[12]

With the escalating rates of poverty, the city of Brooklyn Park also saw rates of violent crime rising in ways that justified housing advocates' concerns—and that put the rest of the community, especially those that had been there for decades—on full watch. By 2007, in fact (just in the middle of the Sophomore Academy years, that is), community members were coming together to better understand both where the crime was coming from and what they could possibly do to slow crime rates that had rocketed well past Hennepin County averages.[13] The first decade of the 2000s was so tough in Brooklyn Park, in fact, that the city actively sought to rebuild its image within the metro. In the 2010s, it embarked on an aggressive 'rebranding' campaign to let outsiders know that Brooklyn Park was indeed a good place to visit and do business.[14]

In all, the Brooklyn Park side of the Osseo school district at this time began presenting challenges and needs that the community—and most definitely its schools—hadn't been all that used to managing.

The tougher economic circumstances, new languages being spoken, and wider range of cultural and religious backgrounds, and so on, that were coming in from the eastern end were creating more issues in a short period of time than the city could effectively accommodate. In effect, the suburb of Brooklyn Park was growing into a bona fide *urban center*, in stark contrast to Maple Grove's growing white affluence and Osseo's small-town stability.

And yet again, my interest in sports ties me in personally here—both to Brooklyn Park's new realities and to grasping how unique Brooklyn Park's transformation was in regard to the surrounding metro. More specifically, I was hired away from Osseo Senior's football staff in 2000 to coach for four years at Park Center Senior High (the Osseo district's easternmost high school, which draws primarily from the city of Brooklyn Park).[15] Long-time staff at Park Center could tell me a lot about how the players' lives and our barriers to success had changed over recent years: we suddenly had many more players with transportation issues, conflicts due to younger siblings' childcare, abrupt withdrawals from the team due to parents' relocation, and so on. Also, I could tell on sight alone that we were the only school of our kind whenever we faced our Northwest Suburban Conference opponents, which included major Twin Cities suburbs like Anoka, Blaine, and Coon Rapids. Where the teams we faced had only occasional players of color on their teams and in their stands, our sideline and bleachers were veritable rainbows of backgrounds and creeds.

School matters: New accountabilities, old habits

Not surprisingly, these expanding populations and new diversities of community needs also sent shockwaves through the Osseo Public School District. Fairly unused to the profound needs now coming at them (or at least to the frequency with which they were suddenly being presented), the district—and especially on its east, 'newly urban' end—was a more than a little caught off-guard. Staffed largely with long-veteran teachers, many who'd taught for multiple decades in the Osseo district and who'd been unaccustomed to the new populations' new needs and expectations,[16] Osseo's schools were suddenly scrambling a bit to provide effective learning environments.

And while this scramble to learn quickly and adapt to new needs was particularly pronounced on the district's east side in the late 1990s-early 2000s, all of Osseo Public Schools was actively working to regulate itself within the wide range of new realities.

In a very practical way, for instance, the district had to figure out how it was going to become more uniform in terms of curriculum and programming to account for in-district transfers. The district now featured three large high schools (Osseo Senior, Maple Grove Senior, and Park Center Senior) and four large junior high schools (Osseo Junior, Maple Grove Junior, Brooklyn Junior, and North View Junior), all with decidedly differing characters, environments, and academic opportunities—a reality that would likely accelerate transfer rates as students moved toward individual best fits.

This meant that the secondary schools had to work together in ways they hadn't before to ensure that students moving from school to school didn't fall irreparably off their academic tracks, a definite challenge in light of the aforementioned staff-longevities. And as the district's schools had run fairly autonomously for decades (with each school being able to operate largely according to chosen instructional identity, priorities, and preferences), bringing things into tighter district-wide alignments would involve great amounts of compromise and conciliation.

Over the top of this local concern, the state of Minnesota had gone to great pains in the 1990s to construct and articulate new statewide requirements for graduation. For all Minnesota students entering the 9th grade in the 1996-97 school year and afterward, basic standards tests would be administered in areas of math and reading (and, for students entering 10th grade in 1997-98 and onward, written composition), and basic proficiency marks were to be achieved in order to earn graduation. A second tier of graduation requirements, called the Profile of Learning, required students to expand their knowledge and skills beyond the mandatory basic standards, demonstrating them through appropriate performance tasks determined at district levels.[17]

To bring these cross-district differences closer together and align the whole to the requirements of the state, the Osseo district typically brought teams of teacher leaders together to assist with design and, later, district-wide messaging. And in yet another illustration of my 'I learned a lot because I happened to be in the right place at the right time' theme, I was tabbed by Osseo Senior to sit on one of these cross-district teams when I was in just my second year at the school. More specifically, I was asked to be part of the secondary English Language Arts group tasked with constructing the secondary curriculum—first to align with the new state graduation requirements, and then to create clearer paths of requirements for greater in-district uniformity.

It wasn't *writing* a curriculum, per se, as we had to stay within the instructional resources (e.g. textbooks, novels, instructional aids, and so on) available across the district. Very definitely, however, the team ultimately made some choices that pretty well tore down some teachers' long-preferred instructional choices in the name of standardization. In creating standard World Literature, American Literature, and British Literature categories respectively across grades 10, 11, and 12, for example, some Shakespeare-loving teachers saw that they'd have to switch the courses they taught if they wanted to continue teaching the bard.

In all, I count my few days of debate and compromise with that team of teachers—and certainly the subsequent communication to ELA teachers across the district—among the most instructive experiences of my early career. Through that process, I got very intimate looks at just how entrenched many teachers' practices and content preferences were, how protective those teachers can be about those practices and content preferences, the histories of how such entrenchment and protection got there to begin with, and how it all was playing against the growing pressures from the community.

Then, pretty well just as we'd gotten our things together as a district with regard to Minnesota's Profile of Learning, the federal government's No Child Left Behind (NCLB) legislation came along in 2001 to change everything yet again.

NCLB required annual measurements of student achievement via standardized tests and subsequently tied unprecedented consequences to these metrics. For an endpoint, NCLB specified that schools set their proficiency targets to 100% by the 2013-14 academic year. NCLB guidelines also outlined how student results could get schools officially and publicly labeled as failures, and they prescribed an escalating series of improvement actions for schools with chronically low results. At the highest end of this escalator—that is, for schools receiving federal Title I funds, five consecutive years of missing Annual Yearly Progress (AYP) targets—a school could be dismantled and restructured: all staff let go and required to reapply for their positions, for instance, or the school converted into a charter school.

In short, NCLB was a reform that wasn't going to care very much about parental pressures from the Osseo district's west side or the ballooning numbers of immigrant populations from its east, nor about the performance tasks the state of Minnesota had worked to make graduation requirements and all the work teachers did to integrate them across their schools and districts. NCLB wanted proficiencies on tests, and it wanted to see them going up over time. That was all. And if it didn't get them, NCLB could make schools and educators pay in resources, autonomy, and even their jobs.[18]

As it did very frequently across American education in the first decade of the 2000s, NCLB's new measurements and potential consequences kicked off a whole different kind of professional-development model in the Osseo district's schools. Teachers were organized into teams or Professional Learning Communities (PLCs) that met to review student data and to set SMART goals (for Specific, Measurable, Attainable, Relevant, and Time-bound) toward achievement targets, then expected to continually push each other on how to reach those goals. Though it took a few years of NCLB-type measurements and actions to get rolling, the Osseo district adopted such PLC expectations—with teachers expected to attend both department-level and cross-district committees—across the district by 2004.

* * *

Taken all together, the Osseo Public School District in the late 1990s/early 2000s was an exciting—and, no doubt, frustrating—place to be. Its communities were at once becoming more diverse and more demanding, and U.S. education reform attempts were setting much tighter rules. In building schools and learning experiences that best prepared students for the world, the educators working within this emerging grid were greatly tested—both to create effective solutions and to keep their chosen improvements 'within the lines'.

In the next three chapters I'll explore further how one such improvement, the Sophomore Academy, was imagined and built up at Osseo Senior High in an attempt to improve the school's graduation statistics.

Endnotes

1. The Osseo Public School District provides service to Osseo and parts of several nearby communities including Brooklyn Park, Maple Grove, Brooklyn Center, Plymouth, Corcoran, and Dayton.

2. Stewart, C. (2011) 'Census of Population and Housing'. U.S. Census Bureau Publications. Available at: https://www.census.gov/prod/www/decennial.html

3. More specifically, based on U.S. Census data from 1990 and 2000 and the Census Bureau's American Community Survey of 2006-10, the Census administrations framing the Sophomore Academy's years of operation (2004-2008), Osseo's median household income raised 33.3% between the 1990 and 2006-2010 samples. In light of the surrounding Hennepin County's rate of 71.7% and Minneapolis-St. Paul (the metro's two anchor cities)'s rate of 78.1% over the same time period, Osseo's economic growth can fairly be considered stable bordering on stagnant. State of Minnesota Metropolitan Council (2018) 'Community Profiles: Community Profile for Twin Cities Region'. Available at: https://stats.metc.state.mn.us/profile/detail.aspx

4. Again, these statistics are taken from 1990 and 2000 U.S. Census and the Census Bureau's American Community Survey of 2006-10, the Census administrations framing the Sophomore Academy's years of operation (2004-2008). See State of Minnesota Metropolitan Council (2018) 'Community Profiles: Community Profile for Maple Grove'. Available at: https://stats.metc.state.mn.us/profile/detail.aspx

5. According to aforementioned 2000 and 2010 censuses, the town consistently hovered around 85% white.

6. Kaszuba, M. (16 March 1997) 'Maple Grove Again Confronts the Issue of Affordable Housing'. Minneapolis, MN: Star Tribune.

7. Lerner, S. (19 December 2001) 'The Sex-Ed Divide', The American Prospect. Available at: https://prospect.org/article/sex-ed-divide

8. Pascopella, A. (29 September 2011) 'Districts Re-Evaluate Sex Education Programs', District Administration Magazine. Available at: https://www.districtadministration.com/article/districts-re-evaluate-sex-education-programs

9. State of Minnesota Metropolitan Council (2018) 'Community Profiles: Community Profile for Brooklyn Park'. Available at: https://stats.metc.state.mn.us/profile/detail.aspx

10. Ibid.

11. Hurley, A., K. (24 February 2016) 'Why Brooklyn Park, Minnesota, Is the New Face of Suburbia'. CityLab. Available at: www.citylab.com/equity/2016/02/brooklyn-park-minnesota-suburbia-affordable-housing/461955/

12. Ibid.

13. Adams, J. (4 December 2007) 'Conditions in 2 Suburbs Invite Crime, Experts Say'. Minneapolis, MN: Star Tribune.

14. Prather, S. (1 December 2015) 'After $150K Campaign, Brooklyn Park's Reputation Improving'. Minneapolis, MN: Star Tribune.

15. Incidentally, I was pulled away from the Osseo Senior staff to join Park Center by my one-time cooperating teacher at Maple Grove Senior.

16. When I joined the staff of Osseo Senior High in 1998, for example, I and one other rookie teacher were hired in the same year to replace two English department retirees. Of the 12 others, only one had taught fewer than 20 years. This reality caused my cooperating teacher from Maple Grove Senior High (mentioned earlier in this chapter) to congratulate me for 'making it onto Mount Rushmore'.

17. Larson, L. (November 1998) 'Profile of Learning and the State's High School Graduation Rule'. Information Brief. St. Paul, MN: Minnesota State House of Representatives.

18. This section adapted from Kalenze, E. (2014) *Education Is Upside-Down: Reframing Reform to Focus on the Right Problems*. Lanham, MD: Rowman & Littlefield, pp. 101-103.

Chapter 3

Making it Happen, Part 1: Putting in the Foundation

'Strategy is, at some level, the ability to predict what's going to happen, but it's also about understanding the context in which it is being formulated. And then you have to be open-minded to the fact that you're not going to get it right at the very beginning.'

– Martin Dempsey

'It is not the beauty of the building you should look at; it's the construction of the foundation that will stand the test of time.'

– David Allan Coe

Wish changes like those described in the previous chapter charging through U.S. education and the attendance area of Osseo Senior High in the early 2000s, the school was fortunate to be led at the time by a seasoned, measured principal like Dr. Robert Perdaems. Not all schools were so lucky, after all, and some of the least lucky saw their operations and practices undergo considerable—if not very results-positive—shifts.

Nationally, for example, many school leaders were responding to their student-achievement challenges by swerving their schools into various bold (but costly, difficult-to-implement, and ultimately low-impact) comprehensive school reforms.[1] Hoping they could improve everything from test scores to student behavior to teachers' collaboration routines, these leaders brought in all manners of packaged programming and professional development.

In 2009 the federal government took comprehensive solutions even further for persistently lower-achieving schools, allocating funds under the American Recovery and Reinvestment Act to spur rapid improvement according to a prescribed set of intervention models. While these SIG (for School Improvement Grant) or 'turnaround' schools received dramatic increases in funding and did indeed make considerable changes to their operations, staffs, and structures, their results were in the main no more successful than others' attempts at comprehensive reform. In 2017, the U.S. Department of Education's Institute of Education Sciences issued an executive summary of the SIG program's impact that showed 'no significant impacts on math or reading test scores, high school graduation, or college enrollment' (among other embarrassing no-effects)[2], leading some prominent American education wonks to wonder if the SIG might be the U.S. Department of Education's biggest failure *ever*.[3]

Even locally, the Osseo Area Schools district chose just such a comprehensive option with Park Center Senior High, Osseo Senior's in-district neighbor to the east, when it re-structured the school as an

International Baccalaureate (IB) site around this time.[4] Though this move required remarkable amounts of staff training and restructuring of matters like schedules and student requirements, it didn't do much to change Park Center's profile within the district. To this day, in fact, the school is still the Osseo Public School District's lowest-performing high school. Over ten years after the decision to re-structure as IB, the percentages of proficient students as measured by Minnesota's annual standardized tests remain below state averages in all subjects.

Despite these field-wide tendencies, Dr. Bob preferred simple, sensible, and staff-sensitive improvement strategies over all the pre-constructed and rash—and, again, not particularly effective—ones flying all about. And as this book intends to illustrate, Dr. Bob's preferences ultimately enabled Osseo Senior to steadily add school-appropriate, student-beneficial improvements even as the waves of new accountabilities, populations, and politics kept crashing into the school. Additionally, as Dr. Bob's improvement strategies empowered his staff to be true—not merely symbolic—leaders, the initiatives he enabled eventually proved to be remarkably durable and wide-reaching. These approaches even inspired some under him to learn even more deeply and to expand their leadership more broadly, igniting effects well beyond Osseo Senior's immediate needs and realities. (For more on the career arcs of teacher-leaders who grew under Dr. Bob, see Chapters 11 and 12.)

Plainly, as the early 2000s were filled with so many new pressures and uncertainties, and as the composition of the Osseo Senior High professional staff was concurrently making its way through a substantial and challenging turnover (many in the very veteran staff Dr. Bob had inherited were reaching retirement and exiting), Dr. Bob's methods of school-improvement were exactly what the school needed. If his approach had been significantly less reasoned or overly directive or standardized, the improvements he ultimately made soar would very likely have never achieved lift off.

Though I left the classroom for other work in education over ten years ago, Dr. Bob and I still meet every few months at a Brooklyn Park pizza joint for a beer. Now retired (he left education after the 2014-15 school year), he spends a good deal of each year traveling with his wife Linda, who is also a retired principal—and who also worked in the Osseo district. He doesn't keep up with or get as actively frustrated by various educational goings-on as I do since his retirement (I'll be honest, he always approached such with a much cooler head than I did to start with), but he has a timeless sense about teachers, students, and the various angles of school leadership. And while I've never been able to get him to take proper credit for the positive school climate he had a way of creating, I love watching how, when I ask him about leading a school, he switches fully *on*. Getting to interview him straight-on about such matters for this book, then, and about a time we both knew well, was a real joy for me.

When I asked Dr. Bob (yes, at our usual pizza joint) about the leadership philosophy that was so effective at Osseo Senior High in the early 2000s, he said he always did what he could to move school-improvement efforts according to a clear set of basic principles, if not according to precise sequences, formulas, or directives of grafted-on programs. No matter what the challenge was, he said, he always found it important to follow basic *principles* of identifying problems accurately, matching the right people to each improvement initiative, giving those people active roles in initiatives' design and communication, and respectfully building and maintaining school-community-wide harmony.

It's a set of guiding principles he worked up over a wide range of professional experiences, including teaching music/directing school choirs (early 1970s), serving as principal in a rural-Minnesota high school (early 1980s), opening a large South Dakota high school and acting as Director of Personnel (early 1990s), and leading a large, diverse high school in a metro's inner-ring suburbs—Osseo Senior's neighboring Park Center Senior High, that is (1996-2000).

By the time he reached the Osseo district, and particularly by the time he arrived to Osseo Senior in 2000 (where he was shifted a mid-year by the district's central office to replace a principal who'd moved into an assistant superintendent position), Dr. Bob's district-level supervisors trusted him enough to put these principles to work. Recalling this period, Dr. Bob said that the district's upper-level administrators never discouraged his leadership vision and methods. His superiors at the district valued his vision and methods highly, in fact, as they were able to keep the school moving forward without the district needing to provide substantial financial support for new programming, personnel, or professional learning.

'At least for me,' Dr. Bob said, 'my bosses at the district always wanted to know what was going on and they always wanted to weigh in, but they didn't tell me very often that "Bob, you can't do that". What they *would* say,' he continued with a laugh, 'is, "Bob, *you can't spend any money on that*." I did what I could, then, to incorporate new ideas into the school without spending additional money. With something like the Sophomore Academy, for example, I knew I wouldn't get any budget consideration to go out and buy something like AVID,[5] so it meant we'd have to do it from within. I could make it happen, but I knew my processes and my communication with staff about trade-offs and objectives was critical to get right.'

Having this kind of trust and support from district-level superiors may seem unusual to some principals, especially in the highly monitored improvement environments that became so typical after NCLB. The trust and support is even more surprising in light of the limited experience Dr. Bob had at the time leading demographically diverse metro schools. (The four years he spent at Park Center, after all, were his only such exposure before his 2000 appointment to Osseo Senior.) As it turned out, however, the stint at Park Center provided a uniquely concentrated dose of professional learning and development for Dr. Bob.

And by the time he was tabbed as Osseo Senior's principal, he felt as confident as central office did that he was well-suited for the school's emerging challenges—and that his leadership style and principles could help the school build effective improvements from the classroom up.

While Park Center's rapid changes of population and according school realities were vital to Dr. Bob's preparation for the Osseo post, he pointed out that most of the credit should go to his Park Center staff at the time. More specifically, he said that the staff's exceptional team mentality and its collective approach to handling emerging school issues left the biggest impressions on him as a school leader—first for giving him what he needed to stay afloat there, and next for providing an exemplary model that he could aim toward and compare against in future work.

'At Park Center I was the beneficiary of the right staff at the right time,' Dr. Bob said. 'During that time, when everything was changing around us, we talked a lot about the same types of things we eventually did at Osseo Senior: about kids who came to us every day with school being the fourth or fifth thing on their mind. We asked ourselves, "What are *we* going to do with that kid?" And Park Center was the first place I really started to see how important that "*we*" was—how our sense of community was going to have to be if we were going to change conditions in each classroom.

'More than anything, my time at Park Center taught me how important it was for the principal to personalize the school-improvement process. It's where I figured out that people will believe in you when you show that you believe in them, and that only happens through a personal connection.'

Dr. Bob said this realization pushed him to get better at building these personal connections, both through how he spent his time each day (e.g., visiting classrooms to casually observe lessons or just to have short conversations about non-school matters—without, of course, committing the cardinal sin of eating up teachers' prep times) and through how staff input was brought into various improvement decisions.

Looking over the whole of how his tenure at Park Center Senior High prepared him for leading Osseo Senior, he said, 'I always joked that at Park Center I learned how to be a principal, and at Osseo I actually *was* one. I mean, I felt I was a pretty good principal before those two stops, and I knew that community and getting people on the same page was important going all the way back to my time as a choral director. But by the time I got to those fifteen years at Osseo I was able to get it all together—to put all I'd learned into play—and it really *worked.*'

The Sophomore Academy stands as a prime example of an improvement initiative that 'came together and really worked' for Dr. Bob at Osseo Senior High. A purely classroom-up improvement that had impact well beyond its classrooms, it was guided from idea to inception to implementation by the improvement principles Dr. Bob had spent a career perfecting. Later chapters of this book will visit and expand on other improvements launched under Dr. Bob's leadership, and a concluding section will include a number of generalized recommendations and lessons for the field distilled from the Sophomore Academy and other improvement initiatives from this period.

This chapter, however, will show just what was involved to put the Sophomore Academy's foundation in place. It should be an instructive view for all educators, as it shows the kinds of vision, research, consistency of focus, logistical design work, and politicking necessary to drum up the elusive 'staff buy-in' so necessary for successful school improvements. (Frankly, in researching this section, I was actually a little surprised to learn how much front-end work went into the Academy's build-up.)

Subsequently, chapter four will follow on to show how the Sophomore Academy team built upward from the foundation set by Dr. Bob and his co-administrators.

Phase one: Addressing a need, considering right solutions

In the early 2000s, Osseo Senior High School needed to increase the attention they gave to the issue of students either dropping out before graduating or needing time beyond their senior years to earn diplomas. For though they, like all high schools, had always been concerned with improving their graduation rates, this period saw new accountabilities being attached: The No Child Left Behind (NCLB) Act of 2001 deemed that high schools report their graduation rates (in addition to test scores in English Language Arts, Math, and—beginning in 2007-08—Science) as an indicator of their Annual Yearly Progress (AYP), and any high school not meeting such progress standards could be designated as a 'School in Need of Improvement' (SINI).[6]

While SINI-designated schools stood to have more and more of their improvement actions prescribed to them by local and state education agencies (with conditions compounding progressively with each consecutive year not meeting AYP), a school like Osseo Senior was also driven by sheer competition for students. Seated where it is in the Twin Cities metro (it's located within short drives of options like Maple Grove Senior High, Park Center Senior, Champlin Park Senior, and others), a 'Did Not Make AYP'-type stain could've costed the school in the form of enrollment—and, in turn, resources, staffing, programs, and so on.

With these realities and new accountabilities in mind, Dr. Bob knew he had to make some changes to how Osseo Senior approached its on-time graduation rates. Going about it as they typically had been, after all (e.g. locating credit-short students in their senior years and doing everything in their power to get them across required finish lines), wasn't creating much change from year to year.

Early in the 2003-04 school year, then, Dr. Bob began pushing his fellow administrators, Assistant Principals Peg Vickerman and Brian

Chance, on the graduation-rate question in their weekly team meetings, and they focused their attention on the earlier—as opposed to the 'too-late'—parts of students' paths through high school.

Focusing here proved difficult to plan solutions around, though, partially because the typical 'at-risk student' was so hard to get under the microscope. While lots of students were waylaid by the new pace and expectations upon entering Osseo Senior, for example (perhaps indicating a mismatch between the school and its junior high feeders), the great majority managed the transition just fine. Dr. Bob knew the dropout risks were in there. But they remained in hiding, camouflaged by some combination of personality, capability, and circumstance. Until the end of the term, of course, when the Fs showed up and it was too late to intervene. Course failures in multiple core classes instantly became credits to make up, and the gears of administrative process began to grind.

The trick, they decided, was going to be in using statistics and searching for predictors that would make these students more visible, earlier in their high school careers. The administrative team continued in this direction, moving to find out more about their dropouts' true natures. They turned their attention to causes and effects, and Vickerman volunteered to dig into some previous years' dropout statistics for answers. What she found was revelatory, and it proved vital to all other action that followed.

Looking over the sample of dropouts and late graduates in regard to students who'd graduated on time, Vickerman identified the second academic term of sophomore year as a kind of 'hinge point'. If by this point of the sophomore year, in other words, a student had failed to earn credits in three or more core classes (and this included their credits earned in ninth grade), his chances of dropping out or not graduating on time increased significantly. Of students who ultimately dropped out of school altogether or needed time beyond their senior years to complete their diploma, an overwhelming majority fell below this credit threshold at this point of their high school career.

This hinge point located, Dr. Bob found it encouraging that the number of students meeting such 'at-risk' criteria each year was fairly manageable: at somewhere between 50 and 100 students total per class (in classes of approximately 600 students), the number seemed feasible to serve with some re-structuring of current personnel and schedules.

Looking over the names of students who'd been below the crucial credit threshold at that hinge point in recent years, though, the team saw still another level of challenge. The list of names included some of Osseo Senior's most difficult students in recent memory, and for every reason imaginable: low/no work completion, volatile/violent behavior, so introverted as to be essentially invisible, spotty attendance, difficult family history, and on and on.

To put it another way, looking over the names let the team know this wouldn't just be a matter of providing 'extra academic help,' 'more social supports,' or whatever other clean, non-confrontational answer might be out there. A great many factors were pushing kids toward this empirical 'at-risk' designation, so Dr. Bob and his co-administrators knew the strategies they ultimately chose would have to have broad academic and managerial reach.

Still, now aware of this credit threshold and the critical time indicator of mid-sophomore-year, Dr. Bob and his administrative team began thinking of how they might interrupt the track these kids were on, but that they couldn't yet see for themselves. Their question went from the very broad—'What can we actively do about our dropouts and late graduates?'—to 'What can we do to make sure those kids who come in shaky from our feeder junior highs fail the fewest number of classes early in their sophomore years?'

In addition to these sessions with his administrative team, Dr. Bob went into the professional trade literature to see what other leaders and schools were doing around the country to get ahead of their dropout concerns. Through this study he became intrigued by school-within-a-school models for graduation-tenuous or 'at-risk' students, as it seemed a feasible way to aim preventive measures at the mid-sophomore-year 'hinge point'. Plus, the literature alerted him to several key factors he realized Osseo Senior wasn't yet attacking in any sufficiently meaningful ways.

First, the Association for Supervision and Curriculum Development (ASCD) and the National Association of Secondary School Principals (NASSP) seemed to affirm the data dive: Osseo's current dropout-slowing efforts weren't happening at the right times to do much good. Students who eventually drop out don't typically decide to do so as academic rigor goes up and slows their early momentum. Rather, most kids who ultimately end up dropping out do so because of core-course failures incurred *early* in their high school careers. They fall behind on credits in these first years and, no matter how mature they may become over the course of high school, find themselves in holes too deep—and with too many classes to make up among other requirements—to bother fighting their way out.[7]

In other words, the gap between the enormity of the challenge and the time and effort needed to overcome it was simply impossible to confront. If these kids failed one or two core classes in their sophomore year, they could always postpone electives or use summer school to recover them. Neither of those options was ever easy, but they were at least do-able. If they failed four, five, or six, though, dropping out becomes the most realistic path to follow. Which was exactly what Dr. Bob wanted to avoid.

Also, Dr. Bob found the idea of the school-within-a-school even more compelling when his study showed him how Osseo Senior's interventions for off-track students were missing a crucial piece. Namely, for all the work they were doing to reach kids, nothing they were doing was going far enough to 'make the large school smaller' for the kids of greatest concern. At class sizes hovering around 30 students in all core classes at that time, it was just easy for some kids—especially those who might not have been real invested in their educations to begin with—to get lost.

This realization took on new life when he reviewed in particular recent studies about the benefits of small schools and, where total school restructuring was not an option, concentrated learning communities within larger schools.[8] Looking at these, Dr. Bob was especially drawn to what researchers were saying about how small schools and schools-within-schools seemed to be of particular benefit to at-risk students. Students in these settings reported higher senses of belonging in school and, as these schools simply had fewer moving parts, students were just easier to 'catch' academically if they attempted to slink off through the cracks.

Osseo Senior, however, had nothing like this in operation at the time. Though the school was building sound habits of reviewing student data and was sending various adults to descend on individual students in academic or social freefalls, it had no structures for authentically and systematically supporting large chunks of students who were socially and/or academically slipping away. In light of the wide range of academic, social, and emotional needs he knew his strategy would be called to address, the school-within-a-school concept's ability to 'make the school smaller' became even more intriguing.

Balanced among all these revelations, however, Dr. Bob maintained some reservations when it came to the idea of grouping students as such. If a school-within-a-school could be created at Osseo Senior High to make sure at-risk sophomores were being held up socially and academically, he knew it absolutely could not devolve into a situation where students were receiving sub-standard preparation for their subsequent years at the school and beyond. The potentially harmful effects of ability grouping and academic tracking had been studied and debated for some time[9], so Dr. Bob knew he had to treat the idea with care. Though the goal was to see that at-risk kids weren't falling behind on credits, after all, he knew it wouldn't do much good to those students' future prospects if the smaller setting he was considering just gave the credits away. More ideally, he wanted to create a setting where sliding students could re-assess their course and permanently turn things around.

In sum, Dr. Bob's work with his administrative team and his independent study of the school-within-a-school model convinced him that it could be an effective piece of Osseo Senior's grad-rate-improvement strategy, addressing issues at root-levels that existing interventions had never quite reached. Plus, though the eventual school-within-a-school's composition still had to be thought through carefully and some clear guidelines had to be put in place about its operations, he had little doubt that the overall strategy was at once feasible and sensible enough to take the next steps forward on.

Phase two: Exploring logistics

So convinced of a school-within-a-school's potential to help with improving Osseo Senior High's graduation rate, Dr. Bob and his team still had some surveying to do before they could get to any real groundbreaking or digging. For no matter how powerful and appropriate *they* viewed the initiative, jumping straight to the business of identifying its students, securing its staff, designing its operations, and so forth would all be wasted if what they had in mind couldn't actually exist within Osseo Senior High School's infrastructure and ecosystem.

For their next step, then, they turned to strategically exploring and investigating questions like these:

- If a group of 50-100 incoming sophomores could be pre-identified as at-risk, would proper space exist in the master schedule for this group to move between their four core classes and still be able to access required sophomore-year electives?

- Though the school-within-a-school would dictate lower-than-average class sizes (for reference, class sizes were averaging in the high 20s-low 30s at the time for Osseo Senior's required or 'core' classes) to get students the ideal levels of support and attention, would creating multiple sections of lower class set off a chain of far-too-lopsided class sizes throughout the rest of the sophomore teachers' days?

- Would the team of school-within-a-school teachers be able to have shared preparation time within the day to consistently update one another on their students and design responses that could 'make the school smaller' as intended?

- Could an appropriate balance be struck between upholding the principles of behavior the school had so painstakingly established and enforced in preceding years and keeping the envisioned school-within-a-school kids in class where they belonged? ('Basically,' Dr. Bob recalled, 'I was asking Brian [Chance, Assistant Principal/Student Services] if he could put some elastic into his assistant-principal tenets. We knew that for the types of kids we envisioned placing into this school-within-a-school, there was no way for them to be successful in school if they *weren't in school*—and that meant figuring out what to do with perhaps-suspendable offenses in a way that wouldn't look like we were playing favorites or being inconsistent.')

Having clearer ideas on these kinds of questions, after all, would be critical for the phase to follow: getting Osseo Senior's faculty at large to accept the various shifts to schedules and class sizes. For as compelling as Dr. Bob's rationales may have been, they alone would never have had the torque to move staff minds and hearts en masse. And going back to Dr. Bob's improvement principles of staff understanding, harmony, and collective investment, this was far from a small matter. He believed deeply that faculty's collective acceptance and agreement would be needed in order for initiatives like the school-within-a-school to function and thrive, but was realistic about how such acceptance and agreement could be tricky to secure. In short, he knew to be respectful and rational in how to ask his staff at large to take on more work.

As creating multiple sections of smaller classes would also mean sending ripples of work increases and shifts outward into the rest of the school, in other words, Dr. Bob knew he'd have to have the clearest vision possible of what he was asking his faculty to sign off on and support.

To get a better look at the student requirements- and registration-related questions, Dr. Bob again turned to Assistant Principal Peg Vickerman. Then in charge of managing the academic side of Osseo Senior's administrative org chart (e.g., matters like grading policies, student registration, and, crucially in this case, master scheduling), Vickerman was—in addition to being Dr. Bob's main resource for previously analyzing historical GPA-to-retention statistics—the school's best resource when it came to crunching enrollment forecasts, total numbers of sections necessary per course, teachers' preferred prep periods, and all other master-scheduling variables.

Though the 2003-04 school year was only around the halfway point when she was given this task, Vickerman pushed the various puzzle pieces around to see if the school-within-a-school could fit. This was particularly challenging, as she was yet without crucial information on matters like the incoming sophomore class's enrollment numbers, adjustments to the school's operating budget, changes in the school's course catalog, and the like. Still, she prepared some preliminary models using her best estimations, and she ultimately found that the school-within-a-school could indeed fit. It would mean some teachers were going to have to push their ideal days around a bit, but the sections appeared to be there.

Also—and importantly—Vickerman's exploratory exercise produced an ideal range for the size of the school-within-a-school's sections. She recommended that class sizes aim for between 18-25 students, as much lower would create excessively over-loaded class sizes for other teachers. These low- and top-end class-size boundaries later proved essential for selecting the school-within-a-school's students.

Before moving into the team's next steps, which involved canvassing the school staff to inform of the initiative being researched and secure their support/agreement, please observe this Brief Note on Master Scheduling (and on Appreciating Schedulers Like Peg Vickerman): While the master schedule might seem a rudimentary technical detail to someone looking in from the outside at education (or, indeed, to someone within education that has not had to manage all its moving parts), it is actually among schools' most complicated and most essential systems.

To the matter of its complexity and potential complications, consider all a school's master schedule must simultaneously account for: sufficient accessibility for students to complete their state-, district-, and/or school-mandated graduation requirements; teachers' course offerings, which are available according to professional qualifications, intra-departmental preferences, and funding-dictated time allotments (to name just three); ebbs and flows in student-enrollment numbers from year to year; demand for schools' various elective courses and intervention/enrichment opportunities, which rise from faculty, school- and district-administrative, community, parental, and even outside-organizational priorities; classes' uses of shared activity spaces and/or available instructional resources; lunchtime flows, cafeteria capacities, and available staff coverage for lunches/recesses; and so on, and so on. And believe me, the 'so on' here is *considerable*. Throw in special days like late-start professional-development bell schedules on the day the football team plays in the state semifinals and the benchmark-testing window is closing (and yes, there are at least one of these per month in any given school year), and the complexity multiplies even *further*.

It should also be noted that while the above considerations vary by weight and proportion from school to school, the task is almost always similarly challenging: scheduling is not necessarily easier for schools with fewer students, for example, as they also have fewer teachers to work with and more limited facilities but generally the same state-guided graduation requirements that must be offered.

Though several within and outside education like to imagine what schools *should* be doing, basically, I'm quite sure they aren't fully aware of how jammed master schedules already are and how difficult it is, either for students to nimbly dance through them to meet requirements or for administrators to make changes to them. Tight as they often are, something as 'simple' as opening an additional section of English 9 to make all the other sections a bit smaller can have 'butterfly effect'-like ramifications that impact every grade and every part of the school day.[10]

Here's what it looks like: first, the school has to find a teacher for the new section. Then that teacher must be paid. (This is important, obviously.) Now we need to assign a classroom. But the new section's being taught by our previously-0.8 FTE building sub who has no classroom of his own, and no classrooms in the English hallway are free that hour. Let's see…looks like 241, the big science lab, is open that hour. Great. Now let's put some 9th graders in that classroom. Hang on, is this during freshman band/choir? We can't pull kids from *there*! That's their one arts elective! What other classes meet that hour? Spanish and health. OK, this could work. If we pull four from Ms. Bakke's health class, I can just re-assign them to health in another period. Wait, what? We only have one section of Health 9 meeting this term? *You get the idea.*

Look, I've been there. If you've been there too, I'm sorry if I triggered your PTSD. The point is that master scheduling is a lot harder than it may look or seem.

Having acknowledged master schedules' inherent challenges and complexities, they should also be recognized as one of the foremost keys to any kind of school-improvement planning. It's more than a day- and activities-organizer, after all. Indeed, as the master schedule orders everything flowing through a school, it is at once an expression of the school's vision, values, and realities. And as such, it can either merely *keep up with* students (and teachers) or actively open and guide them to new possibilities and growth opportunities.

The Education Trust's Karin Chenoweth, a writer who has studied 'beating the odds' schools for over a decade, highlighted precisely this in her 2017 book *Schools that Succeed: How Educators Marshal the Power of Systems for Improvement*. Though several schools and school-leaders are presented throughout the book, the master schedule emerges over and over as a system each leader actively marshaled on their ways to creating continuous, sustained improvements. In the 'Systems to Note' bullet points that conclude and summarize each of the book's chapters, in fact, Chenoweth points out specifically how each school leader leveraged their schools' master schedules to make sure students were receiving appropriate support and enrichment, teachers were given opportunities to continually learn about and improve upon their practice, and/ or schools' various time and human resources were being used to maximum effects.[11] As hard as the master schedule may be to wrangle, in other words, many exceptional school leaders have figured out that doing it well—and actually putting it to work for their continuous school improvement—should be a priority, right up near quality hiring and wise financial management.

Bringing all this back to the school-within-a-school that was being explored by Osseo Senior High's leadership at this time, the initiative (and, indeed, the entire school community) was fortunate to have Vickerman aboard. The preliminary models she drew up—all without exact enrollment figures or even a sense of how many students the eventual school-within-a-school would seat and serve—brought a clarity to the proposal that made Dr. Bob's next job much easier (if not, of course, *easy*).

Phase three: Sharing the plan, securing buy-in

In my interviews with him, Dr. Bob remembered what came next—informing faculty leaders of his intent and securing their buy-in—as one of the largest hurdles he faced in bringing the initiative fully to life. For while he'd been at the school a few years by this point and accumulated a good amount of capital and trust, he knew at the time that he have to pull from all that capital and trust to get the staff where he needed them to be on his school-within-a-school.

The proposal, after all, asked the staff for a lot. It was going to increase class loads for many teachers and, conversely, reduce them for a select few others (the school-within-a-school teachers, that is), which risked creating perceived 'chosen ones' within the staff—always dangerous territory for leaders working on healthy staff cultures. Plus, the school-within-a-school was going to shift master-scheduling pieces around in ways that would cause several teachers to give up preferred free periods and/or courses-taught—considerable sacrifices indeed, especially to make way for an untested strategy that would (perhaps) rescue 40-50 verified-wobbly students per year. As the staff at the time was still deeply veteran, wary of Big Top-Down Changes, protective of its working preferences, and well-practiced in the arts of preference-defense, Dr. Bob knew when he set out that he was in for a lot of tough conversations.

He knew that if he wasn't careful, all the capital, trust, and relationships he'd so painstakingly stocked up over three years as principal could take a real hit. And if *that* happened, he knew he'd have a tough time moving improvements according to his essential principles.

'It was a really important part of making everything work,' Dr. Bob remembered. 'It meant I had to work much more closely with—and sometimes be more directive with—department chairs than I ever had about the schedule. When I got to Osseo Senior, teachers were used to putting down what their ideal teaching day would be and getting it. Once we added in the variable of a group of kids that would be together for four periods of the day, and who needed credit-earning classes available to them in non-core hours so they could stay on track to graduate, we had to tell those teachers things were going to change.'

True to his principles of transparency and respect, Dr. Bob set about communicating these changes one teacher at a time. Over a period of several weeks, he went up and down the school to personally engage department heads and other faculty leaders about the school-within-a-school, hoping to secure their support. Knowing that issuing his decision to the faculty at large would likely cause a storm of questions and pushbacks, he chose a more time-intensive—but sincerely two-way—approach to more respectfully 'seed' the idea among the staff. He individually and informally talked with several staffers about the initiative's rationales, the study he and his team had conducted to solidify them, how it all could work within the schedule, and so on, always reminding them of what he saw as an attractive trade.

It didn't always work, Dr. Bob told me, but it wasn't so much that people didn't like the idea. More so, department heads tended to look out for their people—and they sure didn't want to be the ones who said to the principal: 'Sure, it'll be fine to raise our class sizes, go ahead!' To Dr. Bob, the good news was that he wasn't getting much outright pushback and rejection. He felt he could work with that. Again, he pushed the notion of an attractive trade-off.

'I tried to see my job as soft-selling it to make sure it could happen,' Dr. Bob said. 'I'd plant the seeds, but then bring up the question of, "How would you feel about having more kids in your classroom but fewer kids who give you trouble in your classroom? You know, so you could more fully focus on those kids who come to school ready to learn right out of the chute?" And most of them thought that sounded like a pretty good trade.

'Years afterward and after we had the Academy running, people were still picking out how having the Academy gave them the chance to do things in their classes they never could—how thankful they were that they didn't have to deal with those two or three kids per class that had a way of holding things up.

'Politically,' he continued, 'any time you're going to market a change to the status quo to the people who aren't directly involved in making it happen, it's very important that you give them a reason to support it.'

And ultimately, Dr. Bob's staff felt comfortable enough with the school-within-a-school to let him know they'd be behind it, sacrifices and all.

The foundation work, in other words, was coming along very well.

Secure in his rationales, some rough logistics, and the larger staff's commitment and support, Dr. Bob turned his attention to what this school-within-a-school would actually look like. There was no strict playbook or program to be executed with fidelity, no trainings to send staff off to, no new curricula or technology to be brought in, or anything of the sort. He had some non-negotiable objectives and some school-infrastructural space to work with, and not really much more. From this point, the matter of what his school-within-a-school initiative would look like, day in and day out, would largely be up to the team of teachers he chose to work in it.

The next chapter will focus on this school-within-a-school team: why Dr. Bob selected them, how he approached them, and the design space he gave them to begin building upward from the foundation he and his administrative team set.

Endnotes

1. Vernez, G., Karam, R., Mariano, L. and DeMartini, C. (2006) 'Evaluating Comprehensive School Reform Models at Scale', in *Focus on Implementation*. Santa Monica, CA: RAND Corporation. Available at: www.rand.org/pubs/monographs/MG546.html

2. Dragoset, L., Thomas, J., Herrmann, M., Deke, J., James-Burdumy, S., Graczewski, C., Boyle, A., Upton, R., Tanenbaum, C. and Giffin, J. (2017) 'School Improvement Grants: Implementation and Effectiveness: Executive Summary'. Washington, DC: U.S. Department of Education. Available at: www.ies.ed.gov/ncee/pubs/20174013/pdf/20174012.pdf

3. Smarick, A. (23 January 2017) 'The $7 Billion School Improvement Grant Program: Greatest Failure in the History of U.S. Department of Education?' EducationNext. Available at: www.educationnext.org/the-7-billion-school-improvement-grant-program-greatest-failure-in-the-history-of-the-u-s-department-of-education/

4. Park Center Senior High officially became an International Baccalaureate school in 2007.

5. AVID, or Advancement Via Individual Determination, is a program of professional learning and curriculum dedicated to strengthening students' persistence through school and readiness for college.

6. United States Department of Education. (21 June 2005) 'NCLB Part A—Improving Basic Programs Operated by Local Education Agencies, Section 1111.' *NCLB Part A—Improving Basic Programs Operated by Local Educational Agencies.* Washington, DC: United States Department of Education. States designed their own SINI designations, with Minnesota labeling struggling schools as 'Focus' or 'Priority' according to the degrees of their performance gaps.

7. Though Dr. Bob did not provide exact titles, resources like these are indicative of how ASCD and NASSP were addressing the issue of at-risk students around the time of his study. See: Allen, R. (December 2002) 'Keeping Kids in School', in *Education Update: Taking Up the Challenge*, 44 (8) or: National Association of Secondary School Principals. (2004) *Breaking Ranks II: Strategies for Leading High School Reform.* Brown University, RI: The Education Alliance.

8. Similar to the previous note, exact titles are missing here. For an illustration the type of reports Dr. Perdaems would have accessed in those years, see this literature review: Slate, J., R. and Jones, C., H. (2005). 'Effects of school size: A review of the literature with recommendations', in *Essays in Education*, 13.

9. National Education Association of the United States. (31 May 1990) 'Academic Tracking: Report of the NEA Executive Committee/Subcommittee on Academic Tracking', in *ERIC – Education Resources Information Center*. Washington, DC: National Education Association, Instruction and Professional Development. Available at: www.eric.ed.gov/?id=ED322642

10. For more in-depth analysis of schools' already-crowded schedules and how they got that way, see my previous book's chapter nine, 'Too Scattered to Matter'. Kalenze, E. (2014) 'Too Scattered to Matter', in *Education is Upside-Down: Reframing Reform to Focus on the Right Problems*. Lanham, MD: Rowman & Littlefield, pp. 133-141.

11. Chenoweth, K. (2017) *Schools that Succeed: How Educators Marshal the Power of Systems for Improvement*. Harvard Education Press. For referenced 'Systems to Note', see pp. 33, 54, 81, 103, 140, 167.

Chapter 4

Making it Happen, Part 2: The Right Team

'My philosophy is that you don't motivate
players with speeches; you have motivated
players that you draft. That's where they come
in, and those are the guys that are competitive.
You cannot teach competitiveness.'

– Phil Jackson

It was Dr. Bob and his fellow administrators who did all of the surveying and excavating for this project. They explored ideal options for scheduling, measured logistical realities, and checked in with key staff to gauge reactions. With the school more or less on board, they had their permits in order and could begin construction on the school-within-a-school they believed would improve Osseo Senior High's late-graduate/dropout statistics.

Actual construction presented a whole new challenge. Remember, the initiative Dr. Bob had in mind was large and open-ended. He wasn't 'implementing a program/curriculum', 'providing additional training', or 'acquiring and maintaining hardware/software'. He was attempting something that had not been done before.

What would it look like? How would it 'phase in'? Who would figure out how to build it? While Dr. Bob had read a lot about the school-within-a-school concept and its benefits, there wasn't a blueprint for any of this.

More to the point, Dr. Bob was operating with little more than his studies of factors predicting on-time graduation, how schools-within-schools had shown promise with regard to addressing early high school credit deficits, and the pros/cons of ability tracking. In accord, he also had a set of critical objectives and boundaries for the initiative (e.g. keep the identified at-risk kids from slipping through sophomore-year cracks, make those kids feel like they belong to something at the school, never dial the academic rigor down too low). The operational particulars would up to the team enlisted to design and build it. So that team had to be just right. As hard as Dr. Bob and his administrative team had worked to create the space for the initiative, it was crucial for him to assemble a team that could, with no additional tools, gimmicks, or funding, pull it all off.

He was confident the envisioned learning environment would take shape, though, if he could bring together a group of teachers with qualities like these: savvy enough to recognize when kids were heading the wrong way; assertive enough to block kids from continuing down such paths; sincere enough to win kids' trust; engaging enough to capture and hold kids' attention; collaborative enough to come up with consistent solutions across the team; malleable/adaptive enough to switch up solutions when new challenges arose; instructionally sharp enough to engage kids and provide the right kind of support for kids struggling over obstacles; confident and firm enough to hold ground (with kids and colleagues); and, dedicated/stubborn enough to keep teaching their hardest through the challenges the school-within-a-school's students (and maybe some school staff) were likely to present.

In short, Dr. Bob needed a group of teachers that were confident with their subject matter and classroom-management, plus able to work well across disciplines and who had earned reputations in the school community as 'kid magnets'.

No problem, right?

Still, it's not a stretch to say that the success of the initiative—most especially in its first design/prototype year—was hanging on the team he chose. As faculty throughout the building had agreed to take on larger class sizes and re-shuffled teaching assignments to make the school-within-a-school work, more was at stake than simply success with kids in the initiative's classrooms.

Indeed, for all of the larger convenience the broader staff had given up to make this thing happen, Dr. Bob knew the rest of the school would be watching closely—and that he could lose virtually all of the trust-capital he accumulated if it started disastrously.

As you can imagine, quite a few things could go wrong. The school-within-a-school's classrooms could lose control, channeling at-risk kids back into other teachers' classrooms, increasing already-stretched class sizes. The chosen teachers could get frustrated and withdraw from the program after one year—or, worst case scenario, midyear—to escape the intense conditions. These kinds of systemic breakdowns would have real, troubling consequences on neighboring staff. Dr. Bob had to be sure the teachers he selected would be strong enough—and stubborn enough—to stick with it, even if it got rough. The risk of failure was too high. Failure would not only doom the at-risk kids. It could permanently hobble future improvements.

Despite these pressures, Dr. Bob knew it would be a mistake to micro-manage or be too prescriptive about the school-within-a-school's design. In line with his basic improvement principles, he truly believed that for this initiative to work, the teachers running it would have to make the design decisions. The school-within-a-school he pictured was about connecting to, pushing, and supporting a group of challenging kids in a truly authentic way. But you can't prescribe authenticity. The teachers were going to have to do it themselves, in whatever way came most naturally, or *authentically*, to them. Anything else would not only be phony—it wouldn't work. If he chose the team well, though, this would be a non-issue. They would have the capability to design a system that made sense to them and, ultimately, to run it day to day.

Getting his own level of management right was a big deal in Dr. Bob's methods of building school improvements. When asking staff to take a chance on something so uncharted and pressure-filled, the keys were more to empower, challenge, and support the team he'd chosen— not to simply assign them the task, provide firm guidelines, and expect improved outcomes. In short, he kept in mind that he'd have to do some corrective steering from time to time, but from this point he didn't really see himself as 'driving'.

'I believed the group I wanted to be a part of this experiment would arrive at building the right kind of program,' Dr. Bob said, 'because I took some things into consideration before going and talking to any of them.

'I also held out the last piece, though, which was where I'd have to ask some questions if I saw they were going the wrong way with it. They were going to be held professionally responsible for all of it—by me, of course, but by everyone else in the school as a result of their class sizes—so I had to choose the right people, give just enough direction, then really just be a blocking back for them while they focused on the inner-workings and end goals of this initiative. That's what I saw my main jobs as.'

Identifying and engaging the school-within-a-school team

With his candidates in mind, Dr. Bob set out to begin his conversations with them. We'll get to know more about each individual's instructional and management beliefs in the next chapter (and, indeed, in subsequent chapters about the school's operation), but for now the focus will be most on Dr. Bob's rationales for targeting them.

First, Dr. Bob went to the person he had projected as the school-within-a-school's English teacher: me, Mr. Eric Kalenze.[1] I was not his top priority based on my strong skill, reputation, or profile within the school, though. Rather, Dr. Bob targeted me first because he had been concerned about my job satisfaction. Having detected some unhappiness in me over the past year or so, he thought something like this might get me a change of scenery and a different kind of professional/personal challenge.

'I deliberately sought you out first,' he told me, 'because I knew you had been frustrated by the way your department was functioning, by regulations you were being constrained by, and other things, and were having some second thoughts about staying with us. I thought this might be a good way to bring a change in your teaching life that would make things work better for you.'

Strategically, then, bringing me into the fold helped with multiple issues.

First, it secured an English teacher who was experienced with the sophomore-year curriculum.

Next, it brought in a teacher who had a reputation for working well with challenging students. Dr. Bob had a unique perspective on my classroom climate and regimen, because I taught two of his stepchildren, Blake and Sara, some years before.[2] Dr. Bob's kids were nowhere close to being challenging or difficult students. They got to see first-hand, though, how I would halt class to settle a distracting rift between students, or how I justified my tough lines on things like late work (accepted, but it'll cost you dearly) and extra credit (none, ever). I can only assume they shared stories like these with Dr. Bob, for better or worse.

Finally, it plugged me into a new team and a new teaching challenge he expected to recharge my enthusiasm for working at Osseo Senior. And I have to hand it to Dr. Bob here, as he absolutely nailed my struggles at the time: I had indeed been quite frustrated, and I'd very nearly taken a position at another school the previous spring.

Next, Dr. Bob targeted his social studies teacher, Mr. Gerry Zelenak, a caffeinated, spiky-haired dynamo who's quick with wisecracks and celebrity impressions. Zelenak had transferred into Osseo Senior from Maple Grove Junior High at the beginning of the school year. Before his Maple Grove Junior stint, however, he'd started his teaching career at neighboring Park Center Senior High—which was also his alma mater. In his short time at Osseo Senior, his huge personality and passion for the job had already made an impression on the school's students. No matter when he saw him, Dr. Bob said, Zelenak seemed always to be surrounded by happy kids.

In more strategic terms, though, Dr. Bob valued Zelenak's recent experience working in the junior high school: first because he was one of the few people at all of Osseo Senior who had any such experience, and second because he felt the junior-high perspective and attitude would be critical to the overall success of the school-within-a-school and its goals. Where high school teachers can tend toward being rigid with behavior expectations and primarily content-focused, Dr. Bob thought that someone like Zelenak would help to keep the new team grounded with regards to students' cues, needs, and prior expectations. Of all the teachers he planned to approach for this effort, none had such a keen take on the expectations and cultures of junior high schools or on the concerns, fears, and mindsets of junior high-aged students. And as valuable as this set of perspectives would be for kids in the new school-within-a-school, it would also go far to keeping the team of teachers in check.

For the science position (biology, that was, as it was the standard core course for sophomores at that time), Dr. Bob targeted Mr. Eric Ruska. Then in his third year at Osseo Senior (but fourth year teaching—he had been cut a year prior when his department reduced; then, after a year teaching in Spooner, Wisconsin, came back to Osseo Senior in 2003), Ruska was a multiple-sport coach and a veteran of teaching the science department's adjusted biology course—a modified-curriculum offering designed for students who were struggling with the pace and expectations of the mainstream biology class.

Again from a strategic, overall-program-strengthening standpoint (to go with refreshing my enthusiasm with a new challenge and leveraging Zelenak's understanding of junior-high settings and students), Ruska's experience with adjusted biology gave him the team's deepest knowledge of how to get the most out of behaviorally challenging and/or academically unmotivated students. Where I'd taught the standard English 10 class for several years and thus managed classes filled with wide ranges of student abilities and engagement-levels (plus plenty of very motivated students in the elective journalism classes I'd taught), and where Zelenak was still getting his high-school legs back under him after several years in the junior high, Ruska's time teaching the adjusted course made him well-used to working with entire sections of reluctant learners—a handy skill-set for sure, considering the projected enrollment.

Plus, thanks to his experience as a coach, Ruska's management skills went beyond how to work a challenging classroom. He'd proven over his time at the school that he could collaborate with fellow coaches, plus manage delicate matters like parent complaints, player squabbles, and project details at very high levels. After head-coaching varsity girls hockey (in Minnesota, to boot) and varsity softball, he had seen the full range of teenage (and parental) drama, from screaming matches to the silent treatment. As all of these were premium strengths to have aboard (especially when Zelenak was still fairly new to Osseo Senior and I, admittedly, still had some growing to do in my collaborative and diplomatic areas), Ruska was a natural fit.

After initial conversations with these three teachers to explain rationales and work through each's questions and reservations, Dr. Bob was feeling pretty good about how things were falling together. There were no snags or lingering hesitations, and each teacher seemed up for the school-within-a-school's new frontier.

He was still one teacher short of a full instructional team, though, and the final seat was going to take a bit more doing. 'I felt like I got lucky that you all said yes,' Dr. Bob recalled to me. '*Then* came the hard one.'

More specifically, the 'hard one' was filling the final seat of math teacher. For this position, Dr. Bob was going to have to work a bit harder than he'd had to for his English, social studies, and science teachers.

For starters, he didn't have an obvious candidate. As he viewed many in his math department as a potential good fit, his first challenge was working his way down to a single person. Rather than identifying an ideal and chatting with that person about rationales and reservations, as he had for the first three spots, Dr. Bob first had to go through the math department's roster, teacher by teacher, and weigh each with regard to current workloads, responsibilities, and potential limitations.

The backstory will be familiar to any teacher. The chair of the department at that time was Dr. Bob's first choice, but pioneering the school-within-a-school while managing the entire math department would be asking too much. His second choice was head coach for multiple sports and would be similarly overburdened. Other candidates who were well-known 'kid magnets' or excellent teacher-leaders couldn't do it for other reasons: they didn't have sufficient experience with sophomore curriculum, had already committed to teaching classes that others couldn't cover, and all of the usual scheduling complexities.

After some time walking through this process of elimination, Dr. Bob got to a candidate that intrigued him, Ms. Kelly Klecker.[3] While Klecker knew the sophomore-year math classes well (including lower levels, where several of the initiative's students were likely to be placed) and had no massively deal-breaking conflicts, Dr. Bob admitted to me that he just didn't know enough about her at the time to make a firm decision. He only had limited contact with her to that point (a rarity for him), and he simply couldn't say one way or the other if she would fit well with the team members already aboard—or, crucially, if such a prospect would even interest her.

True to his pattern, then, he set to finding out for himself first-hand.

'I started talking to her. I'd just stop by to watch her class, chat with her, get a feel for what she considered important in teaching, that kind of thing,' Dr. Bob said. 'And after some time, I learned enough about her that I thought she could have a unique kind of compassion for—and insight into—the kind of "outlier" kids we were thinking of bringing on to this thing.

'Also,' he added with his characteristic knowing grin, 'she was a strong figure in her classroom. I knew she could show you guys a thing or two.'

After securing Klecker's commitment, Dr. Bob's team of teachers (and, concurrently, the team of *program designers*) was complete.

Alongside the four teachers, Dr. Bob arranged additional support for the nascent program from the counseling office. Knowing that we would need quick access to students' data—and quick access to matters deeper than just assessment results—to make effective decisions, and knowing as well as that the school's students were likely to require higher levels of responsiveness and counselor care, he retained the counseling of Ms. Jackie Trzynka to fully round out the team. He consulted informally with Trzynka behind the scenes through all phases of his construction to this point, and he knew her abilities and perspectives would bring an additional layer of strength and value.

The logistical foundation laid and the practical pieces now fully in place, the work of designing the school-within-a-school—how it would actually look from day to day—could finally begin.

For that design work, Dr. Bob arranged for the new team to have two full days of planning time in the spring of 2004, moving the project from concept into practice. The next chapter will go into greater depth with that initial planning meeting: more about the team members' professional assets, plus more about how they negotiated those assets within their shared mission to put in the school-within-a-school's pillars.

Finally, and of note: gradually over the course of the listening/marketing/discussion tour detailed in the past two chapters, in which Dr. Bob used several months to visit all points of the school talking about all aspects of his idea and how it seemed worth giving a shot, he began referring to the initiative as the 'Sophomore Academy'. It fit more easily into sentences than 'school-within-a-school' did, and it set a placeholder for something catchier or flashier if the team of teacher-designers eventually decided they wanted something they thought fit better.

We didn't. The placeholder stuck. From that first meeting to today, we were the Sophomore Academy.

Endnotes

1. For more on this conversation and his rationale for selecting me, see Chapter 1.

2. Sara, in fact, was in my class when planes hit the World Trade Center on 9/11—which also marked the one and only time I ever used the 'F' word in front of kids. That, though, is a story for another time. Look for it in a future book from me, *Classroom Management Techniques That Work, But That You've Never Thought Of.*

3. Now Kelly Skare-Klecker.

Chapter 5

Making it Happen, Part 3: Installing the Pillars

'As you navigate through the rest of your life, be open to collaboration. Other people and other people's ideas are often better than your own. Find a group of people who challenge and inspire you, spend a lot of time with them, and it will change your life.'

– Amy Poehler

With so much build-up leading to this two-day planning session, I'd love to report to education's continuous-improvers, improvement-scientists, and seekers-of-scalable-solutions[1] that it was a perfect, replicable mix of inspirational learning, professional and personal epiphanies, and all the rest. I'd love to report that all the chart paper we filled and markers we burned through in our sequence of thoughtful reflections, data dives, root-cause analyses, driver diagrams, and strategic-planning exercises utterly parted the clouds for us, ultimately giving us a clear roadmap for how the Sophomore Academy would look each day, how it would measure its progress, and how it would continually and cyclically adjust its operations. I'd love to announce how the process we followed on that day was what made all the difference, and then share exactly what schools can do to magically organize their own improvement efforts as such.

But I can't.

This wasn't how we—and Dr. Bob, especially—did things in the Sophomore Academy, at all, from the beginning.

Here's exactly what Dr. Bob did to get us rolling in this, his vision, his special project, the one he bet so much leadership capital against and spent months working on:

- He called us to order and had us introduce ourselves to one another.
- He re-familiarized us with work he and his team had done to identify the issue, shared data to underscore why this work was important to the school, and reminded us that we were personally picked for this charge for specific, strategic reasons.
- He restated the initiative's mission and vision, plus its most basic boundaries—things we should keep in mind, basically, as we worked toward any of our team decisions: creating a culture that would accelerate a sense of belonging to Osseo Senior, not just one or two classes; keeping managerial and academic rigor

high enough to prepare kids for success throughout high school, not just giving them a kinder, gentler 10th grade experience; following the same basic curricular expectations expected by our departments, but with more discretionary flexibility.

- He told us to use the next two days as we pleased, and that he would drop in occasionally to see how things were progressing and to challenge our thinking as needed.
- He asked us if we had any questions, and he said he was looking forward to seeing what we came up with.
- He left the room.

All of this took about 30 minutes. Then he was gone.

We looked at each other, not knowing what to say.

Dr. Bob didn't provide a playbook, any concrete directives, or any kind of facilitation guidance. Just a problem to be solved, some structure and space to work within, a restatement of our mission, a few explicit things to avoid (no dumbing-down of expectations/content, no giving up on kids or recommending they be transferred out), and lots and lots of trust in the team.

In other words, it was all on us. We had no pre-packaged content, formulaic plan, or step-by-step approach to follow. While intensive sessions like this Academy design meeting had clear objectives, and while the involved teams of teachers' thoughts were most certainly pushed, Dr. Bob never used a strict or explicit improvement process to keep things moving ahead.

In his view, it wasn't necessary because he knew the people he enlisted would (or *should*, anyway—recall that he reserved the right to 'correct steering' as needed) produce what needed to be produced. It was why he put all the thought and time into selecting just these team members. The improvement principles introduced in Chapter 3—

1. *Identify problems accurately.*
2. *Create appropriate solutions, and match the right people to them.*

3. *Give those people active roles in initiatives' design and communication.*

4. *Respectfully build and maintain school-community-wide consensus around initiative.*

—defined all phases of construction, but worked together so practitioners could concentrate fully on their practices.

To put it another way: All the research, politicking, and legwork Dr. Bob and his administrative team did in the run-up to this crucial planning session were essentially taking care of principles 1, 2, and 4 so the carefully selected practical experts could work on principle 3, planning the Sophomore Academy's teaching and management.[2]

This planning session, then, wasn't really to be about 'engaging teacher-stakeholders to study data, determine root causes, and plan interventions'. More so, it was rather like a football team's huddle just before running a play: a place where the on-field athletes (the football-playing experts, in other words) receive a common strategy from the sideline based on what the sideline coaching staff has deemed most effective in light of their study of the opponent, their understanding of their own personnel, and the current game situation. All players emerge from such huddles with their own responsibilities and play-making strengths, but they are expected to execute them within a common, coaching-staff-directed—read: *not co-created*—objective.

The situation had been assessed, and a theoretical means for making progress on it had been declared. The Academy teachers' only real charges for this two-day 'huddle' were turning the theory into action. Their tasks, simply, were figuring out how they were going to work together and mapping out the to-dos and support needs between now and the beginning of the next school year.

The team's first order of business was getting to know each other better.

In a school like Osseo Senior High, after all, which has a large population and an equally large physical footprint, it's not uncommon for teachers to section off by department and be generally unaware of one another. To wit: my third-floor classroom at one end of the school was nearly a half-mile walk from Kelly Klecker's math classroom in the opposite wing. As a result of this distance (and, flatly, our disciplines' differing 'wirings'), I had never actually been to her classroom before working with her in the Academy—and I was a *six-year* veteran of the school by that point. Before our group could come together on things like unifying philosophies and policies, we had to give one another some background on who we were as professionals and as people.

In lieu of any real structure or directives, we chose to start by sharing with one another why we thought Dr. Bob picked us in the first place: we shared with one another how we did our work with kids, what we found important to uphold in our classrooms and why, and, simply, more in general about what made us tick as people.

To that end, let's meet the Sophomore Academy team, in alphabetical order. (Because I'm an English teacher.)

English: Eric Kalenze (me)

When the Academy team came together in 2004 I was in my sixth year of teaching, and all of them had been at Osseo Senior High. I'd taught English 10 for all of those years and done some comprehensive curriculum- and program-design work for the district, so I was well-familiar with the instructional program's texts and tasks.

As I said, I'm a football guy. (Go Pack Go.) I played offensive line in high school and college, and at the time the Sophomore Academy got going I was a varsity football coach at Park Center Senior High, Osseo Senior's in-district neighbor to the east. (In 2005, though, I returned to Osseo and united my coaching and teaching lives.) Though I recently dropped it to make more time for family and for coaching, I spent my first five years as the school's journalism teacher and newspaper adviser.

I also worked for the Osseo district teaching in the Adult Degree Program a couple nights a week for two years. Though I mainly did it as a way to earn some extra money for my young family (my wife and I had our daughters in 1999 and 2003), this experience turned out to have a remarkable impact on my professional philosophies, instructional expectations, and classroom-managerial policies. For in the Adult Degree Program, I actually had the chance to work with and pick the brains of adults who dropped out of high school and were actively and independently seeking to make up for that choice. At bottom, teaching in the Adult Degree Program removed 'high school dropout' from the abstract and statistical for me, giving me up-close access to these (usually young, but not always) adults' motivations, their post-dropout paths/difficulties, their regrets, their re-awakened academic work ethics, and their view of the world.

Within Osseo Senior's school community, though, I was admittedly a bit difficult to work with. For one thing, I wasn't particularly keen on collaborative teacher planning. The school had recently begun a program of 'collaborative job-embedded professional development' using a Professional Learning Community format (the now-ubiquitous 'PLC', but before consultants like Richard DuFour and his Solution Tree conglomerate helped it catch fire across education[3]), I found the methods and structures more frustrating than fulfilling, and I was the kind of staff member to make my frustrations known—hence Dr. Bob's aforementioned concern for my job satisfaction.

It wasn't so much that I was against collaborating or goal-setting, however. The issue was more that I wasn't appreciating our move to greater standardization. I'd begun doing a lot of independent research and learning a lot more about evidence-supported practices and approaches, and, as these often didn't jibe with the decidedly *non-*evidence-supported practices and approaches of many of my teammates, I wasn't crazy about doing things more like them. In short: while I may have brought a passion for evidence and a willingness to do research for the Sophomore Academy, I also brought a skeptical, impatient attitude.

And when it came to my classroom-management, I was skeptical it could be done by formula or according to any real 'strategies' at all. Essentially, I just was who I was in the classroom, and there were generally few problems. I didn't really have classroom rules, but more an overriding expectation of all-way—yes, from me included—respect: 'In here, you will respect yourself, your classmates, the physical space, and your teacher,' that kind of thing. I guaranteed the students that I'd treat them like adults until things got disrespectful, and then, as the actual adult responsible for it all, I reserved the right to get things back into a respectful line. I didn't use tips, tricks, or any particular 'model' or 'style'. Rather, I worked on creating a culture with expectations and consistent reactions. Simple as that.

For my pre-professional background, I went into education because my schooling was quite possibly the most defining part of my life. Though I'd never pictured myself as a teacher when growing up in my small northwestern-Minnesota hometown (that part came later, well after receiving my undergraduate degree, actually—I went back for a post-baccalaureate certification four years after my college graduation), I appreciated school as a place where I could improve myself, express myself, and lift myself to a better life. My mother and father had both grown up in large families of limited means, and neither of them had earned college degrees. They often had to scrape and claw to keep our family running, and they always insisted I make the most of the many opportunities school presented. They provided lots of moral support, cheerleading, and advocacy, and in turn expected me to finish what I started and do everything to my fullest ability. I followed their direction and, as they promised, I eventually saw opportunities open up through schooling that forever convinced me of the institution's power to transform lives.

Math: Kelly Klecker

Ms. Kelly Klecker was in her fourth year of teaching in Osseo Senior High's math department and was a track and field coach (and avid high school athlete). She started teaching directly after earning her undergraduate degree at central Minnesota's College of St. Benedict, which made her young enough to regularly be mistaken for a student. However, Klecker had seen considerable changes in the department's curriculum sequence, course progressions, and support structures in these first few years. When she began at the school, she taught within a traditional Algebra I-Geometry-Algebra II sequence, which got switched out for a more integrated, 'reform-based' math sequence a year or two later. Thanks to these diverse experiences, Klecker had already developed deep expertise about both the curriculum and how to support students through variously challenging aspects by the time the Academy began. For the youngest member of the Sophomore Academy team, she possessed a rare mix of approachability and wisdom.

And of all of us, she may well have been the most rigid classroom manager. Without raising her voice or breaking from her gentle positivity, she matter-of-factly ran a highly structured classroom environment, with rules and routines that were far more detailed and advanced than anything I could have imagined. (This contribution was crucial to our ultimate decisions about Academy-wide procedures, which will be given more detail in the pages ahead.)

When asked to elaborate on her basic classroom philosophies and styles, Klecker replied, 'In my classroom I always set a tone by acknowledging them as humans in the learning space. I come out and tell them I'm going to learn their names very quickly—I aim to within the first four days, usually—to show I respect their identities and that I value my relationships with them.

'But the way I run things is very organized. To someone coming in it might seem monotonous and boring, but the goal is to get rid of surprises and distractions for kids so they can concentrate on the learning. After that, I'm going to help kids realize they can do it, but never by giving away the answers. I ask a lot of questions to help them move toward answers on their own.'

Asked to reflect on how she developed her 'no-surprises, no-giveaways' style of instruction and classroom-management, Klecker said it may have been more a matter of necessity than anything else. 'When I started teaching, I had kids who were 18 and I was 22. I felt like I had to be strict, to have a lot of rules, so I wouldn't get overwhelmed. I was still figuring out who I was as a teacher in a lot of ways, but it helped me come up with some things I've found to work and that kids like—I mean, I don't think they always enjoyed it in the moment,' she added, laughing. 'But I've found over time that my kids appreciate it. They come back all the time and tell me how I was strict, but that they really felt they could learn from me.'

Klecker's path into the teaching profession, too, was as definite and linear as her classroom management. Having grown up in a Twin Cities-area suburb, she said she can remember knowing she wanted to be a teacher—a math teacher, even more specifically—in the 7th grade, and she traveled the path directly into her practice at Osseo Senior.

'I loved doing math as a kid, and in junior high I started helping my younger sister, then my older sister, with their math. Like with my students now, I wouldn't just give them the answers. I'd help them learn how to do it, and I realized I really liked it when they told me it was helpful. My dad pointed this out to me and how I was into sports, and said maybe I'd make a good teacher and coach. So that's what I decided to be, just like that. Went to college, then came here to teach and coach.'

Biology: Eric Ruska

Unlike Klecker, Mr. Eric Ruska went into teaching because it was a 'default'. Though he went to college with some ideas of becoming an engineer, he admits that his plans were anything but solid by the time he got there.

After stints studying business and accounting—and even working toward getting into medical school—he ended up, with a young family and at the age of 26, volunteering at Minneapolis's South High School purely to see if a career in education might be for him. He quickly found teaching to be a perfect fit: he loved helping people, he enjoyed talking with the kids from day to day, and he liked leading science labs. He even recalled having fun doing *lunch duty*. After going back to earn his teaching credential, his series of false starts and bounces around the career map ultimately led him to a job at Osseo Senior High in 2000.

Very much *like* Klecker, though, who ran the most regimented and strongly routinized classroom of all the teachers gathered to discuss and design the Sophomore Academy, Ruska's classroom was run according to consistently tight rules and high challenges. A Wisconsin-raised, crew-cut-wearing, self-described 'disciple of the old school', Ruska firmly believed kids could master, not just endure, essential content, and he always held students accountable for their behaviors and work habits. At a time when responsibility for students' results seemed to be turning more and more onto educators alone, Ruska was the type of teacher who wouldn't think twice about giving a student a failing grade if they didn't put in the effort.

Surprisingly, however, Ruska didn't build his classroom culture around these rather hard-nosed classroom premiums because he was a highly structured person himself. Much to the contrary, Ruska considers himself to be the *opposite*. To this day, Ruska describes himself as just having too little discipline all the way around, from being on time for events to sitting through (or even attending) meetings he's not engaged in. 'Basically,' he deadpanned to me in an interview, 'I'm better now, but I've never been real structured when it comes to all kinds of things. My very structured wife has to tell me to get it together a *lot*, for sure.'

At bottom, the structure and personal responsibility that have always anchored Ruska's classroom are more a *rejection* of his preferred settings than a *reflection* of them. Having recognized his own lack of discipline since childhood, and having viewed it as making so many things more difficult for him, it's a quality he wished he would've more fully developed. Figuring many of his students at Osseo Senior were coming from similarly unstructured backgrounds (especially those in his adjusted biology course, which was intended expressly for students struggling in regular 10th grade biology), he knew he could help his students become better prepared for the world after high school by putting down clear structures and sticking to them.

'I grew up in a single-parent home, where in some ways it was like, "Do whatever you want,"' Ruska said. 'My mom had high expectations of me, but we didn't really have a lot of guidelines or boundaries. I found out in college that the less structure I had, the less likely I was to be very successful. I ended up always wishing I had the discipline—wished I'd gone to the military, actually, where I might have taken on some of that.

'And when I got into teaching, I knew the kids I was working with probably were coming from the same place. Making sure they didn't ever feel the way I did, I think that's where the whole structure and discipline piece in my teaching all started.'

In his third year teaching at Osseo Senior and his fourth year overall at the time of our Academy planning meeting,[4] Ruska's in-class principles and style were also heavily influenced by a set of deeply veteran teachers he fell in with around the school and through his various coaching assignments. He saw how well those teachers could both build efficient classroom cultures and cultivate strong relationships with kids through no-nonsense, no-gimmicks methods, and then he decided to take them on as his own.

Of all these influential colleagues, though, Ruska said he learned the most from his neighbor in the science department, the late Mr. Brad

Rosch.[5] For while Rosch didn't coach Ruska too heavily or prescribe any sets of practices, his self-discipline and ability to hold students' attention with his sincerity and humor left a strong impression.

'I would watch [Rosch],' Ruska said, 'and think about how I could do the same thing—and if I ever could, because Brad was such a master storyteller. He'd just tell me to take what I could, but to make sure I made it my own. After a while I think I got it, but I had to start with strong rules and expectations, then work with kids so they knew I was on their side. That I did it this way because I cared for them.'

Counselor: Jackie Trzynka

On her way to her job in the counseling office at Osseo Senior, the Sophomore Academy's dedicated counselor Ms. Jackie Trzynka made a few stops that prepared her well for working with the Academy's students—and, importantly, for the Academy's teachers.

More specifically, she'd actually worked as a teacher (a high school social studies teacher, that is, while her husband completed graduate school in Manhattan, Kansas), an experience that few high school counselors can boast or truly identify with. Her first-hand understanding of classrooms' realities informed her counseling practice by making it work cleanly alongside and/or in support of teachers' objectives, giving her a remarkable amount of clout and credibility with the exceedingly classroom-first Sophomore Academy teachers.

Her path through teaching actually routed her toward counseling, however, in how it defined for her the type of impact she wanted to make as an educator. As a young teaching professional who originally studied to help kids as a child psychologist, Trzynka always found leading a classroom limited her ability to identify the neediest students.

'I was just always drawn to the kid who was always showing up late for class, or coming in and putting their head down,' she told me, 'but it's hard when you have to get to the business of teaching a roomful of kids about economics, say. It was clear to me that I had to take another step toward those kids, and I decided to look into a counseling program. When I got into it, I knew this was it: I'd finally found the sweet spot between academics and support for the kids who needed it most.'

Trzynka said she owes her balance of care-taking and structure in part to her small-town upbringing, and in part to her parents. Her father modeled structure: he was a career-military man who later went into farming before organizing groups of growers around their hometown of Cavalier, North Dakota. Trzynka's mother, a nursing professional and the main nurturer of Trzynka and her two siblings, inspired her to always care for others.

'There was a lot of structure and expectations were high when I was very young,' Trzynka said. 'We always had an awareness of how others would see you—about how things you might do and choices you make might impact the family, like small-town life can be. My dad became a leader with other farmers in the area and my mom was always the caretaker, so I always had that balance. I think I really carried all those kinds of things into my work with young people and into supporting teachers' work with kids.'

Social studies: Gerry Zelenak

Out of all of us, only the Sophomore Academy's social studies teacher, Mr. Gerry Zelenak, went into the job because he loved kids. Remember: Klecker had driven a straight line between gratifying childhood moments of helping siblings with math into a teaching career; I somewhat ambled into the profession, following a hearty appreciation for what education had done for me; Trzynka had tried teaching but found a better fit in counseling; and Ruska had had to find his way to the classroom through a few false-start professional experiences.

Zelenak, though, was brought to education by a sheer passion for helping teenagers and his rather uncanny ability to connect with them.

Of all the Sophomore Academy teachers, however, Zelenak might have been the very *least* inclined to pursue education as a career when he was younger. In fact, if not for a few very unexpected and disappointing life events, Zelenak may never have realized how satisfying he found it to work with young people.

Simply, Zelenak never gave teaching a thought throughout his formative years because he spent them so singularly trained on becoming a pilot in the United States Navy. It was an aspiration he had since he was nine years old, and he can to this day pinpoint the event that kicked off this singular focus: a cheer-up trip with his father to see the Blue Angels, the Navy's flight demonstration squadron. The young Zelenak had just endured a tough summer by any standard, but a *terrible* one for a boy under ten. He went through a hip surgery that came with two months in a body cast, therapy to help him learn to walk again, and a permanent screw in his right leg. Plus, his family moved from North Minneapolis to the suburb of Brooklyn Park (and, incidentally, into the Osseo Public School District—he ultimately graduated from the district's Park Center Senior High in 1986). If any kid deserved to see the Blue Angels dance around in the sky, it was the nine-year-old Zelenak.

While it was just meant to cheer him up, the show itself changed him. He didn't just look up at the Blue Angels and see something awesome. The show made him want to *be* a pilot someday.

From that point forward, he put all of his thoughts and energy into someday becoming a pilot in the U.S. military. In high school he met with Navy recruiters instead of college speakers, he opted for taking the military's ASVAB instead of the college-entering ACT, and he signed up with the enlistment office rather than visiting any colleges.

Then, in a deeply ironic twist, Zelenak failed his military physical because of the *screw in his right leg*—the same one that led to him dreaming of being a pilot in the first place.

'I'd put all my eggs into one basket,' Zelenak shared with me. 'And the day of that physical, the whole basket just fell down the hill. Then I bumbled around a couple years, doing various jobs to get by and going to North Hennepin [Community College in Brooklyn Park, MN] because they'd let me in without having to take the ACT. When I was just about done there and not sure what I was going to do, I'd go with the people I worked with out to places like Perkins, a 24-hour coffee shop. They were in high school and I was 21 or so, like this elder-statesman. But with them I started to see I really liked talking to them about the things they were going through personally, at school, or wherever, and I liked helping them see new ways of looking at things. That's the first place it occurred to me that maybe I could make a life out of working with this age group, and I looked into teaching for the first time.'

As working with young people was Zelenak's primary motivation for choosing education, he considered the available disciplines almost as an afterthought. He'd always been drawn to the stories of history, though, so he ultimately made the decision to certify as a social studies teacher and went on to earn his teaching credential at St. Cloud State University about an hour north of the Twin Cities metro.

He got his first teaching job at his high school alma mater, Park Center Senior High, and soon moved to Maple Grove Junior High. While he first thought he'd regret moving to the junior high, Zelenak said the pace, tendencies, and humor of junior high-aged students grew on him pretty rapidly. Working with them, in fact, he was inspired to create many of the novel and clever classroom routines that made his classroom unique and helped him connect better with students. As incentives, for example, he handed out *Z-Bucks*: 'money' he designed and printed, and that students could save and exchange for prizes or classroom privileges. Also (in the pre-interactive-whiteboard classrooms of the 1990s and early 2000s), he built what he called a *Zel-o-Vision 3000*™ system in his classroom: small television sets (that Zelenak picked up at garage sales, by the way) mounted throughout the room and lined together so students could better view classroom visual aids from any seat.

Glad as he was for his time in the junior high and how it helped him expand in these ways, however, he felt it was just time to re-connect with high school-aged students.

'As much as I liked the junior high and loved the kids—and more than I thought I would, for sure,' Zelenak said, 'I was glad to come to Osseo because I was at the point where I just had to have some conversations with people who were closer to adults. People who can keep up with junior high-aged kids for a long time are pretty amazing, but I was running out of the energy to do it.'

Foundational agreements

Once we had a chance to share and process these backgrounds with one another—and, naturally, after an offsite 'team-building' lunch of sub sandwiches—we turned our attention to Dr. Bob's charge: building the Sophomore Academy's premium values.

Drawing from what each of us considered important to running successful classrooms, what we anticipated about the profile of the Academy's students, and what we would need from one another to create an effective learning culture, this part of the strategy session produced the pillars that would hold up the Academy for its duration. While some of these basic values discussions would harden into actual policies and procedures to carry forward into our classroom management, the majority of our work during these two days was directed towards negotiating the key agreements that would guide later decisions and actions (plus reconsiderations and revisions based on new realities as they arose). For while we had no way of knowing what would be in front of us all in our time working together, we knew we'd need a few points to remind ourselves what we were about and what we were out to accomplish if we wanted to make sensible, consistent practice and policy decisions in the future.

Without attempting to recount every detail of that initial planning session, here are some critical points we devoted substantial time/discussion to and achieved definition on.

Uniformity and consistency

With our varied backgrounds and classroom management styles, our team's first point of discussion was around across-Academy rules and expectations—how tightly and how loosely to uphold them from classroom to classroom, and which rules/expectations should warrant various levels of negotiability. As all of us had experience with the downsides of class-to-class differences in behavioral standards and procedures, it was a crucial issue to consider first.

Ask any teacher and they'll tell you: when staying strong on a stance that students don't like, from hats and hoods to cellphones and snacks, or to *whatever* in class, it can be nearly impossible to uphold without reinforcement from your colleagues. ('But Mr. XYZ lets us have snacks! What's your *problem?*') Worse, inconsistently applied rules are one of the surest ways to invite conflicts and confrontations with students.

We knew it was important. Still, it wasn't easy. In fact, it sucked.

For one thing, each of us connected to students and structured our classes differently. Zelenak and I tended to run our classrooms with our 'guts', and Klecker and Ruska were much more structured. Zelenak and I made management decisions very flexibly and in-the-moment according to individual students and situations, believing that no part of classroom management should ever be reduced to flowchart-like logic and efficiency. Klecker and Ruska, on the other hand, were much less relativistic in their classroom decisions. Far more structured and consistent, their classes featured well-defined sets of rules and procedures, attendant consequences to keep things operating by design, and clear systems for pretty well everything between.

Throw in that the four of us were proud teachers who didn't know each other real well, and that we'd to date been given a lot of latitude and autonomy at Osseo Senior (and that I am a flat-out stubborn person), and it should go without saying that becoming more uniform on some things made for a pretty tough conversation.

However, we ultimately landed on that, for the types of kids we were to be serving and our intra-team trust, consistency on at least some matters was not negotiable. On some things, plainly, we'd have to do things like a team. One's own comfort level or teaching style couldn't matter. Simply, we decided this was in the best interest of the kids and our Academy's mission—and, crucially, we agreed that we could *never* openly talk about our differences on these issues with the Academy students.

In reaching this agreement, it is important to include that we did *not* believe we had to create one set of top-to-bottom rules and policies all students had to abide by in all our classes. Indeed, committed as we were to all students' preparation for high school and beyond, we saw it as crucial that we continually worked to build our students' adaptability from situation to situation, teacher to teacher, discipline to discipline, and so on—and we knew that the best way to do this was to exercise these 'switches' via reasonable differences in expectations throughout their days. (With, naturally, lots of supporting messaging, counseling, and reminders. We deliberately agreed to *teach* and *grow* this adaptability, not merely *expect* it.)

At bottom, though, we knew that our classroom policies—and reinforcing them from teacher to teacher—would be the best way to guide students in values and habits we believed were most important. As such, we had to be as uniform on those premium-values-aligned policies as we could, however painful that might be for some of us. Once we came to a team-wide acceptance of this principle, the challenge became deciding which policies/practices had to be expected and carried out non-negotiably in all classes.

Our agreements about Academy-wide consistencies eventually paid off hugely, both in how it united and strengthened us against all manners of student blowback (and there was plenty of blowback—I'll share more in the chapters ahead) and how it actually grew our individual practices. From my perspective, this one decision pushed me to refine my own classroom management in ways I never would have otherwise—and, of course, it allowed me to get a first-hand look at how my preferred ways weren't always successful.

Raising the value of in-class time

Great as our commitment to consistency and uniformity may sound, our resolve was tested almost immediately.

For while we all agreed we had to put a premium on in-class time—attendance, remaining in the classroom, maximizing available class minutes for teaching and learning, and so on—to achieve what we wanted to with the Academy students, we had very different ideas about how to carry it out.

In line with our differing classroom management styles and policies, it turned out that we had very different ways of keeping our students in our classes. Zelenak and I were on one side, continually seeking to incentivize positive class-time usage or make class time more engaging for the Academy's students-to-be, while Klecker and Ruska were squarely on the other. More specifically, Klecker and Ruska thought it might work better to restrict students leaving classes altogether: no locker passes, no bathroom passes.

And their rationale for this rather severe shared policy went like this: if we are putting a premium on gainfully spending every class minute, and if we genuinely want to train our kids to be more prepared and focused in each class, we should force students' hands a bit by taking away the 'outs' of bathroom breaks and locker-runs for forgotten learning materials. Students would have to learn to use their passing times more efficiently or even—*gasp!*—plan ahead a few classes if their lockers and bathrooms were far out of the way of their subsequent classes.

Klecker and Ruska argued that their proposed policies were clear expressions of our mission: give a group of 'at-risk' students sound habits that would ultimately help them succeed as juniors and seniors. And the best way to get them there was not becoming more permissive, letting them out of our sight so they could extend five-minute bathroom breaks into 40 minutes of unsupervised time in the halls, but tightening things a bit and showing them that they did indeed have the discipline necessary to stay in class and learn.

Klecker maintained that a 'closed classroom' had been a key piece of her classroom management for years, and that kids always accepted and met the expectation. While they might not like it at first, she said, it never took long for them to lock into the routine and not question it again—that if it's well-framed and faithfully carried out, the expectation eventually just became part of the way they did things. Of course, the teacher could occasionally bend if it looked like the student was experiencing the kind of discomfort that only a high school cafeteria burrito can deliver. It was meant to be a hard-and-fast rule that improved kids' habits, not one that put them in pain for the sake of becoming more disciplined.

The discussion of these points went on for some time. Zelenak and I couldn't see ourselves mutating into strident rule-enforcers, relying on rigorous structures to deal with situations we were accustomed to managing by sheer feel. Ultimately, however, it started to get a little too cramped and uncomfortable in the school office's conference room, and we still had a lot to cover about how this whole Academy thing was going to look. Maybe it was the crappy air conditioning, or that our first planning day was nearly done and we were getting itchy to see how our substitutes had held up for the day, but at this point Zelenak and I both realized we didn't have a leg to stand on. Klecker and Ruska were absolutely right.

We adopted the 'no leaving' policy because it made such good sense in light of the Academy's objectives. In the name of maintaining consistency and having one another's backs, in other words, I was going to have to grow some new management practices and develop the messages to go with them.

Additionally, once we made our compromises and signed our expectations into Academy 'law', the team imagined a structural change we thought could assist us in carrying out our high premium on in-class time: having my classroom moved from its current place on the third floor to directly across from Zelenak's in the Social Studies wing. This would give our students one very easy transition per day (18 feet—we measured it and later reminded students of it incessantly), essentially leaving them with no good reasons to ever be tardy between those two classes. We raised it to Dr. Bob for approval at the end of our planning session, and he was able to make the move happen in time for our first sections of Sophomore Academy.

Regular collaboration time

If you recall, Dr. Bob had to go through quite a lot—in the forms of schedule arranging, politicking, and marketing—to see that the Sophomore Academy team would have a shared preparation period. He considered it a critical piece of the school-within-a-school's workings, however, in that it would be the one common mechanism constantly and explicitly connecting across the Academy's classrooms. He expected us to make use of that time and space accordingly, to keep our classes and messaging connected. However, in line with his principles, he didn't prescribe or require anything in particular—no meeting structures, no data-review protocols, and no standing agendas.

Our prep was fourth period, so lunch time was built in, offering a much more useful block of time than the typical 55-minute period. To decide how we should use the time, we agreed to use the shared prep period to meet once a week, at minimum. In this weekly meeting, our sole concern would be Academy students: which kids seemed to be struggling in which classes, useful approaches for reaching struggling kids, big flags raising in classes between individuals and/or groups of students, and so on. To guide these conversations, we mutually agreed to bring updated grade books to each meeting. These would allow us to see how students were doing to stay on track with grades, assignments-completed, attendance, and behavior—and, importantly, to notice when a kid was falling off in one class but not others (starting a conversation with the teacher about possible strategies) or falling in all classes at once (starting a conversation about something bigger going on that Trzynka could address).

None of us had yet heard the term, but we were basically planning to execute a 'Response-to-Intervention' (RtI) or 'Multi-Tiered System of Supports' (MTSS) intervention and action-planning process like those so commonly found in U.S. schools today.[6] Our plan was to use objective data to begin our discussion about students, then work to solve problems across the entire Academy group ('Tier 1' for all students, in other words—but technically 'Tier 2' as the Academy itself was already a targeted intervention) or to direct more focused supports directly to individuals ('Tier 3') based on the kids' work-completion, attendance, and behavior rates. In contrast to the structured departmental PLC meetings, which revolved around improving consistency of content requirements (and left me feeling pretty cold), the only content to be discussed in the Academy team's weekly meetings was our *students*.

We didn't have a standard format or meeting protocol we were planning to follow. We didn't need one. The time and the routine were enough, and all kid-related concerns—a free-flowing conversation of academic, behavioral, and social topics—would be in play. We were ready to talk about whatever:

'Angela hasn't turned in an assignment in my class for two weeks. Any of you know what's up with her?'

'Rocco's missed three classes in a row. Is his dad back in the hospital? Can we do anything?'

'I'm just struggling in general right now with second hour. Ever since the fight between Ashely and Ryan, it's like nothing can get done. How are you all handling them?'

At least to start, the idea was to convene, voice our concerns about the kids, and plan next steps or share advice from there. Again, our sole goal was to get together as a team (at a minimum) weekly, and to get our kids—not administrative details or SMART goals or whatever else—on the table to see how we could help them. If it was too free-form or too much like a vent session, we would build in efficiencies later.

While our initial thinking was for this weekly meeting to keep the team connected about strategies and individual student concerns, the connection between us became much more continual and sturdy over time.

Selection of students

After reaching agreement on the above Academy-wide premium and policy points, we wrapped up our planning session with our immediate next steps. As we weren't going to require any additional training, materials integration, or curricular structuring, though, there plainly wasn't a whole lot we could do before the first round of Academy kids got to us in the fall.

Who these kids were going to be, however, was still a major question, so we took some time to figure out just who to bring into the Academy and how we were going to get them there.

Beginning from the basic guidelines we had (e.g. fill two sections of no more than 25 kids per section, locate and serve students identified as at-risk of falling behind on credits), we first established some profile parameters. Doing so was more challenging than we initially anticipated, in that there certainly was no particular *type* of student.

We didn't just want kids with significant histories of behavior issues, for example, as many kids needing the kind of intensive intervention and outreach we were planning didn't have patterns of acting out. Rather, lots of kids in any given high school are at-risk because they so prefer to *not* engage in classes. The kids we sought out were not so much falling through the cracks as running for them. And the range of students was wide. Some kids regularly attend class but only rarely participate. Others only finish learning tasks that fit their narrow interests (art project yes, reading assignment *no way*). Still others go absent for days or weeks at a time. Most of these kids, though, find out how to get by. They learn how much they can push the boundaries, which is precisely what makes them so hard to find—especially if you're only looking at the data. If we started with objective behavior data and chose kids from the most-referred lists, we would miss many opportunities to connect to students who needed our help but didn't always 'show it' on paper.

Similarly, we didn't necessarily target students whom standardized-test data had shown to be significantly behind grade-level or who had very low 9th grade grade point averages; Osseo Senior had remedial courses designed for these students, after all, often with extra in-room support staff (that we in the Academy would not have) to get the students additional academic help, so we didn't want to duplicate existing school structures and/or resources.

Where several U.S. states have instituted early warning systems in the past decade or so to surface kids with various statistical risk factors as they enter high school (from attendance data to socio-economic status to reports of substance abuse and several others),[7] these practices were effectively non-existent—or at least not accessible to our team—at the time. Though they would likely have helped us find the diverse range of kids and sometimes 'data-invisible' risk factors we knew we had to look for in our inaugural group of Academy students, we were more or less on our own.

In short, we weren't *just* looking for the kids who were always acting up or always bombing out academically, though we expected to see plenty of them in our rosters. We also wanted those kids on the bubble. Kids who hadn't really cracked *yet*, but who very well could under a year's worth of high school pressures. Data can't always tell us who these kids are. But teachers always can. So we decided to go straight to the source. We engaged directly with our district's feeder junior high schools.

Rather than ask for a full data dump with comprehensive quantitative information on grades, test scores, attendance, behavior, and so on, though, we determined it'd be best to canvas junior high teachers and counselors using more holistic criteria. We crafted a rough communication that introduced ourselves and the Sophomore Academy we were launching, then made one simple request: 'Please give us the names of a few dozen kids you can see struggling once they reach the high school, each with a brief statement of why you're putting them forward.'

Trzynka coordinated this communication, and we committed to review the lists we got back more thoroughly (i.e. according to various objective data that Trzynka agreed to gather and organize upon receiving a few dozen names from each school) to establish the intended section sizes and right mixes.

In the next section I'll share more about the groups of students we eventually chose from this initial broad-brush request, how we notified them in advance of their placement, and what it all looked like after pulling the classes together.

* * *

While the Academy's initial planning meeting may seem like an awful lot of discussion for matters like hall passes, team meetings, and student selection, it was all critical for the Sophomore Academy. Indeed, the decisions we reached—and the way we reached them—are incredibly relevant to the whole experience, the nature of practical growth and the realities of collective school improvements.

The policy decisions we made together, after all, pushed me out of my comfort zone of preferred practices. I didn't agree with them at first. And, to be honest, I was scared of how *hard* they would be to implement on my own. But my colleagues helped me see that these decisions were good for my kids' growth. I couldn't afford to resist them. And after I made it over that threshold of acceptance, I realized that new ways of handling locker passes or homework assignments or class-wide consequences would indeed not kill me or my students—and that (shocker) they would *help my classroom run more efficiently and safely.*

Some of these classroom-managerial practices were much stricter than what I tended toward in my career to that point, so actually making the shifts would likely never have happened without this process. Once I understood the rationales behind the practices better via the Academy team's process and felt backed-up via our unified approach, though, I was willing to execute them to the best of my ability. (And, thanks to my teammates' continual support and advice as we went along, I was able to refine and strengthen the practices to work for my context—more on those processes in the next section.)

Then, after these kinds of practices took hold in my classroom and I was able to see the stronger structures actually affecting students' choices and behaviors for the better, I came to consider them to be 'right-side-up': classroom-managerial principles and practices that could (somewhat drastically, if necessary) move students toward understandings and behaviors that will help them prepare for the expectations of mainstream institutions.[8]

None of these improvements to my classroom practice could have happened, I've come to realize, without this initial planning session. For truly, it was there that I first came to see that I had not gone far enough in terms of behavioral and classroom-cultural expectations. How much instructional and relationship-building time had I thrown away, for instance, by indiscriminately letting kids leave class to meet (hardly urgent) personal needs? How many students had I allowed to leave a couple times per week, at ten or so minutes per trip, for the vending machine, their locker, the bathroom, or whatever? Not only did my preferred practice take them out of the learning environment, it may have prevented them from establishing sound self-regulation habits. I could have expected more from them. (Eventually, the Academy taught me I should have.)

To put it another way: I was comfortable tweaking my classes' academic demands according to more right-side-up principles thanks to my independent research (particularly on the importance of background knowledge to effective reading comprehension,[9] maintaining academic intensity,[10] and increasing the volume of reading I required of students[11]). But it took the suggestion and reinforcement of my Sophomore Academy teammates to push my classroom-management in a similar direction.

It's an approach to practical and school improvements that checks many crucial 'improvement science' boxes but, as far as schools are concerned and organized, does so far more effectively. All parts of Dr. Bob's improvement principles were informed by his school's data and existing evidence of promising practices, but also by what truly makes teachers tick and how schools actually operate—never according to generalized notions of how large, complex organizations make improvements happen.

Beginning with the next section, I'll share more about how each of the Sophomore Academy educators had their own practices and perspectives pushed by our shared experience, as well as how Dr. Bob replicated other improvement actions throughout Osseo Senior High around the same time.

Taken together, these types of practice-transformations are intended as the main focus of this book. For from an enterprise-wide standpoint, the type of practice-transformation process Dr. Bob enabled at the Sophomore Academy and larger levels is crucially important. Indeed, in light of all the money, time, and angst spent to change educators' day-to-day practices only to produce frustrating and inconsistent returns (see massive teacher-evaluation systems,[12] annual standardized testing,[13] enormous spending on professional development,[14] to name just three), education's decision-makers should be paying close attention to any sequence of events, pressures, compromises, and/or supports that can lead to positive practice changes—at a fraction of the cost.

The next section will focus on the Sophomore Academy years themselves: who the kids were, noteworthy challenges each group (and, naturally, the Academy teachers) had to manage, various victories and setbacks, and lessons carried forward into succeeding years.

I'll also introduce the Continuous School Improvement team (or, affectionately, CSI), a strategic team Dr. Bob assembled in these same years to plan and facilitate practice improvements at larger scales.

Endnotes

1. In recent years, 'improvement science' approaches—which work to solve specific problems of practice via considerable data study and following improvement cycles to develop, test, and refine practical solutions—have made great inroads into education, thanks especially to work by Anthony Bryk at the Carnegie Foundation for the Advancement of Teaching. See: Bryk, A, et al. (2015) *Learning to Improve: How America's Schools Can Get Better at Getting Better.* Cambridge, MA: Harvard Education Press. Though improvement science approaches hardly have a proven track record for enabling meaningful, durable improvements in schools (and I personally believe they will ultimately disappoint the field on this score for many reasons—see this book's final section for a more in-depth commentary), the field should count on only seeing more of the improvement science jargon and methodology in coming years: The Bill and Melinda Gates Foundation, for example, issued a major Request for Proposals in 2018 to fund intermediaries for Networks for School Improvement, all working specifically around a structured continuous improvement process. See: Bill and Melinda Gates Foundation. (2018) 'Glossary: Request for Proposal on Networks for School Improvement (Late 2018)' Available at: www.k12education.gatesfoundation. org/glossary-request-proposal-networks-school-improvement

2. Which, incidentally, is one very worthwhile advantage of Dr. Bob's approach over a typical improvement science approach. Where improvement science takes great pains to have practitioners arrive at root causes together—to fully engage with the process and deeply understand for themselves, apparently—Dr. Bob essentially did all the rationale and justification study before he ever approached the team and the full staff in this case. This allowed the professionals the space they needed to figure out how to execute on the initiative 'mission' and, importantly, didn't open the process to multiple contrasting ideas of what's actually causing the issues we're seeing—a cliff I've watched many well-meaning root-cause analyses tumble off of, and one reason I'm skeptical education will ever get all Bill Gates thinks it will out of the improvement science processes.

3. For an early PLC-describing title, released right around the time the Sophomore Academy was coming together, see: DuFour, R., *et al.* (2004) *Whatever It Takes: How Professional Learning Communities Respond When Kids Don't Learn.* Bloomington, IN: Solution Tree.

4. Ruska started at the school in 2000, was accessed for budget reasons after the 2001-02 school year, then came back in 2003 after a year teaching in nearby Spooner, Wisconsin.

5. In a great blow to the entire Osseo Senior High community, Rosch passed away unexpectedly in 2017, just a few years into his retirement.

6. Samuels, C. (8 February 2017) 'What Are Multitiered Systems of Supports?' Education Week. Available at: www.edweek.org/ew/articles/2016/12/14/what-are-multitiered-systems-of-supports.html

7. U.S. Department of Education. (September 2016) 'Issue Brief: Early Warning Systems.' U.S. Department of Education: Office of Planning, Evaluation and Policy Development. Policy and Program Studies Service. Available at: https://www2.ed.gov/rschstat/eval/high-school/early-warning-systems-brief.pdf

8. Kalenze, E. (2014) *Education is Upside-Down: Reframing Reform to Focus on the Right Problems.* Lanham, MD: Rowman & Littlefield.

9. Hirsch, E., D. (1987) *Cultural Literacy: What Every American Needs to Know,* (Ed.) New York, New York: Random House. See also: Recht, D., R. and Leslie, L. (1988) 'Effect of Prior Knowledge on Good and Poor Readers' Memory of Text', in *Journal of Educational Psychology*, 80 (1), pp. 16-20. Washington, DC: American Psychological Association. See also: Wolfgang, S. and Körkel, J. (1989) 'The knowledge base and text recall: Evidence from a short-term longitudinal study', in *Contemporary Educational Psychology*, 14 (4), pp. 382-93.

10. Adelman, C. (1999) *Answers in the Tool Box: Academic Intensity, Attendance Patterns, and Bachelor's Degree Attainment.* Washington, DC: U.S. Department of Education.

11. Cunningham, A. and Stanovich, K. (1998) 'What Reading Does for the Mind', in *American Educator*, 22 (1-2), pp. 8-15.

12. Kraft, M. and Gilmour, A., F. (1 June 2017) 'Revisiting the Widget Effect: Teacher Evaluation Reforms and the Distribution of Teacher Effectiveness', in *Educational Researcher*, 46 (5), pp. 234-239.

13. McCluskey, N. (9 February 2015) 'Has No Child Left Behind Worked?' Cato Institute. Available at: www.cato.org/publications/testimony/has-no-child-left-behind-worked

14. TNTP (4 August 2015) 'The Mirage: Confronting the Hard Truth About Our Quest for Teacher Development'. Available at: www.tntp.org/publications/view/the-mirage-confronting-the-truth-about-our-quest-for-teacher-development

Part Two

2004-2008: Constructing a Culture

This section focuses on the years 2004-2008, when the Sophomore Academy was in operation at Osseo Senior High. Throughout, I'll give a closer look at the learning culture the Academy teachers, in line with Dr. Bob's improvement vision, created for the variously 'at-risk' kids placed into the Academy. I'll also share how Dr. Bob's philosophies about shared leadership strategically shaped other school improvements.

The next group of chapters focuses on the Academy itself to show what exactly came to life (and how) when the best teachers for this particular job were given the right mix of direction and autonomy. In short, they show what we in the Academy actually did to get our kids *stable*, and what we did to help them become *able*.

The purpose of the Academy, after all, was twofold. It was not simply to provide a softer high school landing spot, one where each year's group of 50 or so students was made properly comfortable or *stable*. Much to the contrary: for us to succeed with the charge Dr. Bob had given us, we'd have to move kids placed in the Academy as far as possible from one state ('likely to struggle', that is, per their junior high histories) to another (passing the sophomore year's core courses, plus equipped to handle the remainder of high school) over the course of the year we had with them. We had to get them stable academically and socially, in other words, but then we had to build up their school-related habits and attitudes so the students would be *able* to succeed in school without an Academy apparatus around them. Much like a building-renovation team, we were eventually going to have to pull down all the stabilizing scaffolds (the 's' in 'stable') and dedicated time (the 't'), and then hope like heck the students would be stronger and better prepared for the rest of high school.

The next group of chapters in this section will be more specific about how we did this, all informed by files from Academy classes, surveys of Academy alumni, and many conversations I conducted with Academy teachers, administrators, and students over the course of 2018—ten years out from when the Academy came to a close. While our collective recall of events is not perfect, and while the sample of Academy students is not fully complete (using social media resources, I was able to make contact with around half of the original Academy students), the chapters here should give a good look at the Academy's learning culture and expectations, as well as how the Academy's students and educators now view the Academy's impact on them as people and professionals.

The main point of these chapters will be to show the Academy classrooms in action, not only in concept. And, of course, with regard to this book's overall arguments about effective school improvement, they are meant to illustrate what the right team of teachers, working on the right issue, and given the right mix of autonomy and support, can accomplish. I'll describe a number of instructional and managerial choices we made to help students genuinely feel they belonged to a community, they were supported, they could (and would) meet academic and behavioral expectations, and that they—no matter what they'd experienced previously inside or outside of school—held the keys to their destinies. You'll see how hard and how continually the Academy teachers had to work to keep things together, as well as how far we sometimes had to go off-script to do so. Also, you'll see how our students (mostly between ages 25-30 as of this writing) now look back on their Academy participation: how it felt to be placed there, what kinds of connections they made within the Academy, what worked out for them, what did not, and more.

Making school improvement a whole-school effort

Aligned with my intent to discuss how school improvements can (and should) build from within schools, the last two chapters of this section will describe the work and impact of Osseo Senior's Continuous School Improvement (CSI) team, a shared-leadership group that played a key role in the school's all-around collaborative improvement culture.

CSI was an improvement-planning body that Dr. Bob identified, invited, and initiated in 2004, the same year the Sophomore Academy opened, and its purpose was to act as a 'kitchen cabinet'-like counterpart to Osseo Senior's existing team of department chairs, the Building Leadership Team (BLT). Where BLT members deliberated changes/updates to school-wide policies, logistics, and operations (often issues of compliance coming from the district's central office or the state department of education) before broadcasting relevant information to their respective departments, the CSI team's explicit purpose was to concentrate on creating and championing school improvements in a more 'classroom-up' direction.

Dr. Bob added the CSI team because he felt that the BLT, by sheer limitations of definition and time (they met for 90 minutes once per month), would never be able to look out further than the school's most pressing administrative matters. To put it another way: where BLT was crucial to Osseo Senior maintaining effective operations in near terms, Dr. Bob felt he needed a CSI-type group dedicated to building new and better operations for the future.

Also, it was about genuinely handing some of the school-design work over to teachers, the same people he always considered to be most important to a school's success. And as many of his staff in the mid-2000s would likely work there long past his retirement (ten years or so from this point, in 2015), Dr. Bob felt it made good sense to get teachers in on the improvement-construction team. 'Of course I want CSI to think about what we can get better at now,' Dr. Bob would say to the team, 'but always think out to a time when I'm not here. Try to think about making the school you all want to work in someday. Let's think about how we can start doing some of those things.'

And in doing so, Dr. Bob instituted and coordinated a type of shared school leadership and data-driven school improvement that was well ahead of curves now well-grooved into the education enterprise. (Only, of course, much less formulaic and much more authentically teacher-designed and effective than the ones so often operating today—precisely why the CSI model is worth looking at.)

CSI's part in this overall story took a while to reach an impactful level, though, as they didn't seem sure what they should be working on. (It's something I feel comfortable saying as, full disclosure, I was one of CSI's charter members. So, too, was Academy social studies teacher Gerry Zelenak.) They mainly spent their first year or so working on superficial issues of staff morale, organizing 'improvements' like social events and scavenger hunts. (Yes, really. And as such, I'll skip the early part of their story and round back to their contribution a little later in this section.) After the team established a standing set of mission points, though, and began organizing actual improvement work—actions informed by various performance data and the team members' day-to-day observations of school climate, performance, and relationships—it eventually helped the larger staff build practices that were truly woven into the fabric of Osseo Senior High. And in addition, several members of the original CSI team ultimately went on to become leaders themselves—as school administrators in the Osseo district and elsewhere, as activities directors, as education-doctorate holders, and, like me, education researchers/writers.

Plus—and to tie some separate strands of this book together—CSI also occasionally drew up promising practices according to what worked according to what worked in the Sophomore Academy. This was due in part to my and Zelenak's membership on CSI, but more so to the CSI team's general openness to effective approaches. The team was always open to hearing about what was working with our school's neediest kids, and the Sophomore Academy provided a built-in trial environment.

For now, let's look in on that Sophomore Academy itself.

In particular, let's start with how the Academy's students—and, subsequently, the team—dealt with learning they had been placed in our little school-within-a-school. For while we thought it would be a great way to help them get their high school careers off to positive starts, the kids weren't always as enthusiastic about the Academy 'opportunity' as we were.

Chapter 6

Getting Stable

'The beginnings of a forest is one of the
ugliest things on the planet. It's bleak
and your neighbours hate you.'

– Felix Dennis

'You can play hard. You can play aggressive. You can
give 120%. But if one guy is out of position, then
someone is running through the line of scrimmage
and he is going to gain a bunch of yards.'

– Bill Belichick

Near the end of the previous chapter, I explained the mixed-methods selection process we used to populate our rosters of Academy students: part quantitative student performance data, part qualitative recommendations from junior high counselors. I shared how we made our request of junior high counselors rather broad (i.e. 'Please give us the names of a few dozen kids you can see struggling once they reach the high school'), hoping to find more than just serial class-skippers, frequent fighters, or habitual assignment-droppers, and how we did so according to what we knew about typical detection criteria and how they can fall short in identifying the kids we were so hoping to reach. In our experience, some of the kids most in need of extra support do everything they can to *evade* attention, and we were bent on catching those kids too.

At bottom, the Academy was supposed to get to—and, of course, build up—all the credit-risky kids it could. If we only found them after sophomore year, reams of local and national statistics told us it'd be too late to do much about it.

A rough entry

Once this group was selected (via work Jackie Trzynka led with our feeder junior high schools' counseling offices and in consultation with the Academy's teachers) and registered, we welcomed our first Sophomore Academy class in the fall of 2004.

In doing so, though, we chose to forego any kind of fanfare or announcement. Simply, we thought the kids might feel too singled-out or embarrassed if we made too big a deal out of the Academy from the outset, and that was no way to start off the year. Instead, we basically let them show up like they were any other students, and then we set to teaching them. We figured there'd be plenty of time and opportunity in the months ahead to explain how this Academy thing was going to hold together, why we were doing it, and so on. Starting everything that way, though, seemed to us like it would just waste a lot of time and set all the wrong tones.

...and man, did they let us *have it.*

Not right away, of course, as it took them a while to even notice what was going on. But by about fifth period of the first day, when they'd seen three of their five periods contain exactly the same set of classmates[1] —and, of course, that all of those classes featured restrictive behavior expectations like no food/drink, no passes out of class for lockers or bathrooms, and the like—they put it all together. They could see easily that, whatever was going on here, it wasn't anything like the high school experience they'd been picturing for years. Keep in mind, they were sophomores entering their first year of high school. (The Osseo district's junior high included grades 7-9, while high school covered grades 10-12.) They thought they would be treated more like adults. They thought they would meet and mix with all kinds of new kids. This wasn't that.

Looking back on that first day, Kelsey Ubel (née Chapman) recalled how her initial first-day-of-high-school giddiness got jerked up, around, and, finally, down to outright disappointment over the course of that first day. Now a 30-year-old professional and wife (she married her husband Josh in February of 2017), Kelsey has the same blonde hair, big smile, and direct demeanor as she had on that first day. 'I remember talking to people, comparing schedules, being worried about getting to the math hall, that kind of first-day stuff,' Kelsey said, her voice bubbly with remembered excitement. 'When I could see on their schedules that all these people were going to the same classes I was, over and over, I wondered what was going on. I thought it was okay again when I got to my typing class and saw all different people from the Academy kids. For an hour I stopped being scared I was in some "reject class" or something.

'But then by fifth hour, when I saw all the same Academy people again in one big group, I knew what was going on. I felt blindsided. I was actually very pissed off and kind of embarrassed.'

One of Kelsey's classmates, Davar McGee, remembered the Academy's first-day uncertainty similarly: 'At first I thought it was cool because I had all these classes with all kinds of kids I was hanging out with a lot at the time, like Je'Vonne [Woodson] and Abdi [Mohamed]. When I started to think about it, though, I was like, "What kind of *Dangerous Minds*-type stuff is this?"[2] I wasn't too sure about it. I didn't like being thought of as a slow kid, but I didn't rush to hate it.'

Davar's friend Abdi Mohamed, however, did not share Davar's patience. As far as he was concerned, the Academy structure felt a whole lot worse than any hackneyed teacher-as-savior message movie ever could. 'I thought it was really like a prison—or a halfway house, at least,' he said, with a chuckle. 'I was new to high school. I wanted to experience it. Here I was going to have to be with all the same people all day long. And some of them, I already knew from junior high—some I was cool with, but others I knew I didn't get along with, like *really* didn't get along with. When I saw what was going on, I wasn't happy.'

The suspicious and frustrated simmer described by Kelsey, Davar, and Abdi picked up intensity over the course of that day, then boiled fully over in the day's final class, math with Kelly Klecker. There, the students rose together to confront Klecker about just what was going on, barraging her with questions:

'Why are we all in the same classes?!'

'What's with all the strict rules?!'

'How long will this all last?!'

'Why am I *in here*?!'

The kids barraged her with questions she wasn't prepared to answer. She got flustered. So she retreated to what she knew: the Academy's mission. She thought of everything our group had planned out so carefully over the past months. And what came out was:

'Well, you're all just a very, uh, *special* group of students.'

Ouch.

Things got so combative in that period, in fact, that it sticks out in Klecker's memory as one of the more eye-opening moments of the entire

Sophomore Academy experience. Now age 41, Klecker actually sits up a little straighter when she talks about this moment from her mid-20s.

'Until that point I'd taught a lot of lower-level math classes, so I'd seen a lot of kids who had pretty big needs. Not just in math, but in every part of school. I thought I knew how to deal with them,' Klecker said. 'But when that group came that day and started in on me—and it was all of them together, so angry, and I was struggling for answers—I saw for the first time just how tough behavior could be. I knew we were going to have to work together to get a handle on it, or I wouldn't ever get to teaching math.'

In the days that followed (and in part because Klecker unfortunately used the word 'special' in that embattled day-one class discussion—a slip the rest of us teachers in the Academy good-naturedly never let her live down), a number of the Academy's more vocal students began referring to our school-within-a-school as the 'Special Ed Academy'. It was self-effacingly funny on the one hand, but on the other it was meant to continually remind us teachers that their placement into the Academy *hurt*. While many of these kids may have had issues in school before, most of them had never yet been formally singled out as 'slow' or 'needing extra help'. And as such, they definitely didn't appreciate that Osseo Senior had taken it upon itself to levy this designation—or, perhaps more especially, to restrict these students' views of the larger high school as a result. Nobody asked them if they wanted to join an Academy, anyway.

While we Academy teachers generally defrayed the kids' 'Special Ed Academy' talk with assurances about support, the statistically crucial hump of sophomore year, and so on to their faces, we were behind the scenes viewing the kids' branding as a dare of sorts: 'Show us,' they seemed to be saying, 'that we're going to have a positive high-school experience, socially and academically. And don't you *think* of treating us like those special ed kids. We're not them.'

One day in, and we already had a number of challenges piling up: we had to cool the initial heated reaction among the Academy kids, obviously, but we also needed some common big-picture principles and messaging to negate the 'Special Ed Academy' message and perception. If we didn't, we knew it'd be incredibly difficult to get to the jobs of teaching and learning.

Learning to frame

These early challenges made us put our common preparation time and required once-weekly meeting to immediate good use.[3] Unlike the professional learning community (PLC) structure and format Osseo Senior had adopted and that were arranged according to academic department (and that had, you may recall, caused me great frustration), these types of challenges were precisely what our meetings were designed to address: for having no common subject matter or assessments to review to plan around, the Academy team's PLC dealt only with *students, not content*. And as such, we were able to take flare-ups like those that happened in the year's opening weeks and draw up our responsive approaches and strategies.

We had to do all this re-grouping in our classrooms during our shared prep period, which never gave us much time, let alone peace and quiet. The distractions of the day were still there—planning and grading, coaching details, and the like. The hallway din seeped in under the door. And we had to cram ourselves into the students' desks. But we made it work. In the Academy team meetings following that explosive first day, we spent significant amounts of time building clean, consistent messages about what the Academy was going to be and why the students had landed there in the first place. Coming up with a collective message was challenging, because we knew we wanted to play defense and offense simultaneously.

On the more defensive side (and to negate the emerging 'Special Ed Academy' label and mindset), we didn't want the Academy students to believe Osseo Senior as a whole thought less of their abilities. Indeed, we had every intention of getting the best out of these kids, and we felt we were creating an environment where that would happen. But to do so, we were going to have to get across unequivocally that the Academy's design and expectations were put in place because we believed in their strengths, not because the Academy was the school's best strategy for containing their weaknesses.

This was important to get right and to get repeating, mainly because the kids we were dealing with could be so quick to activate complicated defense mechanisms when they felt hurt. The 'Special Ed Academy' label is a perfect example.

In order to protect their own emotions and to carve out definite social spaces for themselves, the students who coined and embraced the 'Special Ed Academy' term essentially converted the school's assessment of them as 'needing extra' into something like a badge of honor, only in reverse—a piece of school-bestowed proof that they were 'bad kids' or 'dumb kids'. They weren't embracing 'bad' or 'dumb' status/identity because they wanted to be thought of that way (in interviews/surveys, most Academy alumni reported feeling hurt by this assessment), of course. Rather, as adolescents, they deeply value having a definite social status/identity—something to help others know who they are and what they are about.[4]

As this was a status/identity they could only live *down* to, though, it was, naturally, the very last thing we teachers wanted. To borrow from *Academic Tenacity: Mindsets and Skills that Promote Long-Term Learning*, a Bill and Melinda Gates Foundation-funded report by psychologists Carol Dweck, Gregory Walton, and Geoffrey Cohen released several years after the Academy concluded, we wanted to motivate Academy students by getting them 'to think of themselves and school in certain ways in order to want to learn and in order to learn successfully...[and to] regulate themselves in ways that promote learning'.[5]

We had to act smart and act fast, though. If we didn't control the message here, the most vocal and most self-defensive among the Academy students absolutely would. We agreed together to play up how the Academy was a protection of their future in high school and beyond, not a punishment of their junior-high pasts—and were explicit to show them how they were receiving the same learning tasks and curricula as non-Academy counterparts in the 10th grade registered for the same course.

When a student felt the need to take a dig at the Academy—to remind me that our collective lack of belief in them was the worst thing we could have done to any kid, and that they were still taking all of this very personally—they would start in with the 'Special Ed Academy' or 'you guys just think we're the stupid kids' routine.

I had to tackle this head on, as the team agreed it that ignoring these remarks wasn't sufficient. We had to actively shut them down.

Robert was a frequent offender in those early days, usually after I called him on a missed assignment or a poor effort. He was plenty smart, but didn't know it yet, and leaning on his 'special' status quickly became a go-to excuse. So when he got revved up, I made a real *show* of it.

'All right, Robert,' I said. 'I know you're going to keep pushing, so let's talk about this.'

I walked over to my daily agenda board. I pointed to the 'regular' English 10 agenda for the day and the 'Sophomore Academy' English 10 one just below it.[6] 'Show me, Robert. If I think you're so *stupid*, why would I have you doing the same thing I have all my 10th graders doing today?'

Robert went silent. He didn't have a leg to stand on, and we both knew it.

But I wasn't quite done with the show.

'Does anyone see a difference here?' I asked. 'Anyone?'

I paused, scanned the room, and made meaningful eye contact with *every student.*

'Again, everyone: We're doing the same thing here the non-Academy kids are. What's "Special Ed" or "slow" about that?'

[Silence.]

'We done here with that, then?'

[Silence.]

'Good. Now, where we left off...'

On the other hand, we most certainly wanted to balance our 'we believe in you, we *promise*' theme with the idea that, like it or not, the actions and attitudes one chooses in life absolutely have consequences. They dared us to hold them to the same standards as all their other sophomore classmates. We double-dared them to act like the near-adults we knew they were.

In our individual classrooms and across the Academy, we considered it a core value that students take personal responsibility for their academic and behavioral actions. We knew the Academy's classrooms would give lots of academic support and build lots of great relationships. It's why the four of us were selected, after all. But hand-in-hand with this, kids in the Academy classrooms would also have no doubts about what their jobs were. To put it another way: at the end of a given grading period, there'd be no question about whom was responsible for the grade logged on one's report card.

With that premium in mind, we wanted to get across to the Academy students—and with complete certainty—that it was their responsibility to address the impressions they'd all made as junior high school students. These impressions were diverse, ranging from academic performance issues to work habits to behavior patterns: class grades not reflecting potential, frequently missing assignments, volatile family/home situations, low standardized test scores, general lack of engagement/drive/self-advocacy, arriving at school inebriated, missing 50 or more school days in the past year, and on and on. To a student, though, the impressions they'd put on paper all said rather loudly that 'success in high school' looked a little dicey.

To this end, we put together actions and messages that told them, in effect, 'These records are indeed yours. Multiple adults at your junior high looked over hundreds of records before recommending *you* for the Sophomore Academy, and we at Osseo Senior confirmed that recommendation. The evidence shows we should be concerned about you. If you don't want to be seen this way, it's on you to change it. How are you planning to do that? Others will judge you based on your record for the rest of your life, whether they've met you or not. Your adult life starts sooner than you think. It's time to be mindful of the impression your high school transcript makes. We're here to help you with that.'

In all, we needed clear, convincing, and coherently shared messaging to bring the Academy students around to what we hoped to accomplish with them. If we could get kids to accept these ideas, we were fairly confident that we could alter students' interpretations and perceptions of our chosen policies and rationales—and then, of course, largely stay the course with those policies and rationales. It was way too early to start thinking of abandoning things we'd put so much thought into, all over an initial burst of blowback.

The inaugural Academy class's resistance forced us to get better at our counter-messaging strategies in a hurry. We hadn't really formed a reaction plan heading in because, frankly, we didn't know what to expect. For all we knew, the kids would see the Sophomore Academy as an awesome deal: smaller classes, familiar faces, and a team of teachers eager to keep them on track. It didn't turn out this way of course, but that first cold splash of reality turned out to be extremely valuable. In fact, collective message-planning turned out to be a primary concern of ours over the Academy's four years. And over time, we actually became quite good at *framing*, or influencing our students' choices and behaviors through the language we used.[7]

We didn't really think of what we were doing as framing in the early days of the Academy, of course. In fact, I don't recall that any of us ever used the term. After the fortuitous release in fall 2004 of cognitive linguist George Lakoff's *Don't Think of an Elephant!: Know Your Values and Frame the Debate* (which I read in a fit of political pique during 2004's presidential election season), though, we realized it's what we'd been doing all along. Lakoff's ideas then guided us, defining and refining the pieces we'd been doing rather by feel to that point.

At bottom—and in line with Lakoff—our goal was never to lie, euphemize, or 'spin'. We had no interest in deceiving students to elicit surface changes as this was not, after all, solely about creating compliant classrooms. Rather, our goal was to get our students to genuinely change their concepts of themselves in regard to their schooling. And in many cases, this meant building entirely *new mental frames* in our students, not simply throwing our facts at their established ways of thinking. From Lakoff, we learned that such an approach as cognitively futile anyway, in that 'to be accepted, the truth must fit people's frames. If the facts do not fit a frame, the frame stays and the facts bounce off.'[8]

As such, we followed Lakoff's four important points—'Show respect, Respond by reframing, Think and talk at the level of values, and Say what you believe'—wherever we could. As with our appeal to students' values of 'definite social identity' and 'reclaiming respect from others' in the examples above, we honestly prepared and packaged our perspectives in ways that aligned to our students' (read: not *our*) values, then aligned messages between ourselves to begin repeating. The process took a good amount of collaborative deliberation, but it was worth it as we watched students come around to the Academy way of seeing and doing things.

(For more examples of how we framed a number of our academic and behavioral expectations in the Academy, see the next chapter.)

A few important reminders about framing

To become good framers, we also had to become good frame-*installers*. Framing, remember, is *not* just good marketing, sloganeering, or 'spin-doctoring'. In order to work as desired, new messages and ideas must fit existing mental frames of message-recipients. (Before proceeding, think: *What do they value and why?*) Otherwise, as Lakoff says, the new ideas simply 'bounce off' and no perceptions or attitudes are changed.

If you are an educator hoping to improve students' motivation through better framing, remember to always start with considering *your kids' values*, not necessarily the new language or slogan itself. Then take time explicitly to install the frames they may not have in place, preferably through identifiable narratives and examples.

In the Sophomore Academy, we found the following frames to resonate particularly strongly across the whole group: 'working hard consistently can earn a person *respect*'; 'the world will rarely come to you, so you have to GOYA for what you want';[9] 'we come to class every day because our different perspectives are important for helping us understand fully'; 'the expectations we have here are to protect our learning environment and your success—not to control you.'

To figure out how to make framing work for us, we generally followed a progression like this:

1. Identify what students valued (e.g. being respected, belonging to a definite group, and eventually attaining the things they desired: money, partners, friends, recognition and safety.)
    Example: *Adolescents value **respect**. Adolescents value belonging to a **group**.*

2. Specify how we wanted students to act, work, or behave on a certain matter. Example: *I want my students to truly engage with reading Chinua Achebe's Things Fall Apart.*

3. Explicitly structure language/rationales that appealed to their values, not ours.

   Example: *First, I showed students multiple publications' 'Best 100 Novels of the 20th Century' lists (which were nearly everywhere in the early 2000s), and showed over and over how* Things Fall Apart *is considered an important, essential text in the last 100 years of world literature. Once this idea was established and accepted, I built my framing accordingly. I communicated how being familiar with* Things Fall Apart *can earn* **respect** *from educated people who know the novel too. Also, if students know it well, they automatically* **belong** *to an international community of learners who appreciate the work as a major literary accomplishment. (Bonus value: I pointed out that other sophomore teachers didn't teach this novel, mainly because they thought sophomores don't get it. I* **respected** *the students' ability so much that I refused to deny you this opportunity. As we read it but other classes didn't—ah, competition—it strengthened our Sophomore Academy's sense of* **belonging** *and group solidarity.)*

When we were building Academy-wide policies or expectations, the team walked through these steps together. Then, we established these new frames with students by explicitly discussing in class. Finally, we repeated messages in our classes and across the Academy to reinforce them.

Example: *Our no-passes policy is not here because we don't trust you, but rather because we are concerned for your—and, more particularly, for your grade's—safety. The decision to have kids present for as many minutes as possible per day is to protect your performance in our classes, not to punish you. (Appealing to adolescents' value of* **feeling safe and secure.***)*

Let's not do that again

No doubt, the first group of Sophomore Academy students' ferocious pushback created urgency among the Academy teachers to become better framers—both to get more thoughtful about the messages we used (particularly in tweaking our messages more toward our kids' values and not our own) and to build greater consistency of such messages across our classrooms.

Our teamwork on this early issue then served us well over the entire life of the Academy, as we were presented with different groups having different dynamics. And after becoming more effective message framers, we were much more able to stay courses on our charted Sophomore Academy principles and their according policies. Indeed, our framing helped us hang on to the expectations we had, and it helped students see that living up to them was in fact feasible and good for them.

With all that in mind, we weren't always above adjusting policies when students' reactions made it clear to us that we'd miscalculated. When we reflected later in the year on the pushback from the first group of Academy students, for example, we decided that our 'no announcement necessary' approach was probably a bit too blind-siding and initially distracting. We then re-thought what entry into the Academy should look like for successive classes, and we decided to give incoming students notification and a bit more context.[10]

To maintain the light touch that was our first impulse, we chose to notify students—and throw in a quick description of the Academy's operations—via a letter from Dr. Bob. Here's the letter we mailed to the families of Academy-placed students the summer prior to their arrival:

Dear OSH Parent/Guardian,

I am writing to both inform you and congratulate you on your son/daughter being recommended for and selected to Sophomore Academy. Academy is a unique learning opportunity available to selected 10th grade students at Osseo Senior High School. Sophomore Academy represents our first attempt to create a smaller, more personalized learning experience for students transitioning into a large, comprehensive high school.

The initial step in identifying students for Sophomore Academy is a series of meetings that occur the spring of the student's 9th grade year. Osseo Senior High School counselors meet with each junior high counseling staff to learn more about students who might benefit from placement in smaller classes that have a strong academic support system in place. We also, with the help of junior high school counselors, analyze student academic achievement, looking at grades and test scores, to identify students who show strong academic promise, but are not yet achieving at the full level of their potential. Students who meet one or both of the above criteria are recommended as candidates for Sophomore Academy.

Logistically, the way it works is fairly simple. Your son/daughter will be placed with the same core group of students four (4) periods each day—for English, mathematics, science, and social studies. They will remain with the four teachers of these classes the entire year. The academic and behavioral expectations for students are identical in each classroom, creating a consistent message for students. The four teachers responsible for Sophomore Academy are among the very finest teachers at Osseo Senior High School. In our previous Academy years, the vast majority of students in Sophomore Academy showed improvement in attendance, grades and feelings toward school.

That's what we want for your son/daughter—to experience success in school. We believe Sophomore Academy will play a significant role in that success.

If you have any questions, please don't hesitate to
contact me.

Thank you.

Sincerely,

Robert Perdaems, Ed.D.

While it didn't erase all the initial hurt and angry feelings, this letter
proved effective in softening the shock a bit for the students after the
first class of Academy students. In interviewing a number of alumni
for this book, several brought up the day they received their letter—the
questions that ran through their minds, how they called their friends
to see if they got a similar one, their parents' reactions, and so on—and
the 'parachute' it created as they entered Osseo Senior and the Academy.

The next few chapters will go a bit deeper on what the Academy looked
like from day to day in terms of academic and managerial expectations—
or, to build on the idea of 'getting students *stable*', what we had to do to
'move students to *able*'. Though there won't be a lot of fireworks or 'cool
practices' (to reiterate: we were just really committed to doing the simple
stuff as hard and as well as we could with regard to kids' preparation),
it should provide a good picture of how the Academy team had to
collaborate and coordinate beyond things like framing/messaging—and,
importantly, what kinds of impacts this coordination produced in the
Academy students.

Endnotes

1. Osseo Senior High's master schedule at the time was based on a six-period day, and the two Academy sections met in hours 2 and 3 (English and social studies, then flipped) and 5 and 6 (math and science, then flipped). For periods 1 and 4, the Academy students were distributed into their other sophomore year required or elective courses like health, physical education, and so on.

2. Davar's reference is to *Dangerous Minds*, a 1995 drama directed by John N. Smith and produced by Don Simpson and Jerry Bruckheimer. Based on an autobiography by retired U.S. Marine-become-teacher LouAnne Johnson called *My Posse Don't Do Homework*, the movie starred Michelle Pfeiffer as a teacher working with a class full of reluctant learners in a segregated, economically deprived community. As Davar is at the time of this writing a budding filmmaker himself (his short film *Suspect?* has received numerous awards of merit in various short film showcases), it didn't surprise me a bit in our interview that he recalled the first Academy scenes in cinematic terms.

3. Recall that Dr. Bob arranged for the Academy team members to have a shared preparation period—fourth period each day, to be more exact. Though we called a standing meeting once weekly for this group, we often went through periods where more meetings would be called on short notice to address persisting issues. The opening weeks of that first year definitely put us in a position to meet more often than once per week.

4. For a bit more on self-esteem-preserving coping mechanisms of adolescents, see the useful literature review in Galanaki, E. and Anne, C. (2011) 'The imaginary audience and the personal fable in relation to the separation-individuation process during adolescence', in *Psychology, The Journal of the Hellenic Psychological Society*, 18 (1), pp. 85-103.

5. Dweck, C., S., Walton, G., M. and Cohen, G., L. (2014) *Academic Tenacity: Mindsets and Skills That Promote Long-Term Learning.* Bill and Melinda Gates Foundation. Available at: www.k12education.gatesfoundation.org/download/?Num=2807&filename=30-Academic-Tenacity.pdf

6. In addition to my two sections of Sophomore Academy English 10, I also taught a section of non-Academy English 10 and two of English 11.

7. A seminal study on framing effects was published in 1981 by psychologists Amos Tversky and Daniel Kahneman. In it, the researchers showed how altering a choice's wording but not its content led subjects to overwhelmingly choose the least risk-averse option. For more, see Tversky, A. and Kahneman, D. (1981) 'The framing of decisions and the psychology of choice', in *Science*, 211, pp. 453-458.

8. Lakoff, G. (2004) *Don't Think of an Elephant! Know Your Values and Frame the Debate.* (Anv. Ed.) White River Junction, VT: Chelsea Green Publishing Company.

9.   It stands for 'Get Off Your Ass'. Yes, I said it all the time—more on this later.

10. We still, though, did not share lots of specific placement information with each student or to do any kind of expressed 'entry counseling' to identify specific areas for growth. After interviewing several Academy alumni a decade or so out, this absence came up regularly enough that I might consider it something we could have done better if starting again.

Moving to Able

'Life is really simple, but we insist
on making it complicated.'

– Confucius

Disclaimer:

The following three chapters show exactly how the Sophomore Academy teachers worked and the kinds of impacts this work had on the Academy students. They do not include any examples of flashy or innovative teaching. (OK, maybe like two.) There are no tips and tricks. You will not find a checklist of cutting-edge strategies, techniques, or programming guaranteed to help you with your own school's at-risk students. What you will find instead are the principles we used every day to help these students as best we could. The technical term for this is 'the point.'

The Sophomore Academy wasn't a school improvement built on formulas or fads. Really, the entire initiative was about some pretty basic education stuff: high expectations for students' commitment and conduct, strong instruction and support, and continual adjustments to students' needs, all designed and supplied by proven, aligned teachers.

While our straightforward beliefs and approaches aren't likely to excite education's more innovation- and scalability-obsessed reformers, the Academy's classroom-up simplicity is precisely what makes it and other school-wide improvements built around this time at Osseo Senior (see Chapters 11 and 12) so instructive for the field. For within the education enterprise's constant scramble to improve outcomes, the idea of paring down to what's most effective is considered far, far too rarely. Unfortunately for education's professionals and taxpayers—and *very* unfortunately for kids, we seem much more inclined to look for approaches that are anything but proven. (The more *innovative*, the better!) We then shove heaps of these unproven but sexy approaches into schools and, when they don't perform as promised, move on to the Next Things That Will Fix Everything. (Which, usually, are just re-packaged, re-named versions of the previous Next Big Things.)[1]

Unlike many of the school improvement strategies U.S. education has seen in the past two decades or so,[2] the Sophomore Academy was never designed to execute some intuitively pleasing and expensive plan scripted by a profit-driven provider from outside the school. We weren't integrating a newfangled technological solution, practicing any new-agey self-regulatory routines, piloting a complex assessment and data-analysis system, or anything of the sort. The individual members of the Academy team were never recruited to deliver an innovative program or technique *with fidelity*, in other words, but to deliver the kind of instruction we were known for within the school.

Long story short, we weren't a particularly gimmicky or experimental group.

We'd achieved our reputations with kids and our superiors over years by sticking to education's fundamentals: we set clear and appropriately challenging expectations for students' performance, effort, and behavior; we constructed thoughtful, rigorous lessons in accord with our respective curricula; we made a point of letting kids know they meant a lot to us as people and that we cared for their success; we worked hard to support students who were struggling; we expected all students to show respect for all parts of our shared learning communities (including, critically, *themselves*); and, finally, we held students accountable when they did not meet the expectations we set.

As you may have noticed, our deepest instructional principles weren't real concerned with things like elevating students' voices, building students' 'agency', creating highly engaging learning environments/experiences, helping students reach self-actualization, or any such like. In educational terms, our approaches were unashamedly much more *traditionalist* than *progressive* (even if we didn't label them such at the time). Our primary goal was to get students better prepared for the world after 10th grade, and we believed the best way to prepare students was to get them to assume more personal responsibility for their learning, however we could. And as we teamed up to work with annual groups of very challenging students, our more traditionalist instructional principles actually got more pronounced across the team.

No matter how the Sophomore Academy might be labeled, though, our approach eventually informed a number of school-wide improvements at Osseo Senior, added new strengths to each of the Academy teachers' professional repertoires, and—most importantly—made scores of the kids we taught *able* to take on the rest of high school where that ability had once been in doubt. Better yet, many of them look back on the Academy experience some years out and feel grateful for having gone through it. (And, believe it or not, a great majority of the former students I talked with and surveyed actually look back on the Academy's environment and expectations quite fondly. Several, in fact, said it was the best part of their high school experience. Imagine that.)

Backward, then, for how it focused on building positive work behaviors and holding kids accountable for their choices? Traditionalist? So be it.

Put all together, the only decidedly innovative or comprehensively programmatic part of the Sophomore Academy was its structure and coordination, which acted to reinforce and amplify each teacher's in-class strategies and strengths. In short, the Academy structure and collaboration made it easier for us teachers to stay focused on the simple stuff we were all already committed to in our classrooms. This was important, too, as the Academy's students pushed us so hard. Very simply: we individually needed all the help we could get, and the Academy structure provided that brilliantly for all of us.

Where the previous chapter focused on how we welcomed students in and did what we could to make them *stable*, the three chapters ahead will share more detail about the principles we followed in the Academy to move students toward becoming *able* high school students and future citizens. You'll see some instructional and managerial premiums we lived by each day and that we found to make differences with the Sophomore Academy students, both when we had them in our classrooms and now, over a decade later. While some of these premiums and practices were informed by research on adolescents and/or learning, it is truer that, at the point of our teaching careers being described, we were mainly going on the kids we saw before us, the goals we had for them, and our agreements about the best ways forward. I will be sure to note where certain research findings pointed us in new directions, as well as where research I and others encountered after the Academy confirmed our approaches as worthwhile.

The premiums and illustrations are arranged here into basic categories and given a chapter apiece: 'Part 1: Building Personal Habits', 'Part 2: Building Academic Abilities', and 'Part 3: In Case of Emergency'. As you go, however, you'll likely detect at least some overlap between the three categories' messages and encouraged outlooks, habits, and mindsets.

My hope is that, whether you concern yourself with big-picture education-improvement issues or more tangible, feasible, and affordable ways to do better things with kids right now, these examples will better illustrate how the Sophomore Academy did what it aimed to do. As things we learned in the Academy helped inform later school-wide actions at Osseo Senior in this time period, the background provided in these chapters will also prove useful in the larger school-improvement matters covered in subsequent chapters.

Endnotes

1. If seeking more background on education reformers' historical preferences for innovative and scalable improvements, many useful histories have been written in recent decades. As starting points, see the following: Ravitch, D. (2001) *Left Back: A Century of Failed School Reforms.* New York, NY: Simon & Schuster. Also: Ravitch, D. (2011) *Death and Life of the Great American School System: How Testing and Choice Are Undermining Education.* New York, NY: Basic Books. See also: Tyack, D. and Cuban, L. (1995) *Tinkering*

Toward Utopia: A Century of Public School Reform. Cambridge, MA: Harvard University Press.

2. For an overview of these types of reform/improvement efforts, see the opening of Chapter 3.

Chapter 7

Moving to Able, Part 1: Building Personal Habits

'You may not control all the events that happen to you, but you can decide not to be reduced by them.'

– Maya Angelou, from *Letter to My Daughter*

Interested as the Sophomore Academy teachers were in improving students' academic capacities and confidences, we believed their success in 10th grade, high school, and the world after high school depended far more on their personal habits, outlooks, and mindsets than any raw academic acumen.

We'd seen quite a few students come and go in our careers, and we had pretty good ideas of the types of qualities necessary to succeed in the classroom and beyond—all well before terms like '21st-century skills' and 'social and emotional learning (SEL)' became buzzy goals of so many education experts. Accordingly, we identified habits/outlooks/mindsets we knew to be fairly required across high school's obstacle course and, in light of the incoming Academy students' junior high records, ones we knew to be in rough shape. From there, we focused on how we might use messaging and policies to shape them across our disciplines.

As a quick and related—and, to us in the Academy at least, entertaining—aside: we were pressed on these beliefs and methods in the Academy's first year, thanks to a chance episode with an up-and-coming education technology pioneer (who will remain nameless, but if you work in education I'll just say it's highly likely you've seen his work). Through a connection with Dr. Bob, this gentleman had heard about the school-within-a-school we were working on and asked if he could collect data on it as part of a research study.

To put it mildly, we did not see eye to eye.

In planning session after planning session, we frustrated the researcher with the types of things we wanted to measure (e.g. measures of students' *commitments* more than their *performance*—things like tardies, discipline incidents, work-completion rates), likely because he knew our chosen outputs wouldn't get peer-review boards', journal editors', and funders' blood pumping. We were aiming at kids' hearts and spirits first, and...well, those don't tend to show up real well in spreadsheets.

Eventually, his obvious frustration with us—and the fact that he could not seem to grasp why we'd prioritize behavior-shaping over raw student achievement—caused us to turn on him. We got pretty juvenile about it, even, nicknaming him 'Statman' and snickering about our spats with him in our team meetings. Eventually, Dr. Bob sensed the tension and asked the researcher to cut the cord.

Taken together, this sometimes-uncomfortable (and yes, not particularly professional on our parts) episode stands as a good symbol of what the Sophomore Academy stood for. As we saw it, our job wasn't to turn our 'D' and 'F' students into 'B' and 'A' students. Rather, and to borrow again from Dweck, Walton, and Cohen's *Academic Intensity*,[1] we were there to help the students in our charge re-conceptualize themselves in regard to their schooling. To help our kids see school as worth their investment and to see themselves as *able students*, for the first time in their life.

To be clear, we did not teach the ideal outlooks/habits/mindsets to students with a skills-based approach. We never, for instance, treated matters like 'persevering through adversity' and 'cooperating with peers' as if they could be demonstrated, practiced, and mastered like shoe-tying or multiplication tables. We had no curriculum to do so, for one thing, and none of us could have fit such teaching in among all the academic content we had to cover.

Our challenge was more about how to intentionally design policies and messages that would continually encourage the desired outlooks, habits, and mindsets in a way that appeared unintentional. We kept students' attention focused on school's academic challenges, then warmly demanded certain outlooks, habits, and mindsets through our policies and messages. We used, as my last book put it, the resistance medium of schooling's *swimming pool* to build strengths that could help kids in life's *marathon*.[2]

It's worth noting here, too, that the approach we employed has been vindicated in post-Academy years by multiple researchers. As the steam for SEL has grown in recent years and more research has been done about what actually seems to work for young people of various ages, not much evidence has shown skills-based approaches to building social and emotional strengths—especially for students in their 'middle-adolescent' years (ages 14-18)—to be particularly effective.[3]

With rationales and illustrations, below are a few personal outlooks, habits, and mindsets—or, as *Education is Upside-Down* called them, 'institutional virtues'[4]—we explicitly worked to strengthen across the Academy students via our messaging, expectations, and policies.

Adaptability

While we Sophomore Academy teachers used common policies and explicit messaging/framing to be sure our most vital principles and expectations defined the Academy's basic culture, our individual approaches differed quite a lot from classroom to classroom. Outside a few common classroom-managerial expectations that ran throughout the Academy (see below), we diverged on all kinds of other matters like late work policies (some accepted no work after its due date, others docked percentages according to how late) and grading scales (an A in one class required a different percentage of possible points earned than an A in others), and we did so intentionally. In fact, we considered this intra-Academy variability to play such a large part in what we set out to accomplish in the first place that we would actively defend one another's approaches to complaining students.

One (perhaps rather obvious) reason for our intentionality was that we were individually proud of how we ran our classrooms. Indeed, we'd been selected by Dr. Bob as the Academy teachers for certain reasons, and we wished to maintain the classroom environments that had earned us the distinction. In other words: as our individual practices could hardly be considered broken, we didn't each do a whole lot to start fixing things or remaking ourselves in the name of consistency alone.

More importantly, though, we resisted too much uniformity because were committed to making the Academy students more *able* (as opposed to simply *stable*) as high-school students/people in the world. Accordingly, we wanted to stress to our students the importance of *adaptability*. And by maintaining our varying approaches and supporting one another's, we hoped students would regularly adjust their behaviors and actions according to present circumstances and expectations—not merely hold general notions of 'fair' or 'right' and expect that this notion be served to them in every situation.

We were communicating to students that they had a direct hand in their own success, and that 'success' was going to look different depending on the setting, whom one was interacting with, the task, and on and on. As rules, expectations, and relationships would differ a lot from teacher to teacher throughout high school (and, indeed, throughout the rest of students' professional and personal lives), we felt this was a key message to send—both through our in-class messages and through our general ways of doing things.

In short, our individual instructional styles and policies were ways of building in students the sense that, as much as we all may want it to, the world doesn't often tailor itself to each of our individual preferences. And then, naturally, we wanted them to strengthen their abilities to read various situations and fit their actions and attitudes to them, as we knew this adaptability to be an institutional virtue that would serve them well throughout high school and beyond.

Self-management and preparation

Unlike with adaptability, building students' institutional virtues of self-management and preparation required much more than subtle class-to-class differences and some uniform messaging.

Indeed, to help students with matters as difficult—and critical—as building their self-management and preparation, we cut way back on any sorts of relativism. Rather than aim for students to gradually understand and accept the intended outlook/habits/mindset, we were very active and prescriptive.

Once again, based on our experience working with Academy-like students, we pre-identified a few areas we knew students were likely to struggle with managing their choices, as well as behaviors that could cause learning-environmental distractions. And from there, we raised our expectations via Academy-consistent classroom policies and required that students meet them or receive consequences.

As we saw it, pushing students to get handles on themselves and the day-in-day-out basics of 'doing school' were that important to their future success, in high school and beyond. We were working intentionally on the 'unobserved characteristics' economists like James Heckman had identified in his studies of GED recipients who were earning less in the workforce than their high school diploma-earning counterparts were.[5] Just as Heckman's work had shown, we knew that being bright doesn't cut it on its own. If one doesn't also know how to 'play the game' of school, of work, or of any institution, really, it was likely to cost them somewhere down the road.

In some ways, we sent this message through fairly low-stakes behavior expectations. For instance, we did not allow the Academy students to have food and/or drink in class. Also, if we as much as saw cellphones out when class was in session, we collected them and made students come to reclaim them at the end of the school day.

We didn't view violations like these as necessitating calls home, discipline referrals, or anything of the sort, first because we weren't particularly anti-food/drink or anti-cellphone of themselves. (If the expectations were repeatedly not met, though, and/or if students became combative when we engaged them about the expectations, that was another matter altogether.) Also, we weren't particularly bent on getting students to 'learn their lesson' after violating these conditions by paying some additional disciplinary toll. More simply, we wanted to communicate that school's work and focus times weren't times for all sorts of other things, and food/drink/cellphones provided good models of 'other things'.

After we chose these target behaviors, we outlined clear cause-and-effect transactions: step outside the (simple and reasonable) classroom guidelines we're setting, and it'll cost you some (simple and reasonable) inconvenience. We did not intend to punish the act itself or put another blot on their records, but rather to send the message—respectfully and definitely—that our learning environment demanded a certain measure of self-control. The goal was consistent reinforcement and self-correction. They had to learn to follow the rules for their own sake. Not surprisingly, this concept had applications everywhere, not just in the classroom. Not many people get formal reprimands at work or home, for instance, for occasionally looking at their phone during meetings or dinner time. Doing so continually or habitually does, however, send a message about one's overall level of engagement. And eventually your boss or the other people in your family are going to take issue.

Because we believed our expectations and consequences were right-side-up with regard to the world our students would eventually inhabit, we made sure to frame those expectations with explicit reminders and *lots* of repetition, all appealing to the students' values of safety and independence. The purpose of our expectations was to *protect* students—their in-class focus and success, their understanding of what others will expect in the future, and so on—*not to control or punish them.*

While the Academy students sometimes considered these policies as Sophomore Academy-exclusive punishments based on what they knew other teachers to permit in their classes (teachers at Osseo Senior were allowed to create policies at their own discretion, so food, drink, and phone use were allowed fairly readily across the school at that time), the overwhelming majority of them had no problem meeting the expectation. Far more often than not, students simply rose to the expected levels in a matter of weeks and moved on. They saw we meant business, and they just adjusted their habits: rather than come to class loaded up on junk food and constantly peeking at their phones, they wolfed their bags of vending-machine Cheetos and caught up on text messages during their own time—passing time, that is, not in class. Done and done.

Full disclosure: the early going can be rough. Kids don't tend to like controlling themselves. None of us do. However, if the rationale for the expectation is sound, the consequences are sensible and respectful, the messages are genuinely presented at the level of students' values, and teachers are consistent, you have everything you need to succeed. I've only seen students rise to the occasion. It takes a while, sure. And you have to account for *all* of the points above, not just a few. But when we did this at the Academy I saw our students—undeniably *tough* students at that—come to accept the expectations as The Way We Do Things Here.

In other ways, though, the Academy-wide policies we designed to shape kids' habits of self-management and preparation really tested them—and *us*.

To further reinforce—or, more appropriately, just plain *force*—the notion that class time was time to focus on working and learning, we did not allow students to leave the room once they were inside. That's right: no lockers, no bathrooms. As with our cellphone and food policies, class time was work and learning time, period.

We were firm on this policy for a few reasons. First, we knew from prior experience that students' restroom breaks could easily become reunion time with friends, sometimes impromptu and sometimes coordinated. And as these reunions could lead to endless strolls through the school's halls, our policy existed to actively curtail this tendency.

The plain expectation was that students would have to plan their restroom breaks around when classes were in session. If teachers could manage this same expectation without having in-class accidents, we reminded them, so could students. Once again: class time was learning time, period.

(We did, of course, leave room for and honor emergencies. As for how one can tell sincere emergency bathroom needs from non-urgent ones, all I can say is that you know it when you see it. And yes, we absolutely gave students grace in such instances. It's hardly rocket science.)

Also, we knew that students would be tempted to abuse locker passes when it came to arriving prepared for each day's learning activities. By removing passes as an option, we were also creating a condition to strengthen Academy kids' between-class routines. We had clear and simple expectations about what 'prepared for class' meant (a sign in my classroom read:

BE PREPARED FOR CLASS. Each day, I expect you to have the following: WRITING UTENSIL, PAPER, MATERIALS FOR DAY'S TASK, WILLING ATTITUDE. NO LOCKER PASSES WILL BE ISSUED.

And it applied every day and in every situation. 'Forgot to bring your notebook on the day of the open-notes quiz? Sure hope you studied!' 'Your group is presenting today but you skipped your locker and the visual aid you prepared is in there? Bummer... better nail all the other parts of the presentation!'

All that said, I'll fully admit: as I'd entered the Sophomore Academy as one of the team's more inherently permissive teachers (along with Zelenak—Klecker and Ruska were the tougher ones), this policy stretched me. From our foundational planning meetings (see Chapter 5) to actually carrying it out, denying students bathroom breaks and locker visits went against so much that came naturally to me and my classroom-management preferences. When I trusted its intents and rationales, though, and I let my fellow Academy teachers' reinforcement of rules in their classrooms hold me up, it actually became something I believed in and could message as sincerely as any of my longest-held classroom-managerial beliefs.

And, just as my tougher colleagues promised, in almost no time the students began to respond to this tougher condition just as they had to more low-stakes ones like no food, drink, or cellphones in class: they adjusted their behaviors to the expectation. They used locker visits wisely, packing up for multiple classes if their next few were spaced too far apart to make locker pit-stops between each. They arrived to class with all they needed for the day's learning activities and, on occasions when they didn't, they resourcefully relied on one another for necessary learning materials.

Eventually, they even began *holding one another* accountable for getting to where they needed to be, and with the right materials in hand. It wasn't at all unusual, for instance, to hear Academy kids urging their friends to 'hurry up, the bell's gonna ring!' or reminding one another to skip the locker visit between classes. (Due to Osseo Senior's size, several students shared lockers, which led to students working out routines for who'd visit the locker during which periods, and who was responsible for bringing which materials to each class.)

And when we could see *these* kinds of developments—kids monitoring *themselves*—we knew we were getting somewhere. And it happened year in and year out.

While the Academy teachers recognized these improvements in real time during the Academy's operation, several Academy alumni I interviewed also noted—when looking back on their Academy tenure—how these structures and expectations impacted them at the time.

Zach Miller, a student from the Academy's fourth year whose current tattoos and piercings echo the Faygo-chugging 'juggalo'[6] he was in high school, vividly remembered how the premium we placed on class time affected his between-class regimen. Recalling what it was like to get to Klecker's math class (which was on the far south end of the school, a challenging walk within a six-minute passing time from Ruska's classroom in the north wing), he described acting with an urgency many might find surprising from a student once labeled as 'at-risk', 'disengaged', or 'lazy'. Through those halls full of kids, in fact, he said he often felt like he was one of the only ones who cared to be on time.

'What you guys expected really made things different,' Zach said. 'I remember I wouldn't even be able to hit my locker. I'd be haulin' ass down the hall to be on time, passing these other kids…you know, just chillin', having conversations, not doing anything, and I'd be like, "*Get outta the way, I'm gonna be late!*"'

In addition to students like Zach, who today can look back and fondly (and entertainingly) recall specific ways their personal school habits changed while they were students in the Academy, my interviews and surveys also raised several memories from alumni about ways they banded together to meet the Academy teachers' raised expectations. Nearly all the conversations I had with our former students included at least some details about classmates looking out for one another, sharing lockers for more ideal between-class positioning, and/or pushing each other to hang in there. It was a simple idea, but it clearly played a big role in how our students framed the Academy, both then and now.

Some even recalled times when Academy classmates helped one another meet the in-class expectations whether those being helped liked it or not. In a spirited, laughter-filled interview with a group of alumni, close friends Anney Yang and Christina Sundberg shared a story about a time they decided to skip class together before I pressured them into coming back—with a crucial assist from their Academy classmates.

'We went to Zelenak's class,' Anney remembered, 'but then we were like, let's just go. It was my birthday, I thought it'd be a good day to not be in school.'

'We used to skip more in junior high,' Christina added, laughing. 'It was hard to get past you guys in the Sophomore Academy because you all talked to each other. That day, though, we just ran for it. We saw Dr. Perdaems in the parking lot, so we had to duck behind cars all the way out until we got to my house. When we got there, we got a call.'

'Yeah, it was on my phone,' Anney said, without missing a beat— picking up where Christina left off, just like the two did 13 years earlier. 'It was a message from you, Kalenze. You were like, "We know you have Sundberg. Both of you get back here. I got your cell number from someone here, I won't tell you who, we just want you to come back." We got all panicked, weren't sure what to do.

'But yeah, we came back. After that, I never skipped again. I learned my lesson. No one in the Academy—teachers *or* kids—was going to let us get away with it!'

Moments like these, in which Academy students worked with teachers to look out for their peers' best interests, happened frequently, and in all kinds of ways. Kids would discreetly share with teachers how a classmate was going through a tough time and needed some help, for instance, or push one another into—and even accompany one another to—our 'Seventh Hour' support period, essentially an ad hoc study hall/ help session the Academy teachers offered that started just after the day's last bell. No matter what form they came in, though, we always celebrated them as signs that we were accomplishing what we set out to. *It's working. Can you believe it? It's working.*

On one hand, we always liked to see peer pressure work toward positive behavior choices. As anyone who's worked with adolescents knows, nothing is more motivating to adolescents than the expectations of their fellow adolescents. With students getting involved in upholding accountabilities, our jobs as teachers were made a whole lot easier.

On the other hand, however, moments like these let us know we were succeeding at one of our most fundamental objectives: creating a place within Osseo Senior High where 'at-risk' students felt without a doubt that they *belonged* to a group—one that was bigger than their own needs, one that they would regularly make sacrifices to support.

It always made us a little giddy to see kids moving through the progression from loosely arriving (with individual concerns across such a wide spectrum) to congealing (so they could rebel against us, mainly—difficult to manage, but useful of itself) to fully adopting our premiums (not even asking to be excused from class, being more disciplined about how they used open times) and to encouraging each other to live by them.

Great as it was see Academy students pressuring one another into changing their daily habits in ways we knew would help them down the line, it was an even bigger deal to see our kids actually giving school—and their concepts of themselves as students—a real chance.

Note to educators:

If you don't believe it can happen (and I've met many, many in schools who would never dream of even going there—'I'm not going to die on that hill,' and all the rest), give your students some credit and at least give it a shot. You may be amazed what your students will accept and rise to if you clearly explain your rationales and follow through on the promised consequences. Be honest—and never disrespectful—about it, and they may surprise you.

Respect for self, others, school

While the above section on self-management and preparation may make it sound like the Sophomore Academy classrooms were stodgy, highly rule-bound environments choked by lists of 'no *this*, no *that*, no X except in instances of Y,' and swift consequences, the opposite was closer to true. All the Academy teachers ran very warm, active, and humorous classrooms, and the alumni regularly remembered as much in my interviews with and surveys of them.

When asked about events and memories that stood out all these years later, for example, Davar McGee from the Academy's first year responded that there were 'too many to count' before telling about an April Fools' Day prank they played. On *me*, that is. And, yes, I too remember it well. Davar and some others rushed into my classroom, breathless and worried. 'Cassie beat somebody up! Cassie beat somebody up!' I was crushed. This was an Academy student we'd all rallied around to keep out of trouble. This would be her second offense, which meant she would be automatically recommended for expulsion. Actually, I was more than crushed. I was pissed. And I let it show, kicking my chair aside and stomping around (and yeah, maybe cursing a little bit). With a huge grin on his face, Davar reminded me what day it was. *Hardy. Freaking. Har.* (Students now rolling on floor laughing.) Yeah, hilarious. Now help me get my desk back together...

Similarly, Latosha Conners (née Hayes) from the Academy's fourth year remarked about how 'my classmates and some of teachers made the experience really fun. I grew to really love the Academy and really missed being in the classes after that year', and Anney Yang from the Academy's second year said, 'All my memories from high school come from Sophomore Academy. I don't even remember anything else.' (Yes, even after getting busted skipping class.)

Trust me, I could fill pages with these sorts of quotes—and I think you'd agree that they're hardly the types of things you'd hear from a bunch of kids who were strapped into their desks, holding back tears as our rule systems were hammering them into compliant automatons.

Still, it's a conclusion far too many in education jump to: impose lots of structure onto kids—especially needy ones who have performed poorly in the past—and you'll suck all the joy out of learning; you'll turn kids into uncritical robots whose only possible option is getting in line to feed The System. As you'll see, time and again, that just wasn't the case.

* * *

Let's take a step back and revisit framing, because it was critical to these efforts. We were able to pull off all this additional structure in the Sophomore Academy, though, because of how we *framed* it. From the outset of our classes, we explained that the structures we were putting in place were necessary because we *respected* each and every student as an individual who wanted the best for themselves and their futures, and we were *protecting* them from anything that might knock them off-track.

The structures, we said, are like traffic laws. They are designed to make sure everyone gets where they want to go as safely and as efficiently as possible. 'The rules of the road aren't always fun to follow and they don't always fit our individual preferences, especially on days when things aren't going our way,' we'd say. 'But try to imagine the traffic system without any guidelines. If cities removed them, they'd actually be showing very little *respect* to all their drivers. The fastest and most selfish drivers would dictate the terms to all others.'

In our classrooms, in other words, the teachers' main functions were to determine what was necessary for—then doggedly defend—the safe and successful 'travel' of all the students—because, once again (in framing, remember, repetition is just as important as the idea), we just plain *respected* them and wished to *protect* them.

In accord with framing our classroom-management policies and routines as based in *respect for and protection of students*, not *control of students*, we made it an Academy-wide expectation that students respect equally their classmates, their classrooms, their teachers, and themselves. Carrying out the 'rules of the road' metaphor, we explained that even the most stringent rules and enforcements won't mean a whole lot if the drivers themselves don't do their part and respect all the other things happening on the road around them—in our case, the backgrounds, circumstances and dreams of their fellow students, the conditions of the classroom's resources, and the orderliness of the learning environment.

In short, we were telling them that we can be as tough as we want to with our guidelines, but none of this 'safe and successful travel' stuff is going to work if you all don't jump in and respect right along with us.

I spelled this expectation out in my own class syllabus, even, describing it as my classroom's only actual rule (set within the Academy-wide 'traffic laws' we'd set to shape students' self-management and preparation, of course). Here's the very text I used:

Respect equally your classmates, your classroom, your teacher, and yourself.

- That's right, one rule. In my mind, this one rule covers about everything. If you find yourself in a situation where you think you might be breaking our rule, ask yourself, 'is this behavior respectful?' I trust each of you to be mature enough to be able to answer the question for yourselves and to choose respectful over disrespectful behavior. If you demonstrate that you are unable to tell the difference, however, I will intervene to assist you, and consequences will be assigned.
- Some examples of disrespectful behavior should be singled out:
  - Put-downs or harassing behaviors (disrespecting others)
  - Damage of classroom materials (disrespecting classroom)
  - Ignoring or disregarding teacher instructions (disrespecting self, teacher, others, classroom)
  - Classroom cleanliness (disrespecting classroom, teacher, others, self)
  - In-class discussion about illegal or inappropriate behavior (disrespecting classroom, teacher, others, self)

And on the first day of every new academic term, my routine was to go over this expectation explicitly and to illustrate with examples of accepted and not-accepted behaviors taken straight from my classroom—including how I chose to deal with each. (Presenting this way proved handy, as well: while I would often remind kids that they only had one rule in my classroom, this 'respect' rule really covered about everything that one wouldn't want their students to do. I did not, of course, let them in on that.)

As the school year was in session, all the Academy teachers would regularly invoke respect—not just rule-following because we said so—in classroom-management situations that warranted it: getting classes back on task, resolving student conflicts, and so on. If a small group of students kept talking to one another during what was supposed to be a quiet work time, for example, we'd work to keep our intervention centered on being respectful to one another—not just, 'Be quiet you guys!' Plus, we didn't just *tell*, we *asked*—not for permission, of course, but for whether or not they'd call what they were doing respectful to themselves, their classmates, me, and so on. It might look like this:

A group of four boys are talking and laughing during 15 minutes of reading time designed to give everyone a head-start on tomorrow's assignment.

Me: 'Guys. Seriously. Keep it down, okay?'

The students become quiet in response. The room returns to silent work. Two minutes pass. One of the talkers whispers something, and the group *explodes* with laughter. A couple other students shift in their seats. They look over at the laughers—who are now doubling over in their desks—then back over at me.

I move closer to the boys, who straighten in their desks. One starts saying, 'Sorry, but he said…', but I hold up my hand to stop him.

'I don't need an explanation. Don't worry. I'm sure it was funny. Still, you guys know how hard it is to get your reading done at home sometimes, right? Everyone here does. Now when you do that, are you respecting your classmates? Take a look at all the readers in here right now. If you don't want to do it, it's your choice, I suppose. You can just do it at home. But in here, respect your classmates who need this time. Deal?'

It was really very simple to do, because the Academy students were generally more responsive to interactions centered on *respect* than they were to those centered on *obeying*. And they were also much more responsive when we didn't *order* them to be respectful, but instead questioned them pointedly, asking 'Do you know what being respectful looks like?' and 'Is what you're doing right now respectful to yourself, and to others?' They know the difference. Our approach helped them practice respecting one another—and us—in the ways they wanted to be respected themselves.

In a survey response about Academy-related memories, Joe Anderson, a student from the Academy's fourth year who is now a lead field technician in the wind turbine industry, recalled one particular example of us explicitly talking about respect, as well as the impression it left on him at the time.

'I specifically remember when Kalenze and Ruska both had separate conversations with the students about respect, reacting to the way that kids have begun to be more and more disrespectful of teachers and the teaching process,' Joe wrote in his survey response. 'Times like these showed me that teachers do care enough, but they just don't have the time or ability to give specific attention to each student unless they need it. This shift in mind let me see their efforts in a different light. From then on I did actually appreciate the fact that I had teachers that cared, a school system I could participate in, and peers that felt the same way I did about the whole thing. Before Sophomore Academy, I had an attitude that the staff in the school system were just doing their job and didn't care about me.'

Personal accountability

While Osseo Senior had mechanisms in place for checking on students' academic progress throughout a trimester and building students' personal accountability—namely mid-trimester updates executed through the school's Advisory class[7]—we decided in the Academy to take those processes up a few levels.

While the school's once-every-six-weeks check-in was somewhat effective, we built on it by having our students complete a similar, Academy-classes-only, report every two weeks. It was partly fun, thanks to a treatment by the ever-witty and technically savvy Zelenak, who took pictures of the Academy teachers and built a stylized progress report with the Academy teachers looking off seriously into the distance at the top.

It was also quite serious, though, in that Academy students were expected to have us each update them with current class grades and notes in much more frequent increments. We would review these individually with students to see what support they needed—and, of course, to jolt them into turning things around when necessary—but also collect them so we could review them as a group.

This simple protocol allowed us both to keep tabs on kids' struggles and to build cross-Academy awareness of particularly challenging stretches in one another's classes. If progress reports were showing large numbers of grade-dips in one class or another, it allowed us a chance to speak with one another about what was tripping kids up and what messages and allowances might work most effectively to position kids for success. For instance, if I knew via the progress reports that large numbers of kids had struggled with learning mitosis in Ruska's biology class or with states and capitals in Zelenak's geography class, I might allow them some extra group-study time in my class to help them prepare for big assessments.

In interviews with and surveys of Academy alumni, these accountability checks and one-to-one follow-ups came up very frequently and positively. Over and over, alums recalled how systems like these made them aware just how invested the Academy adults were in their success—a concept that was new to them. In short, our former students had no doubt that our progress report protocol was as much about helping us do a better job as it was about holding them accountable.

Some alumni, though, remarked in particular about the types of one-to-one conversations we had with them based on these reports. Second-year Academy student Jade Taylor (née Templeton), for example, even reported how follow-ups like these helped her turn her academic approach fully around. Asked about what she remembered most from her time in the Sophomore Academy, Jade—a mother of a two-year-old daughter and an early childhood teacher at the time of this writing—remembered an interaction I had with her quite vividly.

'What I remembered most was that time you pulled me aside because I wasn't getting my homework turned in. You told me to get my crap together and that you believed in me. And from then on you became my favorite teacher. I saw I actually had a teacher who cared about me, and I actually wanted to do good in school after that. Where I thought I hated reading before that, I gave it a chance after that and ended up really liking it.'

Over the course of our first Academy year, we realized how unfortunate it was that the check-in protocols and personal-touch pressures we were able to apply with students like Jade (and others—several alumni recalled turnaround moments like Jade's in surveys and interviews) would pretty well dissolve after their year with us.

In hopes that we could extend these positively accountable relationships with students into their junior and senior years, we approached Dr. Bob to see if the Sophomore Academy students could become our Advisory students. And though it again required a good amount of master schedule-shuffling (students were usually assigned to teachers' Advisories in equal chunks by alphabetical order), Dr. Bob agreed that the Advisory's three-year relationship with students was worth the effort and set about to making the re-schedule happen. While the first year of Academy students remained in their originally assigned

Advisory groups, years two through four were assigned to Advisories taught by Academy teachers and followed throughout the remainder of their high school careers.

'Learning hungry'

In interviews and surveys of Academy alumni and talking to them about memories from their time with us, I was a little surprised to see how multiple students recalled one particular—and to me rather insignificant—moment from my classroom: that moment when, as fourth-year Academy student Andy Martin (now a professional wilderness guide in upstate New York) put it, 'Tyler Miller jaunted up to grab a five dollar bill from Kalenze's hand.' (You may recall the tattooed and jocular former juggalo Zach Miller quoted earlier. Tyler is his identical twin brother, right down to the Twiztid concert tees.)

This moment was part of a demonstration called 'GOYA' (for 'Get Off Your Ass'), and I got it from my college football coach. It goes like this:

- Students are being lazy, wanting everything done for them, at a time when going through the learning exercise is an essential part of the process. Students ask (usually in a very whiny voice): 'Just *give* us the chapter summary so we can study it but don't have to *talk* about it or *look everything up.* This is so *pointless!*'
- Teacher finds any bill larger than a dollar. In my case, a five.
- Teacher stands in front of room, holds the bill up, says: 'Who wants this? You can have it,' then simply waits.
- Students cycle through a wide range of emotions (desire, anxiety, confusion, anger) and behaviors (nervous laughter, raising hands, begging please, jumping up and down), usually for about one minute, two tops.
- One student (always *one student*—trust me) gets it, walks to the front of the room, and takes it from the teacher. (And yes, that student gets to keep it. Choose your bill wisely.)

- Teacher uses what just transpired as an object lesson in how many of us would rather not *get off our asses* when opportunity is right in front of us. For some reason we'd rather sit in our seats and question it, raise our hands and plead for it to come to us, and so on, while one of us—the one who gets off his or her ass—will get the prize. And when it comes to learning, actually sending that information to our long-term memory, we have to get off our asses and do the work. Those that do will gain. Those that do not, well...
- Teacher resumes the previous activity, telling students they should do a better job of GOYA-ing when it comes to learning, earning, and succeeding.

For how the impactful part can be given away, it's a demonstration I'd recommend using sparingly. (In fact, I only remember doing it two or three times in my entire ten-year classroom career. It can, by the way, be adjusted to GOOYS for 'get out of your seat'. It doesn't tend to stick in the minds of teenagers as well as GOYA, however.)

Object lessons like GOYA weren't just for fun or effect, however, but part of a larger piece we in the Academy were committed to instilling in Academy students the outlook/habit/mindset of *learning hungry*.

Put another way, we hoped to make our students much more active in their approach to their schooling. We encouraged the Academy kids to stop sitting back and letting their education just happen (or, perhaps more accurately, *not* happen) to them, and instead to *attack* their schooling experience—or, to again borrow from Dweck/Walton/Cohen's *Academic Tenacity* report, to be *tenacious* about their schooling experience.

Interestingly, the US-wide KIPP (Knowledge Is Power Program) charter-school chain today calls out this very quality (which they term 'zest', meaning 'enthusiastic and energetic participation in life') among the Character Strengths it explicitly aspires to build in its students.[8]

While we in the Academy didn't go as far as to grade students on their zest indices as KIPP does, we could absolutely see why KIPP later considered 'zest' or 'learning hungry' as crucial to students' success and their re-conceptualization of themselves with regard to schooling, and it was absolutely something we sought to get our students to be continually monitoring and improving.

Ultimately, we wanted to help the kids who had always felt marginalized within school to stop accepting these feelings and—crucially—stop giving up in response to them. We told the students that it wasn't always a guarantee that they were going to have aligned advocates and cheerleaders like they did in the Sophomore Academy, so it was in their best interest to reverse their feelings—and, in turn, schools' perceptions of them as students—by taking charge. We wanted them to see their success in school with a sense of real purpose, and then to pull from that purpose wherever they could.

And to help insulate them for the times when they wouldn't readily have Academy-like supports, we again framed learning hungry into a matter of *respect*: that as one's schooling can earn or cost you respect in the world (not just college entry or future income, say), it is well worth the energy and attention. Such framing would pop up in moments like these:

- *Students questioning why they had to learn about a particular historical event in social studies*: 'No matter how much you'll earn or what kind of job title you have later in life, if you know things and can have reasonable discussions with people about those things, you stand a good chance of winning those people's respect, no matter what else they might have on you.'
- *Students threatening to give up on a task or pull out of school*: Don't consider pulling out of schooling or disengaging from it, as you might miss out on learning about things that people could forever look down on and disrespect you—talking badly about you, turning you down for a job you want—for not knowing.

It's not a cheap tactic, remember, as these messages are *true*. They were just a bit more careful about which values they appealed to in our students (e.g. in this case *respect*, as opposed to 'you'll need this someday' or 'you'll need this for a class next year'). For argument's sake: if you work with adolescents, consider for a moment how they tend to react when they feel they've been disrespected. It's pretty intense, isn't it? With that in mind, wouldn't you consider the value teenagers place on being respected—which even developmental psychologists like David Yeager have noted as common in studies of adolescent choices and behaviors[9]— as a frame worth building messages and expectations around?

As not every occasion could fit in a GOYA-like interruption of class time, we had more succinct, sloganized versions of these themes for quick access. When relevant, for example, we urged the kids to do things like 'learn with a chip on your shoulder', to 'show everyone who recommended you for the Academy what you've really got', to 'stand up for your education, it's your chance to earn respect', to 'remember that just because you might not *have things* doesn't mean you shouldn't work to *get things*', and so on.

We did not hide our personal histories in this respect. Each of us would openly share about our own upbringings and educational/ professional experiences (covered briefly in Chapter 5) to show how we dealt with family hardships, teachers who didn't understand us or treat us fairly, content that was too difficult at first, and so forth, all to illuminate two crucial things: the proactive steps people have to take to get over obstacles, and that yes, we were living proof that all of this absolutely can be done.

In addition, we readily encouraged competition among the Academy students. While many progressive education experts recoil in horror at this idea, considering it a threat to students' self-esteem,[10] we actually viewed competition between students as a highly underrated third rail: it got kids charged up about coming to class and it motivated them to do better (which meant studying harder, staying after class for support, and completing work more thoroughly, among other things), which were all behaviors we wanted our previously disaffected, 'at-risk' Academy students to start displaying more regularly.

While the Alfie Kohns of the education world worry about how competition might rob our kids of self-esteem or the joy they get from learning, we only saw competition bring out the best in our Sophomore Academy kids. In fact, owing a great deal to their competition with one another, they seemed on sight to be *learning hungrier* (just as we wanted) and to be getting all kinds of joy out of learning (again, just as we wanted). If it meant having to pit them against an academic rival or two to get these kinds of academic hunger or tenacity, so be it. We Academy teachers didn't actively seek to stop it, that's for sure.

And even now, almost 15 years later, one of the first things Academy alumni recalled in interviews was their academic competition. Selam Yimer, now a politically passionate mom and voracious reader living in Brooklyn Park, believes that developing an academic competitive streak defined her as a person and learner. 'Some people in the Academy, they had to learn to *do school*, but they never came to value academics,' Selam said. 'Me, I always knew how to get by in school, but then I started to get into it with one person—Abdi, it was [Mohamed, quoted in a previous chapter]—and we started going toe to toe with our grades. We'd run into your classes on the days grades were posted to compare where we were. That kept me going. Helped me understand what I was strong in, too, because I could see where I was pulling ahead.'

In short, we never took a skills-based approach to building school-effective personal habits or institutional virtues. We didn't select and assign a 'study skills' or 'communication skills' curriculum or program, in other words, as we didn't have the resources and we didn't really believe it would work anyway. We did believe these virtues were worth emphasizing and building if we could, though, so we always thought hard as a team about how we could do so through our policies and messages. Then, of course, we made sure to immerse our students in these messages and policies as they worked through our academic exercises.

In the next chapter, 'Moving To Able, Part 2', I'll share more details about the academic approaches we committed to and carried out to best support our students as they re-conceptualized themselves within the tasks and expectations of schooling.

Endnotes

1. Dweck, C., S., Walton, G., M. and Cohen, G., L. (2014) *Academic Tenacity: Mindsets and Skills That Promote Long-Term Learning*. Bill and Melinda Gates Foundation. Available at: www.k12education.gatesfoundation.org/download/?Num=2807&filename=30-Academic-Tenacity.pdf

2. In my previous book, *Education is Upside-Down*, the swimming pool-marathon metaphor is used to explain how schooling should see—but really hasn't to date—academic tasks with regard to building non-cognitive or social-emotional strengths. For more, see Kalenze, E. (2014) *Education Is Upside-Down: Reframing Reform to Focus on the Right Problems*. Lanham, MD: Rowman & Littlefield, pp. 79-95.

3. Numerous researchers across several fields have noted the general ineffectiveness of skills-based social and emotional learning programs for adolescents in recent years. See, for instance, economists Heckman, J. and Kautz, T. (2013) 'Fostering and Measuring Skills: Interventions That Improve Character and Cognition', working paper no. 7750, Cambridge, MA: National Bureau of Economic Research, 35. See also developmental psychologist Yeager, D. (2017) 'Social-Emotional Learning Programs for Adolescents', in *The Future of Children*, 27 (1), p. 31.

4. In *Education is Upside-Down*, I use the term 'institutional virtues' to describe the qualities commonly considered 'non-cognitive skills', 'soft skills', 'character strengths', '21st century skills', and so on. I prefer 'institutional virtues' to these for a number of reasons: first because qualities like grit, perseverance, teamwork, self-restraint, and so forth are not technically *skills*. Also, as they are indeed qualities that enhance individuals' eventual abilities to thrive within mainstream institutions, the term *virtues* is more appropriate than merely *qualities*—all without the ethical/moral connotations accompanying *character*. For more detail, see *Education Is Upside-Down: Reframing Reform to Focus on the Right Problems*, pp. 84-85.

5. Heckman, J., J. (2000) 'The GED is a Mixed Signal: The effect of cognitive and non-cognitive skills on human capital and labor market outcomes.' Chicago, IL: University of Chicago.

6. A 'juggalo' is a fan of the band Insane Clown Posse or other bands on ICP's Psychopathic Records label. And yes, Zach—and his twin brother Tyler— were very committed juggalos.

7. 'Advisory' at the time was the name of Osseo Senior's 'homeroom' class. While it provided a home base through which to carry out more school-wide logistical issues for students (e.g. lockers, emergency information, and so on), it also had some light college- and career-preparatory functions (like ASVAB and ACT's PLAN tests and volunteer opportunities) and academic check-ins (like the aforementioned mid-trimester reports). As a group of students remained with their Advisory teacher for all their years at Osseo Senior (and actually had their name called by that teacher as they walked across the graduation stage), it was also a good place for creating strong relationships.

8. Blad, E. (6 June 2017) 'Is Your Child Showing Grit? School Report Cards Rate Students' Soft Skills.' Education Week. Available at: www.edweek.org/ ew/articles/2017/05/31/is-your-child-showing-grit-school-report.html

9. Yeager, D., S., *et al.* (2017) 'Why Interventions to Influence Adolescent Behavior Often Fail but Could Succeed', in *Perspectives on Psychological Science*, 13 (1), pp. 101–122.

10. In the late 1980s and early 1990s, educationists like Alfie Kohn caused many in more progressive education circles to question and resist—and even try to get students to unlearn—competitive mindsets, saying they could cause harm to children's self-esteem. For a sample of Kohn's ideas on the matter, see 'The Case Against Competition' at www.alfiekohn.org/article/case-competition/ (originally running in *Working Mother* magazine, Sept 1987) or his book, *No Contest: the Case against Competition* (Houghton Mifflin, 1st edition, 1986).

Chapter 8

Moving to Able, Part 2: Building Academic Abilities

'Without language, one cannot talk to people and understand them; one cannot share their hopes and aspirations, grasp their history, appreciate their poetry, or savor their songs.'

– Nelson Mandela, from *Long Walk to Freedom*

We Sophomore Academy teachers placed a great deal of emphasis on building students' institutional virtues—the personal outlooks, habits, and mindsets necessary for success in school and most mainstream institutions. Strangely, however, we didn't do much strategizing together about our academic content areas. There wasn't much we *could* do, really, as each of us taught a different discipline. I wouldn't have been much help to Kelly Klecker, for example, about how to assist her math students in analyzing functions, and she likely wouldn't have had much to say about texts I'd chosen to supplement my teaching of *Things Fall Apart*.

Quite literally, the only content we shared was our *kids*. We all knew their beliefs about themselves and school, their persisting and immediate obstacles, and their work habits. As a result, we poured our combined energy and ideas into them.

Still, if we wanted to meet our goal of getting students to re-conceptualize themselves with regard to their schooling, we needed to be at the top of our content-practical game. Our first goal was getting these kids *stable*, helping them feel they truly belonged to a larger community and that they were respected members of Osseo Senior High School. But we did not want to stop there. We were also doggedly committed to helping the Academy kids become fully *able* students, set up for academic success in high school and beyond, if they chose to pursue post-secondary education. That meant creating a whole other set of targets.

Making students *able*, or getting them to adopt certain habits, outlooks, and mindsets is certainly *part* of the deal. But it's definitely not all there is to academic success. Those other pieces—knowing how classes and teachers work, having the knowledge and skills necessary to make it through subsequent levels—deserve their own attention and emphasis. The institutional virtues we continually emphasized go a long way, but truly successful students also understand the nuances of academic life. For example, what teachers mean when they say the class is about to prepare a lab report. Or write a literary analysis essay. Or work on a math concept that builds on an idea from last year's course.

In short, character alone wouldn't cut it.

If we truly wanted to help the Academy kids to become able high school students, we had to help them learn as much as we could about the paces, terminology, and expectations of high school-level academics. To borrow the essence of this chapter's epigraph, we had to do the best job possible teaching them the *language* of high school so they could experience school in a meaningful way and succeed this year and beyond.

To teach them this language, we had to do the basics really well. Our academic expectations had to be fair and challenging, our trajectories of learning had to be reasonable and rigorous, our means of supporting students through difficulty had to be strong and consistent, and our feedback had to be specific and useful to their improvement. And all at a pace that didn't overwhelm them as they rebuilt (or *established*) their academic confidence.

Also, we were well aware that the window to teach them this language wouldn't be open forever. Many of our kids had spent their junior high years becoming jaded, and they were accustomed to 'checking out' when school became too complicated. We knew that even if the Academy kids trusted us enough to take a chance on our experiment, their patience was not unlimited. We were on the clock. We had a strict time limit within which to convince them their new investment was worth it. If we weren't grading students sensibly, if the work we assigned felt pointless or 'busy', if students didn't feel supported through challenging learning tasks, they would slam the window shut on us and the opportunity to intervene would be lost for good.

In short, while thoughtful framing might be good for influencing students to put in the initial effort, it would take much more than deliberate messaging to get students to *continue* investing—especially when the subject matter at hand wasn't terribly thrilling to them, or when the challenging concepts and learning tasks started piling up.

Running alongside these challenges, we were always very mindful of how we handled the idea of 'student engagement'. If we dialed our expectations' and/or our content's rigor down too far in order to keep the kids engaged, we knew we wouldn't be setting students up for the challenges they would inevitably face later in their academic careers. Highly engaging activities and subject matter might keep some students interested and attending. But that 'learning' would be meaningless if everything from the Academy onward felt shockingly difficult. Indeed, prioritizing engagement over preparation would certainly not help students become *able*.

This chapter will share more about how we managed these academic aspirations and challenges, focusing especially on the idea of how we built and maintained student engagement without losing the handle on our commitment to making our students more academically *able*. These positions and practices are culled from themes that rose repeatedly when I asked Academy teachers, administrators, and alumni about what had the greatest impact on students' learning—of content and skills, of course, but also about themselves as able high school-level learners and as people.

We very consciously used the academic resistance medium to strengthen students' non-cognitive awareness and strength (as, again, using a swimming pool to build strengths for running a marathon[1]). So there will naturally be some overlap between this chapter's 'academic ability-building' and the 'character strength-building' discussed previously. My hope is that you'll see how we were able to help students learn some important lessons about their 'character' choices and habits (and adjust them when necessary, of course) via academic pursuits, all without explicitly separating the academic from the purely social and emotional.[2]

You may also notice that the positions and practices shared here fit well under the disclaimer that began these 'Moving to Able' chapters, in that they are tied to some pretty basic—'old-school' even, if you must—instructional wisdom. Admittedly (and, indeed, unashamedly), our instructional and managerial preferences were fairly *traditionalist* in nature, even if none of us would have used that term to describe ourselves at the time.[3]

Simply, when we considered what the Academy kids' really needed, it was clear that the fundamentals—practice, accountability, knowledge-building, discipline, and so on—were the top priority, and we believed in attacking those fundamentals as hard as we could. If you came seeking something flashier, or ideas based in a more progressive-educational philosophy, I hope this chapter will convince you why our traditionalist instructional orientation was absolutely necessary.

* * *

As I'm on this note, though, I'll make a brief detour to stress a crucial point. Namely, that we weren't adhering to traditionalist instructional playbooks out of a stubborn loyalty to old-fashioned preferences or a general lack of capacity.

I, for one, was moving in a much more traditionalist direction during the Academy years thanks to study I'd begun doing of education-historical, cognitive-scientific, reading-instructional, and linguistic research literatures.

Prior to this independent study, I spent my years in the classroom following the advice of my progressively oriented teacher-certification program and my school's continuing professional development. As a result, my classroom had many of the typical progressive education-inspired hallmarks: I gave students lots of choices with the types of assessments they could do, I checked myself to limit the amounts of my 'teacher talk' so students could do more of the talking and (purportedly) create their own understanding, I had students work in groups to complete projects (that were frankly more 'art' than 'language arts') fairly often, and so on.

Over that early period of my career, though, I had to be honest with myself: based on my students' grades in my classes, the quality of their products, and various standardized test results, I really wasn't moving my kids as well as I wanted to academically. I had little question about whether kids were *happy* and *engaged* in my classroom in this period, but I was nowhere near as sure about if my kids' reading, writing, speaking, and listening abilities—*the abilities my English class existed to improve*—were growing in accord.

I began my independent study simply because I wished to bring my instructional game into better alignment with the positive classroom culture and relationships I had created. And because I was well aware of the kinds of recommendations I'd receive if I went deeper into the experts I already knew (and, again, because I wasn't thrilled with the results they were producing in my classroom), I decided to explore all the content my teacher-preparation program had ignored.

Rather than read more John Dewey, for instance, who philosophized about the nature of the child a century ago, I read histories of education's last century: Diane Ravitch's *Left Back: A Century of Failed School Reforms*, for example, and David Tyack/Larry Cuban's *Tinkering Toward Utopia*. Also, I dove into education theorists and researchers that my ed-school professors generally told me and my fellow teachers-in-training weren't worth knowing: figures like E. D. Hirsch, Jeanne Chall, Lisa Delpit, Siegfried Engelmann, and others

And once I got into such study, I started to see that the more progressive-educational approach might not be best for my kids' growth and preparation. Here are just a few notions my independent research confirmed: that novice learners absolutely can't think like—and thus shouldn't be treated like—expert learners;[4] that allowing kids to discover their own learning was a verifiably bad idea;[5] and that possessing background knowledge is a whole lot more important to reading comprehension and critical thinking than some common taxonomies of intellectual activity would lead us to believe.[6]

While these are all crucial matters of teaching and learning, they were new to me. More than that, these ideas actually ran *directly counter to* what I had been trained to accept and enact.

Also, spending more time with these ideas really made it dawn on me how 'upside-down' much of the progressive education-oriented practice was with regard to post-K-12 expectations. After all, in many, many 'real world' institutions (and I don't just mean an institution like *college*, but institutions in a more general, sociological sense—the economy, home-ownership, marriage, community participation), it *can* actually cost a person something if they can't meet due dates. Similarly, there are actually lots (and *lots*) of situations where one will be required to demonstrate their proficiency at something in a very specific and bound way, not one fully left up to the demonstrator. One can't pass their driver's test with an interpretive dance, for example, or submit a short film in lieu of a form 1040. In fact, some people lose their jobs—or their homes, or their life partners—when they don't meet certain expectations.

I could continue here, but you get the idea.

In short, my educational research at this time showed me that I had planned a cognitively and institutionally upside-down classroom for the first five years of my career, 'preparing' kids in ways that were plainly out of step with how humans learn and the world these kids would one day join. It wasn't a particularly comfortable realization, as you might imagine.

I couldn't take all of the blame, however, for having done things this way. I designed and delivered my instruction like this because I had lots of people—education-school professors, professional-development consultants, administrators, colleagues—tell me practices like these were best for kids' healthy development and learning. I didn't always feel quite right about it, because I knew *I* didn't learn best in these ways. But I took their word for it. I guess I figured that all these smart people couldn't possibly be wrong, so I did my best to practice as they recommended. Not to mention, I practiced this way to make sure I could get and hold a teaching job in the first place. It's hard to get a job in education unless you subscribe to these 'right things', after all. And as an early-career teaching professional with a young family at home, job security was a highly motivating factor.

Finally, and troublingly in still another way, I learned through my research that a lot of what I had been advised to do by so many education professors and experts had very little evidence to support it. Indeed, many of the practices I had been told were 'best' were really based in ideals, philosophies, and outright junk science, some going back a century or more.[7] When I recognized this, I realized that I hadn't been making classroom-practical decisions very *professionally* at all.

When I learned how little actual evidence supported these recommended practices, in fact, it made me angry and upset. Here's how I thought about it: if I went to my doctor with a broken arm, how would I feel if my doctor bypassed the evidence-based practices of medical science and relied instead on *philosophies* about 'how patients heal best'? By any account, this would be unacceptable.

As an early career educator who was starting to turn an eye toward the bigger picture of my profession's public esteem, it sure didn't sit very well with me to learn that my field was making so many decisions about our craft—and, hence, kids' preparation for the world—in ways that were so patently unprofessional.

Without question, my personal research and subsequent reflection at the time told me I was going to have to bring new and different practices into my classroom. Based on my new awareness of evidence, though, the 'new and different practices' turned out to be more traditionalist and 'old school'. In short: my independent research in this period taught me that, to borrow from formative assessment guru Dylan Wiliam, I 'need[ed] to stop looking for the next big thing, and instead do the last big thing properly.'[8]

And yet I still did not consider myself a pure *traditionalist*. Doing so, after all, implies a commitment to traditionalist practices in and of themselves, and I had no such commitment. I just wanted classroom practices and policies that would prepare my kids for the world after high school. And based on the evidence I saw, more traditional practices seemed better matched to my kids' needs than those I'd previously subscribed to.

In other words, I never went full-traditionalist, changing every practice to fit my new identification. My instruction wasn't 100% lecture based, for example, because I knew collegiate literature courses (and, in the workplace, staff meetings) would feature all kinds of discussion. Kids needed to be prepared for this. I didn't fully eliminate group work, because I knew my kids would have to work in teams someday. I did, however, change structures, incentives, and consequences of group work to better reflect post-high school realities. Students not holding their own, for example, could get fired from a group—yes, *fired*—and have to work through assignments on their own. Again, kids needed to be prepared for this.

In full, if I had to name the educational philosophy/identity that emerged for me around the time of the Academy, I would say that I became an education *preparationist*. It is, by the way, how I define my educational philosophy to this day.

In the Academy, I wasn't alone in my traditionally methodological *preparationism*. Zelenak—who, like me, relied heavily on the power of positive relationships and saw himself as fairly permissive from a classroom-management standpoint—was also a decidedly traditional instructor, relying heavily on lecture and student reading to get his content across. Also like me, his reasons for using traditionalist methods were thoroughly considered and deliberately chosen over a number of years and professional experiences.

When I spoke to him recently about his instructional philosophies and practices, Zelenak admitted that he hadn't always made sound content-learning his main focus. He began his career with a strong content emphasis but changed this approach when he started teaching junior high. There, he said, 'It couldn't be about content so much, or at least I had really convinced myself of that. I'd really started to think things like, "Does it really matter about the outcome of the War of 1812?" At that point of my career it was more about creating engaging lessons, getting kids to develop good habits. I did always put a lot of emphasis on student reading, and I always had a textbook—even as "textbook" was becoming a dirty word in social studies. I just made it really important to read, even if I had to spend a lot of my time and energy *convincing* them to read.'

Over this period, Zelenak said his traditionalist/preparationist instructional inclinations got a jump-start from the educational philosophies of Michael Hartoonian, a one-time president for the National Council for the Social Studies who taught at the University of Minnesota at the time. Hartoonian's bold beliefs about the mission of schooling, students' responsibilities as learners, and teachers' according roles rang loudly for Zelenak, and the impact on his classroom design and delivery soon followed. 'I started to see my role as a social studies teacher and kids' responsibilities of being learners in social studies differently,' he said. 'It changed a lot of what I do and why.'

Incidentally, a few major premiums of Hartoonian's are that the social studies act as a training ground for developing 'loving critics of our society',[9] that 'learning is the responsibility of the student',[10] and that schools should never be considered customer-service entities with the students acting as consumers.[11] Definitely not what one usually associated with progressive education philosophy.

Though teaching and learning in the sciences happen differently than they do in the humanities, Klecker went about her math instruction fairly traditionally during the Academy. She was fiercely committed to putting the hard parts of learning onto students and, as she put it to me, 'Never taking the pencil out of kids' hands to show them how it's done.

They have to work it out, or the learning doesn't happen.'

And while she could have gone to all kinds of lengths in her instruction to make it more hands-on or engaging, she found that much of the advice suggested by math education gurus got in the way of building kids' math abilities and their confidence with math. She tried math manipulatives (i.e. objects used by math instructors so students can have a physical, hands-on representation of the math concept being studied), collaborative problem-solving exercises, and so on, but ultimately they didn't produce as promised. She doesn't count herself as a teacher who opposes these practices altogether, but admits they aren't always the most effective choice.

'In some cases,' Klecker said, 'I saw that introducing more *stuff* into math really just makes kids more frustrated. I tried it—having them connect this triangle-like thing we'd just made, say, to what we were doing algebraically—and they'd be like, "So…why'd you have me do that?"'

'In the end,' she continued, 'I've found it more effective to explain the concepts, let kids practice them, then introduce harder and harder problems. And always—*always*—I let *them* do the work.'

We were not, in other words, stuck teaching in the ways we were taught, uninformed about the 'latest innovations', dedicated to upholding patriarchal institutions, or whatever other insult is commonly lobbed at teachers who choose traditionalist practices and policies. We tried other ways, thanks, and then moved over to more traditional practices very consciously and studiously. From our perspective, doing so was just plain better for our kids.

In all, the instructional philosophies and positions of my Academy teammates helped me to complete the practical turn my independent research suggested. If I hadn't been working alongside these teachers and with these kids, I'm not sure it would have happened. Ask any teacher who's ever attempted to go against the grain of their school, and they'll tell you that it's very hard to see it through—with everything from collegial peer pressure to evaluation rubrics presenting obstacles.

My Academy teammates constantly helped me keep the wheel turning, and in multiple ways. First, they always helped me with ideas about how to message and 'sell' my practical changes to kids and, naturally, with how to adjust them when things didn't exactly work out. As I learned more about their own instructional choices and rationales in our ongoing formal and informal team conversations, my teammates helped to remind me that my intended practical changes were indeed sound and appropriate, not too harsh or 'backward'.

The support and guidance my Academy teammates provided me through this point turned out to be critical for my day-to-day classroom performance and my overall professional growth. And that's the main reason for this detour into *preparationism*. For as helpful as the Academy's structures were toward more uniformly and efficiently messaging our instructional choices to Academy students, these structures also provided us with ways to check, question, and deepen *our own* understandings and rationales. In an education environment that always seemed to favor the progressive-educational, overly sentimental, and faddish, the Sophomore Academy was like a refuge—a place where we could identify, question, hone, and reinforce the operations we chose, based soley on what *we* agreed was most important for the kids we served.

One final point: we weren't in a professional 'bubble', exempt from everything else in the school and able to play by our own rules. Much to the contrary, our ideas were regularly challenged—and, on occasion, contradicted or outright rejected—by Dr. Bob. The Academy's structure, however, definitely gave us a space where we could tune out much of the noise and refine our policies and practices with less interference.

Based on the results we generated and the quite consistent qualitative evidence I collected from Sophomore Academy alumni about our methods' effectiveness and impact, it would seem that our choice to teach more traditionally didn't compromise our students' relationships with us, their engagement with content, or success within school and beyond. In fact, after speaking with so many of these students, I'm even more committed to the idea that our chosen methods were a good fit for our mission.

* * *

Now let's get into those academic-practical positions.

One final caveat: this will not be a blow-by-blow, day-in-day-out memoir of how the practices looked in action. Going into that kind of detail would not only be tedious, it would distract from the much more important issue of comprehensive school improvement. Plus, as complex as teaching and learning is, it would likely take an entire other book to describe all the actions and rationales that flew around within one of our classrooms, much less four. The main point is to show how the Sophomore Academy team aligned on vital instructional premiums and expressed them practically within our individual subject areas, all thanks to the provided structures and supports.

To bind this discussion more tightly, then, I'll focus on student engagement: how we thought about it in general terms as a team, as well as some strategies, practices, and messages we used to create and maintain students' engagement to academic tasks across the Sophomore Academy.

Student engagement: Keeping the academic over the academic-*like*

To start, I'll elaborate on and qualify my initial assertions about the complex (and massive) issue of student engagement. Based on what I've written so far, you may have the impression that the Academy teachers didn't care about student engagement at all—that, as neo-traditionalists, we believed engagement was not our problem but the kids' alone. But there's a quite a lot more to it than that.

First, we did believe student engagement with our content and learning activities was important. We went to considerable lengths to engage students to our respective contents and learning activities, and I have no problem saying that kids actually liked being in our classes as a result. In 2005-06, in fact, I was voted 'Most Inspiring Teacher' by Osseo Senior High's student body, a distinction I'm quite sure came because Sophomore Academy kids stuffed the voting boxes. (Thanks, guys.) I don't mention it to boast, but rather to make a point: 'Most Inspiring Teacher' is hardly the kind of honor hundreds of students would bestow on an unreasonably demanding, disrespectful, 'engagement-is-your-problem' drudge.

Finally, we all took pride in our ability to design engaging instruction. Yes, we *liked* that kids thought our classrooms were productive and fun. (That 'Most Inspiring Teacher' recognition, for instance? I count it as one of the achievements I am proudest of in this world—personal, professional, or otherwise—and I suspect I always will.)

Very plainly, though, we never let ourselves believe that 'traditional' and 'engaging' were diametrically opposed. Instead, we brought these concepts together by keeping them in proper balance. We absolutely believed that building student engagement was a crucial piece of effective instruction. The difference was we saw engagement as a *means* to effective teaching and learning, never an end in itself.

Indeed, piquing our students' interest was a standard part of our planning. Strictly speaking, though, we did this so kids would dig into difficult content more actively and come away with the intended learning. Doing anything else would be more academic-*like* than academic,[12] and it would hardly be an adequate way to make students *able* to handle future academic challenges.

In short, if the more engaging pieces took too much class time, didn't lead into more substantive learning of future-useful content and/ or skills, or were far out of step with future academic expectations, we didn't see them as worth keeping. While other teachers sought to replace unengaging content with something more attractive when they saw kids checking out—such as watching a film version of *The Crucible* to avoid reading the play's challenging language, or reading a young adult novel about unrequited love instead of *The Great Gatsby*, or completing 'pick-your-own-project' instead of a position paper—we always sought to keep the rigorous content right where it was. 'The kids *loved* it!', in other words, wasn't a very meaningful goal.

To make these choices plain to our students, we often presented them in culinary terms. To us, engagement didn't mean serving snacks and desserts all the time ('The kids loved it?' Y'don't say.). Anyone could do that. The real trick of engagement was serving them healthy food, and figuring out how to make them eat it. It was the same challenge so many parents face at dinner times with their own kids: vegetables, not candy. As we worked in a school, where the mission is always to make kids 'healthy' enough to survive the world they would one day join, serving them 'vegetables' was our *responsibility* more than it was a *choice*. We would prepare the vegetables so they were tastier, of course, but we would only serve candy after a nutritious meal was fully digested. Making healthy food taste better—and reinforcing its long-term value to their systems—was something we were all committed to doing well.

Within our content areas across the Academy, our engagement-building actions looked rather different from classroom to classroom. And, of course, we sometimes had to try several different recipes to get the kids to eat up. As I talked with Academy alumni and staff, though, some unifying themes emerged about how we built student engagement to academic tasks.

Design instruction to coax students into challenging work

One engagement strategy several of us used was to simply keep kids guessing about where class was heading—to plan instructional 'arcs' in ways that revealed more and more as we went along, rather than be completely up front about our goal from the outset.

While this may contradict ideas about how clear *learning objectives* or *learning targets* are essential for keeping students engaged to and focused on various learning activities (e.g. student-friendly, highly visible, and frequently repeated descriptions of what was to be learned or mastered within the span of a given period[13]), we found that *getting kids hunting for* the intended learning was far more effective than *making them keenly aware of it*. And to do this, we built students' appetites for learning material simply by keeping the lesson's learning objectives hidden as long as possible.

It was nothing revolutionary, really. We were just stretching Madeline Hunter's classic concept of the *anticipatory set* to its limit.[14] We began with something that captured students' attention and then stuck with it as long as we could. Rather than kick learning activities off by explaining where we would be going for the day, we systematically coaxed and clued students into what we wanted them to know and be able to do.

This design principle was especially handy for the social studies and English learning environments, where concepts didn't always build logically upon the previous ones, and so Zelenak and I leaned on it quite heavily. When switching gears to a new history unit, reading selection, or writing exercise, we started by asking students to respond to a prompt that seemed purely personal on its face, but was indeed based in the themes of the content that lay just ahead. In my classroom, for instance, I had students respond by writing in their 'Almost-Daily Log'—a routine that proved quite handy for getting students to do lots and lots of informal writing over the course of a grading period. Students' subsequent responses/reactions would in turn fuel a class discussion. And from here, after students were able to air (and, usually, argue about) a range of personal perspectives, class would segue into the particulars of the content at hand.

Here's a step-by-step breakdown of how my classroom tackled Heinrich Böll's short story *The Balek Scales*:

- Without providing any definitions or clarification, I asked students to freely write for five minutes about a time they experienced injustice.

- Next, I directed students to talk in small groups, comparing their tales of injustice. (*Process point: As students shared their log entries with one another, I circulated around the classroom to check a few pieces and to record a small credit for completing, as well as have short discussions with students about their responses.*)

- We conducted open class discussion for 15-20 minutes, highlighting students' definitions of justice and injustice, subtly influencing the conversation toward the question of 'Who defines what is just?', which is of course a key theme of *The Balek Scales*. (Keep in mind, the title of the work has not been mentioned to this point.)

- Building off personal points raised by students, I segued the prelude discussion into the lesson's more explicit-instructional portion using the familiar image/symbol of 'Lady Justice' with her blindfold and scales. I drew this image on the board and explained the symbolism, then shared pictures of where the statue can typically be seen and why. (This is relevant to *The Balek Scales*, as the scales perform a similar symbolic function in the narrative.)

- At this point I turned fully into the study's explicit-instructional portion by sharing more particulars of the story we planned to read. I explained the title of the story and how it fits into the unit of works we were studying; I installed any text-relevant background knowledge about author Heinrich Böll—the period and place he wrote from, his typical writing interests and themes—and took students' questions. I also introduced a set of vocabulary words from the selection that students were unlikely to know—their meanings as well as some example sentences. (*Process point: I prepared these bits of knowledge and vocabulary—ones vital to comprehending the selection's plot and main themes—in advance of class so they could be delivered efficiently via lecture. This explicit emphasis on building essential background knowledge, incidentally, was a practical adjustment that grew directly from my aforementioned independent research—in particular the work of E.D. Hirsch.[15] Students would be expected to record notes on all these pieces into their class notebooks, alongside the log entry they completed, and these assignments would accumulate over time, becoming a quick-reference study guide of the literature unit.*)

- After the intro to Böll, I *shared learning targets* for the period and/or the selection, pulled from the relevant content standards and other guidelines. Some examples: 'Students will be able to recognize relevant symbols in the selection and explain their significance to the overall themes of the selection' and 'Students will be able to use at least three specific examples from the selection in an assessment of the main characters' rebellion strategy'.

- Then we began reading the selection, but only after allowing questions from students about any part of the setup.

All told, the learning targets were kept 'hidden' from students for 30 minutes. It was time well spent, in that it was typically far more engaging than the standard 'What You Will Be Expected to Do Today' jazz. Namely, it built students' appetite for the selection by allowing them to wrestle with some of the story's big themes on their own terms and according to their own experiences. It strengthened students' ability to process and understand the selection by using explicit instruction to install crucial foundational knowledge and vocabulary. While learning targets may have provided clarity of task and kept all parts of the lesson on-track and chugging along, I'm fairly sure they wouldn't have kept the Academy group engaged as well as this sequence. In short, the setup *prepared* them to *engage* with the story while reading it, instead of getting derailed by questions about context, purpose, themes, and unfamiliar vocabulary.

This approach resonated with the kids in the Academy for a different reason as well. Many of them didn't particularly care about what kind of academic ability they would possess by the end of the period, the end of the trimester, or whenever. They most certainly *did* care, though, about that time when a teacher broke up a fight they were in and they got suspended but the other kid didn't. That was *unjust.*

Giving some controlled space to this kind of conversation—followed by some explicit knowledge-building, of course—was all it took to bring my kids from early 21st century Osseo, Brooklyn Park, Maple Grove, or Wherever, Minnesota, all the way into selections like *The Balek Scales*, which was written by an angry German writer from half a century ago. There was no need to sacrifice entire periods with instructionally empty calories to get them engaged—or, worse, to avoid challenging content altogether because kids 'couldn't see themselves' in them.

The science classroom, with its discrete concepts that build on one another, differs quite a lot from the English and social studies settings. But Ruska worked his own brand of 'keep them guessing' to build engagement. In his classroom, it was less within each lesson, and more over the course of entire instructional units.

He continually changed up how students interacted with and accessed content from day to day, having them process the information in multiple ways. 'I always started with this idea that if I could keep their hands busy, I could keep their minds engaged,' he told me. 'Some days we'd diagram and color to show how a certain cellular process worked.

On other days I'd have kids in groups to read about that same process, and then work out a model of that process with some supplies. It was all about keeping them busy at *something*, and then finding leaders within their work groups—kids who were getting it faster than others—to help things make sense to their partners.'

After setting the stage, Ruska would use a more traditionally academic approach to bring all the engagement work into focus. 'After those pieces, there would be note-taking and reading,' he shared with me, 'because those more hands-on activities couldn't quite get at the terms or the actual facts we know about the science. And then they'd have to show me they understood it all, sometimes through a test, sometimes through a presentation.'

In all, Ruska's engagement-through-variety fulfilled much the same purpose as Zelenak's and my focus on students' values and interests. Where Zelenak and I leveraged students' life experiences and perspectives to pique curiosity, Ruska went into his content through students' values of *social interaction*. Plus, by having students work in groups and occasionally present to the class to demonstrate their understanding of content, Ruska ingeniously leveraged a key social value of the adolescent human: preserving status (i.e. *saving face*) among their peers. (Taking a cue from him, by the way, I summarily worked more presentation into my own courses.)

I won't pretend that our 'keep them guessing' strategy was a research-guided practical choice based on multiple cognitive scientists' findings about adolescent learning tendencies or promoted to us by some professional-development trainer. Rather, it came out of observations we made of our kids over the years. With these observed preferences in mind, we knew the 'learning objective' way of keeping kids on track would most likely fall flat as an engagement tactic. We knew the real trick was getting kids to *value* the content we wanted them to learn, practice, and master.

This approach is similar in spirit to the values-based messaging or framing I discussed in the previous chapter. The same way humans have been shown to respond differently to different messages based on how those messages resonate with their deepest values, we saw that students engage to content based on how the content connects to their values. Continually reminding students of what they should learn by the end of a period may lend clarity, but it will not necessarily appeal to a deep adolescent value—especially if the concept is not something the students particularly care to learn.

It doesn't matter how you set expectations and targets, in other words. Write them on the board, do en masse chants of them periodically throughout the class session, brush up the 'student-friendliness' of their language, or whatever. If the students *don't value the concept*, clarity won't keep kids engaged.

But (and I can't say this enough), we never believed in moving the goalposts according to what students valued. We knew that if we chose our content and exercises only according to what our kids valued right now, we would deny them opportunities to learn about worlds outside their own experiences and to grow in new directions. And to us, that was absolutely not acceptable. We sought to make our students more *able*, remember, and that meant *expanding* our students' knowledge and abilities, not just reinforcing their current ones—spending more time looking out the window, in other words, than they were looking in the mirror.

Rather than adjust at the level of the content/exercises, we held firm on our rich content and exercises and did everything we could to bring kids closer to them—even if it meant 'tricking' students into hunting for them.

Engaging to challenging work through explicit priorities

As engaging as it was to route our paths to challenging content and tasks through students' values, we couldn't rely solely on this method. For indeed—and as any high school-level math teacher can most certainly tell you—some subject matter simply doesn't match up real well to kids' inherent values. You can be as clever as you please, in other words, and do whatever kinds of cognitive-linguistic coaxing you like…but when students find out there's no real practical use for quadratic equations after high school, the job of getting adolescents—especially ones who aren't all that keen on school to begin with—to dig into them becomes a *whole* lot more difficult.

It's hard to blame kids for not loving the idea of working hard on things they'll likely never need to know again. So instead of lamenting, resisting, or outright ignoring this reality, we tackled it head-on. We were honest with ourselves about it and, when the subject matter and/or skills to be taught were particularly 'boring-but-important' (to borrow a phrase from David Yeager[16]), we took a number of steps to make sure we could engage our students to them:

- First—and most importantly—we reviewed our scheduled subject matter to make sure we indeed considered it essential, taking Dr. Bob up on his allowance to adjust our course programming as necessary. And yes, we absolutely jettisoned content if, upon this reflection, we found that we could meet standards without them. Thanks to this review, which often led to eliminating legacy content (e.g. a previous teacher's pet unit, a random project that had 'always been in 10th grade geography class', etc.), we focused on what we believed were absolutely essential learning units and activities with regard to kids' preparation, the district's graduation requirements, and the state's content standards.

  Note: This did not mean that we only pruned courses *down* to essential learning priorities. Sometimes, this process helped us add or revise existing units to better reflect Academy premiums. As a result of my review, for instance, I re-worked an existing 'Choice Novel Unit' the 10th grade English team had done for years. While I liked independent reading and student choice, I felt it needed some tweaks—especially in terms of student accountability and text choices, which I tightened up considerably—to make it fit the Academy's logistics and mission. (Incidentally, this Independent Reading Project later informed READvisory, a school-wide reading initiative the Continuous School Improvement [CSI] team designed to target the school's goals around reading improvement. See Chapters 11 and 12 for more.)

- After landing on what we considered to be essential learning priorities, we designed structures—learning activities, in- and out-of-class supports, assessments, and so on—to move students toward mastery of those priorities.

- Having confidence in our leaner and more effective outlines of activities, we prepared our messaging to students about why these subject matter and/or skills were considered essential learning priorities.

This kind of priority-setting and continual expression of rationales turned out to be particularly effective for content and/or skills students needed to *master*—not just 'be exposed to' or 'practice'.

In my case, I prioritized the mastery of basic five-paragraph essay structure because all sophomores had to take the state's Basic Skills Writing Test—a test all Minnesota high school students had to pass in order to earn a diploma at that time. Though my sections of Academy students groaned and most certainly wanted to check out as I drew my mnemonic 'essay train' device on the board and presented a practice prompt for the umpteenth time, they engaged to the task because they were convinced that internalizing the process was a prioritized matter. It was boring, yeah, but they trusted it was important. And as such, they dug deep and found the motivation. (Incidentally, in 2005-06, the second year of the Sophomore Academy, I saw a 100% passage rate on the first attempt from my two Academy sections—a rate I had never seen in any other year, Academy or 'regular' English sections. While no other year ever recorded these types of results, my Academy sections— all identified as 'at risk' for high school, remember—always had success rates that matched my 'regular' English 10 sections. While I wish I had saved the data, I had no idea I would someday be writing a book about it.)

Ruska and Zelenak used priority-setting particularly effectively, identifying a few particularly important concepts in their respective biology and social studies classes and having students repeatedly demonstrate understanding until they reached a minimum bar of mastery.

I can well remember, for instance, stressed-out students cramming in my classroom for yet another crack at the states and capitals assessment in Zelenak's class. While I can't say exactly how he got them to be so engaged, I can absolutely affirm they were fully interested in meeting his expectations. (So much so, in fact, that forcing kids to put their social studies work away in my class became an annual ritual.) In biology, Ruska made it clear that students would not be allowed to move on to successive concepts until they proved they mastered foundational ones.

'We decided there were some key ingredients to all other learning,' Ruska explained to me, 'and we didn't even give grades until kids could prove that they had those key ingredients down. They had to do it and do it and do it. Once they showed they really knew what I needed them to know, they got their grade and could move on.

'I modified it a bit for struggling learners, as I saw they had a tendency to quit. Overall, though, it was designed so they could take the hands-on learning we were doing, put the academic terminology to it, and then show me they'd made the connection. But they weren't just able to do one or the other, not on those key things.'

In Klecker's math classroom, her emphasis was less on concepts to be mastered and more on prioritizing students' responsibilities in the learning process. She sent homework with the students nearly every day, stressing that she needed to see how they made sense of each day's concepts when working independently. When they reported for class each day with proof of how they struggled with practice problems, she could get better a sense of individual and class-wide gaps in understanding.

When all else fails, engage via accountability

A final way we engaged students into doing what was expected was through plain old accountability. When we needed them to do something because we knew it was good for their learning and for productive class sessions, we pushed them—sometimes with simple and sensible points-based incentives and consequences, and sometimes by personally challenging them to do a better job with their assigned learning.

Some of this accountability arched over entire grading periods, like our policies on late work. Though we all came at this a bit differently, we structured our policies and point-penalties to make sure the work got done at some point. Doing the intended learning exercises was the point. We didn't want to get so tough with these policies that kids never did the practice that would help them learn the material. Klecker, for instance, used a simple decimal system to note which assignments had been turned in after their due dates, and others of us allowed work to come in indefinitely at half-credit.

Other accountabilities, though, were more immediate to keep class sessions running as productively for students' learning as possible, and to nudge students into making good choices with their assigned work. We didn't shy away from regular quizzes, for example, to get kids showing up to class prepared.

When teaching a novel in my English class, for example, there was no way I could have learning-productive class sessions each day if too many of my students arrived without having read the assigned homework. I viewed in-class time as time to *learn about* the text, not to *read* it—just as collegiate literature classes would, that is. Class time was for explicit instruction about how the text was working, building background knowledge the author may have omitted, and collaborative processing of the text's themes through group discussion. And as such, the only reading we did in class was illustrative review: to close-read select passages for appreciating authors' artistry, crucial events, arguable interpretations, and so on.

Unlike in college, however, my students weren't always motivated to prepare simply because they were afraid of 'looking dumb' if they couldn't respond when I called on them. Some of them, in fact, had carved out personas based entirely on being unprepared. And while a lot of kids could get pulled into good reading habits through my framing, I designed the simple accountability of daily reading quizzes to jolt resistant kids in a different way.

The quizzes were simple—usually no more than a dozen true/false or multiple-choice items, all very straightforward and even sprinkled with funny answers to keep things light.

The agreement was simple, too. I explained it like this: 'Do the reading, and you'll get 10 to 15 free points every day. Bombing one or two won't kill your grade, but I wouldn't bomb ten or eleven of them if I were you. They're free points! Read your assignment tonight, then take tomorrow's quiz. You'll see how easy it is!'

And they did. Kids who read the assignments did well on the quizzes, because there were no tricks or surprises there.

And when they saw the points piling up—and also noticed that everything we were talking about in class made a whole lot of sense all of a sudden, and that they actually had opinions about a frustrating character here or a confusing event there—they *kept on* doing their reading.

And, as we graded the quizzes together—which provided a built-in comprehension review to start each class period (a bonus benefit I hadn't anticipated)—they even started getting competitive with one another about their score tallies.

Voila! Engagement.

When the outlook was particularly bleak, and the occasional Academy student *still* wasn't doing what they needed to prepare for classes, we got very direct. The teacher team would meet to figure out the best approach, and one of us (or more, if the student was struggling in multiple classes) would go straight to the student to conference with them about it. (For examples of how these conferences looked, note former Academy student Jade Templeton's account of 'get your crap together' talks we had with her in the previous chapter.)

All together, the Academy teachers were really very concerned about the ways we created student engagement to learning. It meant a lot to us, just not so much that we would ever sacrifice the rigor of our course content to make it happen. Very simply, we made 'getting it to happen'— through lesson design or messaging or outright accountability—a constant focus of our work.

To close this chapter on our academic approaches (and echoing some of the behavior expectations I suggested in the previous chapter): if you're an educator reading this and you believe your kids can never fully engage to works that are outside their reading level, their direct interests, or their comfort zones, I urge you to give your students more credit. Be aware that if you deny them the chance to interact with challenging content and master certain skills, you may be limiting what they learn about the world and what they can do within it. Figure out the trick of engaging them, and try a range of approaches, just as we did. I'll tell you right now, your students may surprise you by how interested they get, even when the subject matter isn't dialed exactly to their backgrounds, interests, and ability levels. (And this is coming from someone who did a full about-face on this during his classroom career, remember. Very simply, the Academy taught me it can be done.)

With these ideas firmly in mind, the next chapter will take a look at what we had to do when *none* of the tactics described here worked like we thought they would. For as much as it may seem that we had all the angles figured out, some classes pushed us to get more inventive.

Endnotes

1. See note 4 in Chapter 7.

2. For more on developmental psychologists' recent recommendations about teaching students social and emotional qualities, see discussion in Chapter 7 and that notes 3, 8 and 9 within the same chapter.

3. In the main, teachers are trained—initially and continually—according to *progressive* educational principles and ideals. As Kieran Egan accurately puts it in his 2002 book *Getting it Wrong from the Beginning: Our Progressive Inheritance from Herbert Spencer, John Dewey, and Jean Piaget* (New Haven, CT: Yale University Press, pp. 5-6): 'progressivism's tenets… [are] the conventional wisdom of American education'. The progressive tenets are so accepted as self-evident, in fact, that most teachers would never know they come from a specific tradition. When I say the Sophomore Academy's teachers wouldn't have labeled themselves as 'traditionalist' as opposed to 'progressive', it's because we simply didn't know of such labels or such schools of thought. Where 'trad-versus-prog' arguments break out fairly regularly at this time of writing (2018) on social media outlets like Twitter, we were essentially ignorant of the labels during the Academy years of 2004-2008.

4. National Research Council (2002) 'How Experts Differ from Novices', in *How People Learn: Brain, Mind, Experience, and School*. Washington, DC: National Academies Press.

5. Mayer, R., E. (2004) 'Should There Be a Three-Strikes Rule Against Pure Discovery Learning?', in *American Psychologist*, 59 (1), pp. 14-19.

6. Though much has been written about the crucial ties between background knowledge and successful reading comprehension, E. D. Hirsch stands out as an early champion of the concept. I found these works particularly instructive on the idea around the time of the Sophomore Academy: Hirsch, E., D., *et al.* (1998) *Cultural Literacy: What Every American Needs to Know*. New York, NY: Vintage Books. Also: Hirsch, E., D. (1999) *The Schools We Need: And Why We Don't Have Them*. New York, NY: Anchor Books. Lastly: Hirsch, E., D. (2006) *The Knowledge Deficit: Closing the Shocking Education Gap for American Children*. Boston, MA: Houghton Mifflin. I urge anyone taking up any such study now to visit any of these works by Hirsch, then pad them with pretty well anything by cognitive scientist Daniel Willingham. From there, Alice, enjoy your fall down the rabbit hole.

7. See chapter three in my 2014 book *Education is Upside-Down* (Lanham, MD: Rowman & Littlefield).

8. Ashman, G. (11 August 2018) 'An Interview with Dylan Wiliam.' (Filling the pail). Available at: gregashman.wordpress.com/2018/08/11/an-interview-with-dylan-wiliam/

9. Hartoonian, M. (12 December 2015) 'Courage or Timidity?' (Think. Teach. Inspire.) Available at: thinkteachinspire.com/2011/06/22/courage-or-timidity/

10. Ibid.

11. Hartoonian, M. (1997) 'Education is About Producing, Not Consuming', in *Social Education*, 61 (6), pp. 365-66.

12. For a discussion of 'academic' vs 'academic-like' classroom activities, see pages 127-131 of my 2014 book *Education is Upside-Down*, (Lanham, MD: Rowman & Littlefield).

13. In the past two decades or so of American education, declaring and posting 'learning targets' has emerged as a fairly common expectation for teachers across the enterprise. Though the learning target idea has existed for some time, the practice commonly became a required 'look-for' in evaluative observations carried out by so many administrators and instructional specialists over the past decade or so. (i.e. 'student-friendly descriptions—via words, pictures, actions, or some combination of the three—of what [teachers] intend students to learn or accomplish in a given lesson...shared [to] become actual targets that students can see and direct their efforts toward'; from Moss, C., M. and Brookhart, S., M. [2016] *Learning Targets: Helping Students Aim for Understanding in Today's Lesson*. Victoria, Australia: Hawker Brownlow Education, pp. 9-10)

14. Madeline Hunter was an American educator whose structures and standards for lesson-planning and –execution became widely followed in the late 20ᵗʰ century. About the time the Sophomore Academy teachers were coming into the profession, as a matter of fact, Hunter's ideas were still widely referred to—if, fairly, riding the outwardly swinging pendulum. For a pretty good summary of Hunter's classic lesson plan model, including the anticipatory set concept, see: Wilson, L., O. (No date) 'Madeline Hunter Lesson Plan Model.' (The Second Principle) Available at: thesecondprinciple.com/teaching-essentials/models-of-teaching/madeline-hunter-lesson-plan-model/

15. See note 6, on the previous page.

16. Yeager, D., S., *et al.* (2014) 'Boring but Important: A Self-Transcendent Purpose for Learning Fosters Academic Self-Regulation', in *Journal of Personality and Social Psychology*, 107 (4), pp. 559–580.

Chapter 9

Moving to Able, Part 3: In Case of Emergency…

'Invention, it must be humbly admitted, does not consist in creating out of void but out of chaos.'

– Mary Wollstonecraft Shelley

There were times when all our collaboration, support, framing, expecting, cheerleading, researching, caring, and hustle still didn't get it done.

For all the success we enjoyed in the main, every year brought a few students who were too far away for us to reach—kids with profoundly complicated home situations, kids caught up in highly distracting (and sometimes outright dangerous) activities outside school, and kids who actively prevented us from seeing what they needed. Unfortunately, these exceptionally distant students often didn't make it through their sophomore year, deciding to transfer from or drop out of Osseo Senior. Luckily for the Academy, however, we only saw a few of these cases per year.

(On the off chance one of those students is reading this: wherever you are, know that your Sophomore Academy teachers and peers still think of you fondly. In fact, many of you came up in the interviews for this book. If this book should happen to reach you, feel free to get in touch. I would love to hear from you, and it would be great to hear how your education turned out and how you're doing now.)

In the Academy's third year (2006-07), however, something very, very different happened. We ran into a *wall*.

Specifically, a wall of particularly tough students. As I said, we usually encountered a manageable number of truly resistant students, and most of the time we eventually reached them through continual communication, trying new strategies, and general hard-headedness. But this year they ballooned to numbers that overwhelmed our capabilities. And it was not a case-by-case situation. They were united in their resistance. Many of them knew each other for years before the Academy, so they knew one another's tendencies and personalities—and defended them fiercely. Put another way, they came into the Sophomore Academy's burgeoning culture with their *own* fully realized culture.

This new culture was both self-affirming and self-reinforcing. When they arrived, it quickly became apparent that we needed solutions beyond those that worked in years one and two. If we didn't up our game, the year-three students were going to derail everything we had built, maybe for good.

Interestingly, the year-three students didn't come at us with fire and fury like the inaugural group did.[1] Much to the contrary, this group brought profound *apathy*. In every way imaginable, they *did not care*.

They didn't care about being placed in the Sophomore Academy, they didn't care about how earnestly we wanted to help them overcome whatever rough patches they hit back in junior high, they didn't care about class assignments, they didn't care about our behavioral or work expectations, they didn't care if they earned poor grades on their work, they didn't care about being on time for class, and they didn't care about consequences, whether they applied to one of them or the whole group. Their response to pretty much everything was a shrug, an eye-roll, a slow turn-and-walkaway back to their desk. We tried hard to make them feel they belonged to the larger culture of Osseo Senior High, convincing them to 'learn with chips on their shoulders', showing them they had the ability to succeed. We got zero results. It was as if we weren't needed. Every student in the Academy's year-three wall had their needs met by this long-standing and lethargic group of friends.

They weren't cutting classes, bullying one another, explosively disrupting the learning environment, or making trouble elsewhere in the school. They just didn't want any of what we were offering, *thanks. We're good.*

(If we had the choice, we would have preferred harsh pushback at high volumes. We were all about moving our kids toward mainstream-institution-ready habits via strong structures across our classrooms, and we always saw abundant student brio as a *positive* to harness, not a fault to be squelched. Indeed, we actively encouraged our students to be passionate, as we viewed passion as a raw material loaded with potential. With the right containment and direction, we knew we could get that passion to work wonders for individual students and for overall classroom cultures. The third year of Academy students gave us precisely the opposite.)

While it probably goes without saying, the year-three wall's general and consistent apathy didn't generate much in the way of academic performances over their first few weeks with us. In our progress reports, we saw excessive numbers of missed and late assignments, piles of poor grades on tests/quizzes, and a general lack of effort and attention to detail, all within the first six weeks. At the time, though, we never felt any urgency about the group as a whole—most likely because they weren't making much *trouble*. They weren't reacting in any way.

Several members of this class confirmed their challenging nature and recalled the same slow start, too. In a focus group that included Sophomore Academy students from multiple years, one third-year alumnus, Faith Neumann, described the class as: 'Really bad. Seriously, we were *really* bad. We needed intervention, basically.' (Neumann went on to graduate *magna cum laude* with a degree in Ethnic Studies and to study law. At the time of this writing, she is scheduled to earn her JD in 2020.)

In the moment, of course, we teachers saw it like Faith did. The thing was, though, that we were unsure about how best to intervene. We were well-accustomed to kids not doing what we expected of them. As teachers of teenagers, we knew that was part of the deal. Plus, all the Sophomore Academy classes started with the obstinate knob cranked up a few notches. So yes, we'd been *there*. We were definitely *not* accustomed, however, to having so little to react to—to have nothing tangible, really, that warranted swift, definitive, and visible adult intervention.

And, trust me, it's a lot harder than it looks to design and enact actions that get kids to *care*. It effectively paralyzed our team of committed, creative teachers. And we were only six weeks in.

We ultimately chose to stay true to our processes, hoping to see more and more kids buying in, overall participation in classes and activities ticking upward, and students' performances/results in turn taking care of themselves.

The struggles with the year-three wall went from confounding and paralyzing to four-alarm fire when the first trimester came to a close.[2] When the Academy kids' grades were finalized and we compared them across the team, we saw far more failing, near-failing, and incomplete grades than we could accept.

Our number-one charge, after all, was making sure our students didn't fall behind on credits over the course of their sophomore year. And while a few F's per trimester were inevitable, the numbers we saw across the Academy—and, even more distressingly, the numbers of kids we saw with *multiple* failing grades—made it plain that we couldn't stay the course.

We couldn't, in other words, stick with the tactics that worked well in years one and two. Despite how hard we were pushing those buttons, we clearly weren't getting the effects we were used to seeing. Indeed, even actual *consequences* didn't break their apathy. As the end of the trimester loomed, we watched unusually high numbers of kids with failing grades kind of take their F's with no attempts at late-trimester rallies or desperate extra-credit completion. Even with their high school record hanging in the balance: shrug, eye-roll, walk away.

Surprised as we were by this, we didn't have time to stand and admire the problem. In light of the Academy's mission and the data that supported it, we knew we had an emergency on our hands. If we truly wanted to *move these students to being able*, they absolutely had to understand—and very quickly—that increasing their investment in their own schooling was in their best interests. Based on the attitude, demeanor, and accordingly lame results we'd seen out of them over that first trimester, it was abundantly clear that far too many of that year-three group didn't have what it took to make it out of high school with a diploma.

We needed a radically different approach. What we came up with was the 'Game of Life', an intensive experiential learning exercise that was likely the most innovative and, according to alumni, the single most memorable activity of the entire Sophomore Academy initiative.

Over the rest of this chapter, I'll share more about how the Game of Life was designed, what the Game of Life looked like in action, and all the ways it impacted the third-year Academy students who played it.

As you may expect by now, this examination is not intended as a comprehensive account. Because of the Game of Life's many moving parts and the myriad ways Academy students experienced it, a truly comprehensive record would involve far too much detail. And it would miss the point that a uniquely demanding group required a uniquely creative approach.

The Game of Life: Objectives

During the years the Sophomore Academy was in operation (2004-08), Osseo Senior High ended each trimester with a mark-reporting day. No classes were held, but teachers reported for a wide range of trimester-end business: finishing outstanding trimester grading and recordkeeping, entering students' trimester grades into the school's data system, preparing classrooms for the subsequent trimester, meeting with department teammates to coordinate trimester content schedules, etc.

On the mark-reporting day that concluded 2006-07's first trimester, the Sophomore Academy team met and, based on the aforementioned and deeply concerning end-of-trimester grades, determined that the class in progress needed a drastic intervention.

While it was tempting to view the results as a 'blip' and stick to our usual processes, we didn't have unbounded time. For again, the statistics that bore the Sophomore Academy to begin with were plain: if our students fell below the minimum-credit threshold over the course of this year, the historical data told us that they were essentially guaranteed to drop out or not graduate on time. With a third of the year gone and large numbers of students with failing grades in core classes, we couldn't risk doing more of the same and hope their apathy would somehow work itself out.

It was hard to know where to begin. We had no real sense of what might actually punch through. After all, if the class's indifference was so profound that large numbers of students didn't bother to rescue their own grades, we weren't sure what we could possibly do to create the ideal impression. We talked about a wide range of possible actions, from getting tougher and swifter with consequences to actively and formally showing more care and understanding.

After considerable discussion, however, we didn't see that any new classroom-managerial policies, outward demeanors, or constructed check-in routines would have much impact. None of those options seemed likely to provide the *jolt* we thought they needed.

We needed a quick, concentrated, and definitive disruption. Something that would take the kids out of their usual ways of thinking. Something that would rattle them and maybe leave their ears ringing for a while. While imposing stricter late-work policies or instituting regular one-on-one progress conferences might have had some marginal effect, they were too slow. Those tactics wouldn't shake anything up. And, again, the last thing we could afford was any tactic that got us the dreaded shrug, eye-roll, walk away. If we lost any more time, we would fail at our most foundational mission with these kids.

In all, we knew we needed an intervention that could do all of the following:

- *Send a strong message about the moment's urgency.* The kids had to know we were taking their success in high school and beyond very seriously, even if they weren't. (On this note, we thought it was worth taking Dr. Bob up on his offer to interrupt our normally scheduled curricular programming where necessary. While all of us did this to some degree in our individual classrooms, we thought the kids might get a truer sense of the situation's gravity if they saw us swerve the entire Academy—all four core classes at once—away from business-as-usual.)

- *Give the students a brief, intensive, and explicit course in our prioritized personal habits.* Where we'd previously woven our desired personal habits and mindsets into the fabric of the Academy's policies and messages, we knew with the third-year group we had to be more overt and intense. Such policies and messages had helped shape previous Academy classes' behaviors and attitudes, but their effect was admittedly a little too much like 'water on a stone' for the year-three situation. For the 'stone' year three had lain before us and for how much of the year we'd already spent, we needed a *sledgehammer.*

- *Present the course in a way that didn't feel like schooling as usual.* If students weren't moved by schooling's usual structures and consequences (which, to that point, they certainly hadn't been), we figured there was no use employing and slightly modifying those structures and consequences. To put it another way, the intervention strategies we chose couldn't be incremental adjustments to our current systems; we had to enact something that would feel like a shock to the system.

- *Affect the new trimester's overall grade.* While no academic content would be covered in the intervention we ultimately designed, we needed consequences and incentives of some kind to encourage participation. The point total of the exercise had to be large enough that students would invest effort, but not so large that it could permanently derail kids' grades for the trimester. Also, all points at stake should be on the basis of effort, not demonstration of mastery or proficiency. Whatever we decided to do, we wanted to get across that the institutional basics (e.g. showing up, being prepared, working hard despite immediate levels of interest, working *hungry*, etc.) were of absolute highest importance.

- *Be fully imagined, planned, and ready to execute within the opening weeks of trimester two.* We were out to shock and rattle, and we figured nothing could do so better than an abrupt ambush of their routines. While lazing into second trimester and working slowly up to something drastic *could* have worked, we thought it could cost us the element of surprise. (Also, being honest with ourselves, we knew our best intentions could well have gotten swept up in events if we rolled up to it more slowly. Schools have a way of doing that, as anyone who has ever attempted to make substantial improvements or changes will tell you. To use a familiar saying, it's like changing the tires on a car while it's moving down the highway.)

This was a huge and daunting project we were considering, especially when each of us still had so much individual end-of-trimester business to complete. The way we saw it, though, there wasn't any way we could circle back when the timing was better. For the students (especially those who already missed credits in our core classes), each additional moment lost was crucial.

So resolved, we turned our attention to what this disruptive learning experience might look like.

The Game of Life: Design & Elements

As we began mulling possibilities, Academy social studies teacher Gerry Zelenak half-jokingly suggested that we create some kind of simulation to immerse the students in a miniature world of work: something where the students could get a whole different perspective on the types of behaviors we were asking of them in our classrooms, and that would draw from some rather miserable jobs Zelenak had bounced among in his pre-teaching years—jobs which, as you may recall, helped make him get more serious about choosing a career in education. He offered that it might be a good way to get kids thinking differently about their general lack of passion.

'I think I just thought it was the one thing that might make the break we were after,' Zelenak recalled. 'Like, you know what might get them to understand all we were saying to them? Put 'em to work—like the *world* was going to make them work, not like schools did. Tasks they *wouldn't like*, but that they'd be accountable to doing *anyway*, correctly and on time and no excuses accepted.'

We teased Zelenak's initial idea out, suggesting experiences that such a simulation could contain. At first, our suggestions were mainly for laughs—such as having kids do some really tedious assembly line-like work and putting them on production quotas—because who would really *do* that? And *how*? As we continued describing what it could look like, however, we got more and more intrigued by how it could meet all the criteria we had in mind. It was offbeat, for sure, and it would take a lot of energy and time to assemble quickly. If we could make it work, it could communicate the themes that had thus far not made it through.

We ultimately resolved to go through with it, aiming to launch the simulation in the second week of the new trimester. We called it 'The Game of Life', and its major elements looked like this:

- Interrupt all usual academic programming for one week to immerse Sophomore Academy students fully.
- Use a large venue in the school as the Game of Life's learning arena, wherein all Academy classes would meet for the duration of the game. (Operational note: For this venue, we were able to secure the school auditorium soon after we established our rough plan. This venue turned out to be ideal for other Game of

Life pieces, for reasons that will soon become clear.)

- Convene the two consecutive Academy sections[3] for 110-minute blocks in the learning arena twice per day for the entire week. Over the Game of Life's course, all Academy students would meet in the learning arena for periods two and three (supervised by Zelenak, Kalenze, and Trzynka) and for periods five and six (supervised by Klecker, Ruska, and Trzynka).

- Initiate all Game of Life activities, procedures, and conditions with no advance fanfare or justification. (This was a smaller consideration within the Game of Life experience, but crucial to an effective opening. Essentially, the idea was to whisk students into activities before they could fully understand what was happening and get their guard up.) Accomplish this on the first day with signs on classroom doors directing all students to meet outside the school auditorium. Upon their arrival in the auditorium foyer, give simple directions about immediate tasks and expectations. (Operational note: Zelenak and I were in charge of this. We received all the Academy students in the foyer, then told them only to go inside and await further instructions from Mr. Ronnie King, Osseo Senior's dapper and thickly muscular Assistant Principal of school discipline at the time, whose physical presence perfectly matched the serious impression we aimed to create, by the way. With the impressive, serious, and authoritative Assistant Principal King explaining the Game's opening expectations, we were quite confident there would be no questions asked.)

- Divide the Game of Life learning arena into four sections, with each one representing a different type of employment. The four types—manual labor, office labor, research and development, and executive/creative—must all be openly visible to one another, with executive/creative located in a featured or central position. (In the auditorium, for instance, we placed executive/creative up on the stage.)

- For tasks, each employment level involves the following:

    1. *Manual labor* simulates factory assembly tasks by having students put screws into wood blocks to simulate circuit-board construction. When all boards' pattern templates are filled, students are to 'build circuits' by winding yarn around the screw patterns according to specified directions. When all these 'circuits' are 'built' and all materials have been used, convert the assembly plant into a recycling plant: direct students working at this level to disassemble all 'circuit boards'. Collect teams' results at the end of each work period for shift assessment and to inform discussion of individual workers' re-assignment. (Operational note: For setup, Zelenak and I went to a big-box department store near my home over a weekend for supplies, then cut and marked all the 'circuit templates' by hand in my garage. We brought receipts to Dr. Bob afterward for reimbursement. By my recollection, the screwdrivers, screws, and lumber we bought on this day were the only non-salary monies Osseo Senior ever had to lay out for the Sophomore Academy initiative.)

    2. *Office labor* simulates a shipping-and-receiving department by fulfilling shipping orders from all over the school building. This includes tracking all packages' whereabouts and persons last responsible for packages' whereabouts. Collect teams' results at the end of each work period for shift assessment and to inform discussion of individual workers' re-assignment. (Operational note: For setup, we collected every unused box—*every single box*, of every shape and size—we could find in the school, wrote

random codes on them, placed them in classrooms all throughout the school, and requested that teachers call the auditorium randomly to arrange pickups and deliveries from, to, and between their classrooms.)

3. *Research and development* involves students reading various short informational works and filing short reports on them, with assigned students working toward daily team quotas. Collect teams' results—tallies, plus all reports—at the end of each work period for shift assessment and to inform discussion of individual workers' re-assignment. (Operational note: To set this up, all teachers assembled dozens of short readings, plus a set of basic guiding questions that could apply generally across all to guide the students' report writing.)

4. *Executive/creative* watches documentary films and, like 'research and development', also files reports. In addition, however, this level makes recommendations about how their organization should act on the information presented in the documentaries. In order for all other levels to be able to see the executive/creative team's working conditions, place this team in a central, easily visible location with regard to other employment levels. Collect teams' results—tallies, plus all reports—at the end of each work period for shift assessment and to inform discussion of individual workers' re-assignment. (Operational note: In constructing this workspace we reserved a large TV-VCR cart so all other workers in the auditorium could readily see that the executive/creative team's work involved watching films. We faced the screen away from the audience, however, so they could not see what types of films were showing. Also, we purchased a supply of snack food—popcorn, candy,

soft drinks—that we teachers would periodically and quite *ceremonially* bring across the stage to the workers as 'perks'. As I'm sure you can imagine, this got the full attention of students on the floor of the auditorium as they drudgingly drove screws into boards, ran empty boxes from one location to another, and hurriedly read piles of informational texts to meet quotas.)

- For initial 'job placement', have students complete and submit an application to the Academy teachers for review. To test students' attention to detail, the application forms include standard administrative-paperwork directives like 'Complete in black or blue ink only' and 'For office use only: Do not write in this space'. Include several pencils, brightly colored pens, markers, and so on, alongside the black- and blue-inked pens made available as writing utensils.

- Supply instant feedback to students' applications. Direct them to slide their completed application through a slot made through the auditorium's stage curtains, then declare visibly and definitively whether the student's application moves them on to the interview phase or not. (Operational note: We accomplished this by having Klecker and Ruska behind the curtain to review and announce, respectively. Klecker would review the applications quickly at a detail level only [i.e. were 'office-use-only sections' written in, was application completed with black or blue ink only, were all fields complete] and approve or disapprove. If approved, Ruska boomed—through an amplifier and some sound-processing equipment of mine that lowered his voice several octaves—only the applicant's name and 'ACCEPTED. AWAIT FURTHER INSTRUCTIONS AND PREPARE FOR INTERVIEW.' If *not* approved, though, the application would be crumpled up and vigorously tossed back through the slot onto the front of the stage, with Ruska—again in his 'Wizard of the Academy' voice—only saying the applicant's name and 'DENIED!' With no explanation of why they were denied, students were to start again: take their denied application and a fresh form, determine what they had done incorrectly, and re-apply, as many times as it took to be accepted and moved on. Incidentally, watching initially rejected students' reactions as their crumpled applications bounced back to their feet and Ruska boomed their fate is a memory that has forever burned into my consciousness. The looks on their faces showed clearly that this process was getting through to them like nothing yet had before—which was, of course, precisely why we constructed the Game of Life in the first place. If you may be thinking we were crushing their poor souls by asking them to pay attention to a very reasonable, real-world task, fear not—all students eventually moved on to interviews and all were allowed to join the Game.)

- Interview students individually to discuss application points, but also to go over trimester one performance—attendance, engagement, work completion, and so on—and to make a recommendation for their Game of Life 'initial employment level'. (Operational note: Zelenak and I were in charge of this while Klecker and Ruska reviewed applications. We conducted interviews one-on-one in the auditorium seats as students applied, re-applied, and/or patiently waited.)

- Based on applications, interviews, and trimester one results, place students into employment levels. All Academy teachers work on their shared prep period to work out this placement. (Operational note: By the combined fifth-sixth period of the Game's opening day, we were able to gather all the Academy students and inform them about where they had been placed, to describe each job task to them, and to inform them of what the remainder of the Game of Life week would look like for them—how they could become 'shift managers' within their current employment levels, how they could get promoted and demoted across levels, etc. Per our design premium about the Game of Life counting authentically in the upcoming trimester's grade, we also used this time to explain that their week's participation would be graded out of a possible 200 points that would then be divided four ways and applied across all four Academy classes, with no option for extra credit. Essentially, the grading policy told students they would be consistently rewarded if they showed up every day and did their best. If they did so, they had a chance to start the new trimester with a 50/50 foundation in each class, roughly the same percentage-booster as a perfect score on a significant test. We told them they would be able to opt out of the Game of Life altogether and receive alternative assignments for the week, and this alternative would also be graded out of 200 distributed points. These opt-outs, though, would also be escorted to the office to have one-to-one meetings with the principal, Dr. Bob, to explain why they were choosing to forfeit a healthy trimester-padding cushion they could earn simply by showing up and making an effort. Dr. Bob did actually have a few of these conferences, and he even pulled parents in by phone so the reluctant kids could explain for themselves why they were choosing to not earn what were essentially free points toward their next-trimester grade in four of six classes. Needless to say, all students eventually came back to the auditorium to participate.)

- Reward hard work and displays of employment-level leadership by promoting students through the four employment levels and/ or to shift-management positions within levels. (Operational note: As we moved through the week, all Academy teachers were responsible for observing students in their assigned employment levels and for collecting evidence about their performance. We would note who was working particularly hard and who wasn't, who was urging other level-mates to achieve higher standards and meet level quotas, and so on. We would meet during our shared fourth-hour preparation period and after school to shuffle students among levels and supervisory positions, with new assignments announced at the beginning of each work period. Students placed at certain levels would then be responsible for 'training' and 'onboarding' students who earned promotions.)

- On Friday, the final day of the Game of Life, put students through several processing and reflection activities to assess whether our intended messages about the value of effort and 'doing the right things' in school had hit home or not. (Operational note: We dedicated the first few hours of that final Game morning to a range of guest speakers and discussion leaders: students from previous Academy classes who had epiphanies and turnarounds during their sophomore year, other Osseo Senior students who were well-known in the school community but who had to overcome several obstacles and/or questionable choices. For final exercises, we had students complete a series of reflection questions, sit for individual 1-on-4 debriefing sessions with all the Academy teachers at once, and go to the computer lab to prepare a 'New Trimester Resolution' that would be kept with Academy teachers for the duration of the trimester. To prepare this resolution, students had to reflect on and draw from all elements of their Game of Life experience, their first-trimester performance, and any new realizations they arrived at over the duration of these experiences.)

The Game of Life: Impact

As I mentioned, the exercise had many, many moving parts. Indeed, while putting together the 'Design & Elements' summary, I was still a bit astonished that we took it on and made it all happen. Considering all we had to build and arrange, as well as the limited time we had to work with among our other duties (all Academy teachers taught classes in addition to the two Academy sections per day), it could very easily have been something we brainstormed and believed in but ultimately decided was too overwhelming to pull off.

Heading into second trimester with the apathetic year-three group and all the failed credits that were piling up, the situation was too critical for us to sit and do nothing. And while we could've chosen many, many more conventional interventions, the Game of Life exercise seemed uniquely suited to our crucial objectives. Namely, it broke up the schooling routine; it required kids to pay attention to detail, not simply settle for 'close enough'; it held kids directly accountable in multiple ways, and it openly and immediately rewarded kids for the effort they put in; it pushed kids to work *hungry*—to go and get their success, not expect success to come to them (and/or opt to quit when it didn't); and it gave kids a way to reflect on their first-trimester attitudes and performance outside of the academic context.

Thankfully, too, the Game of Life brought the best out of the year-three kids and reset the tone for the rest of the school year.

Reflecting on what it looked like in the moment, everyone involved recalled how the auditorium absolutely buzzed with activity, focus, and teamwork over the Game of Life's course.

At the time, others from outside the Academy confirmed this for us as well. More specifically, we got objective feedback in the moment from the stream of Osseo Senior High staffers who came down to see what the hell was going on in the auditorium. Drawn to the game during their prep periods because they heard about the crazy thing the Sophomore Academy was doing (or perhaps to see what was causing the frantic, stressed expressions on our 'shipping and receiving' kids' faces as they retrieved empty boxes from their classrooms), they gawked at the Game of Life operations in states that settled somewhere between disbelief, fascination, amusement, and horror. Then they pulled one of us aside to get a full rundown: How did we do it? What's the point supposed to be? Why are the kids listening and doing all this stuff? What are the incentives? What are the stakes?

In these side conversations I always started at the beginning, explaining that the Academy put heavy premiums on building kids' habits, outlooks, and mindsets, but that all our usual means had fallen flat with this group of students. Accordingly, all elements of the Game of Life—its tasks, its manufactured competition, its feedback-and-promotion routines, its bearing on trimester two grades—were intended to impact students' school-related habits, outlooks, and mindsets related to *effort* and *responsibility*. The exercise's main goal was getting kids to *care* about the most basic prerequisites for success.

After that setup, I pointed to the kids before us as evidence that we might actually have found a way through. I noted David here, for example, scribbling away in the research and development group, and explained how he opted out on day one and had to be prodded back into the Game by Dr. Bob and a phone call home. I then pointed out Sheshauna on the stage in the executive/creative workspace, a girl who placed straight into that group on the first day but who was still as focused on day three as she had been on day one—and who even assumed the responsibility of 'training' students recently promoted into her level.

My bottom line to these inquiring teachers was that, counter to what we saw all through the first trimester, laziness and a lack of caring seemed were becoming the exceptions, rather than the rules, in the Game of Life arena, and that kids were demonstrating effort in all kinds of ways.

Though it took a lot of brainstorming, planning, and coordination—and, unlike in our classrooms, a bunch of *completely meaningless tasks* for the students—the kids seemed to have found a productive desire in the Game of Life that they hadn't found in the academic arena.

Better still, in a number of ways the kids were confirming our observations that they were reaching valuable conclusions about the nature of hard work. For example, they were seeing that working hard was not ability-dependent but purely a *choice*; that working hard wasn't actually all that *hard*; and that working hard came more easily if you were hungry; and that, yes, it was completely legit to be hungry for 'not looking dumb in front of my classmates' or 'watching a movie and eating popcorn on the auditorium stage'. While these realizations were difficult to observe, the cumulative impact became more and more visible as the week rolled on.

By Thursday morning of the Game of Life week, for instance, it dawned on us that the 'executive/creative' category (the Game's most prestigious employment level) now included more than half of the students. It took us by surprise at first, likely because we had been working so hard to keep up on all the assessments, promotions, logistics, supervision, and so forth. But sure enough, by the second-to-last day, the Game's highest employment level, which had started with just three kids, had grown to nearly two dozen focused, note-taking, and silent (except when munching popcorn, of course) employees. By the last day, the research and development group—the Game of Life's third-highest employment category—had ten employees. Of the 39 Sophomore Academy students, then, 30 had worked their way into the top two levels—and were enjoying the benefits of their positions.

For the first time since we met them, the year-three kids had by and large done the little-but-crucial things. They were putting in the hard work, day in and day out. And that's all we were after. Plainly and simply, at long last, it looked like we might have actually gotten the year-three kids to *care*. Now that we had seen it—and, importantly, now that our kids had seen it in themselves—we felt we finally had the raw material we could work with for the rest of the year.

In addition to what we could observe and assess daily (or point out to visitors), the records we kept of the Game of Life provide some interesting insights into how the Game changed student attitudes.

The notes we kept and evidence we collected about the students' work habits (which we used to determine how students progressed through employment levels) give a good idea of how driven the kids were, on average, to succeed within the game's parameters. Again, 30 of the 39 Academy students finished with at least 160 of the available 200 points, leaving only 23% of the class scoring a 'C' or lower (140 or less) on the exercise—a figure we were pleased with, considering the 'wall' of students that had us so concerned throughout the first trimester.[4]

Even more interesting, however, were the informal reflection activities all students completed on the final day, which provided qualitative information about how students processed the Game's demands and their individual journeys through it.

While these reflections provide great amounts of information about the kids' outlooks and mindsets as the Game of Life came to a close, the most instructive themes with regard to the Game's impact are these: students remarking on how *proud* they felt to have achieved something they set their mind to, and students clearly understanding what we were hoping to get across about the importance of personal investment in assigned tasks. Below are a few of many notable examples:

- Asked to explain how she felt about the tasks she was given and about the overall design of the exercise, student Bionca Brown (who, at the time of this writing, recently finished a BA in psychology and works as a school paraprofessional) wrote, 'I felt wonderful, because I made it to Level 4! I was thinking to myself I must be trying really hard to make it this far. I felt responsible.' Asked how the overall Game of Life experience made her feel differently about school, Bionca responded, 'It made me change a lot. I feel like I made it to the top and now I realize that I have to do what I gotta do...This is not the streets and outside, it's school. When you come to school you have to do what you gotta do in school.'

- Another student, Siera Walton (who, incidentally, now works as a licensed social worker and case manager), noted some key realizations she made about herself and schooling in her reflection. She wrote: 'I learned about myself that when I want something I will work towards it. Like I said I want to get to Level 4, and I made it there. When I was in the 3rd level I worked extra hard to get promoted. I also learned that if I work hard enough it all will pay off. When I made it to the 4th level I felt like I did something good.'

- Still another, Miranda Thune, put the lessons of the Game of Life into perfectly practical terms, writing, 'Now I know that getting A's and B's really isn't hard at all. If you're in class, do the work, you're good. It's not hard at all.'

Though I won't pretend that the Game of Life made everything perfect, the remainder of that year was much more academically productive—and generally smoother—than the first trimester. We teachers sure didn't feel the need, in other words, to go into 'emergency mode' again.

I also can't say I have thorough data on how this class turned out—enough to know whether the Game of Life corrected students' courses in the long term or not, that is. I can tell you that all the students I was able to contact from this class (right around half, that is) ultimately earned their high school diplomas, even after their rocky start. (One transferred out of Osseo Senior to earn her diploma at another high school, and another needed extra time after withdrawing from school for a time.)

Collecting all the anecdotes, operational records, and qualitative reflections together, however, there are clear indications that the Game of Life jolted the year-three Academy students to make better choices for themselves.

To this book's larger arguments, though, the most valuable part of the Game of Life is how it showed what can be accomplished at the school-site level when a group of practitioners has the right combination of autonomy, operating structures, and administrative support. Emergency situations can indeed be addressed effectively, within mission, but it can be excruciatingly difficult without proper room to move and able helping hands. Within the structures that Dr. Bob created when he commissioned the Sophomore Academy—not an off-the-shelf, comprehensive program, remember—we were given the freedom to make a real difference when it mattered most.

The next chapter will conclude the exploration of the Sophomore Academy initiative, focusing on the effects these actions created among the students and how many of those students look back on the experience ten years or so later.

Endnotes

1. For more on how the first year group challenged us, see Chapter 6, 'Getting Stable'.

2. At the time, Osseo Senior's year was divided into three 12-week trimesters. Trimester one ended in late November.

3. Recall that in the Academy schedule, the two sections of students met in hours 2 and 3 (flip-flopping in English and social studies) and again in hours 5 and 6 (flip-flopping in science and math), with individual class times at 55 minutes each.

4. Incidentally, two 'F' grades—100/200 points—were given. While one opted out for most of the Game of Life, the other 'F' was given to a student whose participation was seriously limited after suffering an injury on the Game of Life's first day. While this may seem a callous decision, the consequence was actually appropriate and realistic with regard to the situation: she sustained her injury while monkeying around *while class was in session,* jumping from an unsafe height in the auditorium.

Chapter 10

They Knew They Belonged

'If you can show me how I can cling to that which is real to me, while teaching me a way into the larger society, then and only then will I drop my defenses and hostility, and I will sing your praises and help you to make the desert bear fruit.'

– Ralph Ellison

'Being a teacher gets overlooked by many, but when I think about inspirational teachers I think about my sophomore teachers. They all possessed the eagerness to see everyone succeed. Something that came naturally to them.'

– Selam Yimer, first-year Sophomore Academy student, in a Facebook post for National Teacher Appreciation Day (8 May 2018)

In this book's very first pages, I dropped you into a fight scene. While reading it, you may have assumed you were about to read a 'from-the-mean-streets' work like *Stand and Deliver* or *Dangerous Minds*.

That scene, which captures a few minutes of an actual day in the Sophomore Academy's first year, connects directly to one of the most important aspects of this enterprise: establishing a sense of *individual belonging* and *shared community*.

I can hardly blame you if that sounds odd, or if you're thinking, 'Wait—he's introducing a chapter on "belonging" by talking about an *assault* the Academy kids planned and carried out?' Indeed, it's hard to see how multiple students beating up another could ever jibe well with concepts like 'community' and 'belonging'.

Before I bring these two opposed elements together, let's be clear: the incident didn't sit well with us at the time. It wasn't the type of thing any of us wanted to see in our school, and it was *very* definitely not something we wanted associated with the Sophomore Academy in that crucial first year. You may recall that our little school-within-a-school caused quite a few changes throughout Osseo Senior's structure, and that meant many of the school's eyes were trained on us. To skeptics, an incident like this could be viewed as a sign that Dr. Bob's grand Sophomore Academy idea—which caused class sizes to increase and teachers' preferred schedules to get shuffled around—was rambling out of control. Because we aimed for the Sophomore Academy to exist without inconveniencing the larger school ecosystem, in other words, the impression this assault could create was definitely one we were hoping to avoid.

All the troubling aspects of the assault aside, however, the incident stands out rather prominently in light of what we hoped to accomplish in the Sophomore Academy. In fact, when it happened we teachers took it as evidence that our combined efforts were creating the *desired* effects in our students. That's right, in many ways, we *liked* what we saw when we viewed the situation in a big-picture sense.

Before I dig too deep a hole for myself, however, some context is necessary. Allow me to back up and share more details about the incident, its origins, and its aftermath. It's appropriate here, as it should shed some light on the net-positive feelings we took away from our kids jumping and beating a fellow student. (Without a doubt, it's hard for me to even write that last sentence.)

Once that context is established, I'll build outward from this single incident to show how it was of a larger narrative emerging in the Academy—a story that, a decade later, many alumni still single out as one of the Academy's greatest successes.

The assault happened during the Academy's first year—a group of students, you may recall, that presented us with intense attitudes and challenges at our outset.[1] The group waiting for me at the bottom of the stairs—the assailants who coordinated every act so they could get an adult to hear them—included five Academy girls.[2]

That day, when I asked them about what happened upstairs a few minutes prior, the girls *exploded*. Shouting all at once, they explained how another of their Academy classmates, Kelsey, who had recently missed numerous days of class, had been the target of intense bullying by a group of senior girls for the last month or so. And though she had covered her absences by claiming illness or that she was 'dealing with stuff at home', she had in reality been skipping school to avoid the torment.

When I asked them to be more specific about what Kelsey had been going through, the girls explained that the bullies had been working a kind of under-the-radar psychological warfare, the kind portrayed so well in movies like *Mean Girls* and *Pretty in Pink* and, undoubtedly, experienced by thousands of high-schoolers every day. They told me the bullies would very suddenly silence themselves and stare at their target as Kelsey passed them in the hallways or the lunchroom, for example, as well as broadcast horrible rumors about her.

By all accounts, the girls doing the bullying were skilled. As seasoned teenaged bullies tend to be, they were masters of tactics that were wildly effective at driving their targets crazy with adolescent self-consciousness and incredibly hard for teachers and administrators to see, much less prosecute. And because no grown-ups were doing anything about it, the Academy girls believed it was up to them to make it stop. They picked one of the senior bullies (the most popular and high-profile one, of course), and decided to send her and her cohorts a message—one that was clearer than any they had ever received.

I was a bit confused at this point, to be honest. The victim they said they were defending wasn't someone this particular group of girls ran with. I'd barely seen them interact with her in class, and I knew the group of them didn't have history with her going back to junior high. I was doing my best to make sense of their story, so I pressed them on this very point. Essentially, I asked them, 'Why are you so interested all of a sudden in defending Kelsey? I've hardly seen you guys talk to her.'

Their response has always stuck with me:

'She's *Academy*! We weren't going to let her get *punked* like that!'

It hit me hard. It was one of the first and clearest signs any of us in the Academy had received that what we were doing was working. It gave me chills. (And it still does today.)

Before we go any further, let's get back to the bottom of the stairs. In that moment, I didn't have time to be jubilant or moved or anything else besides a cool-headed adult. A popular senior girl was upstairs with Sharpie scrawled on one side of her face and an ice pack on the other. Word was rocketing through the senior class that a bunch of sophomore thugs had mercilessly jumped and beaten one of their own. Five of my students needed administrative consequences (and, frankly, to be ushered out of the building as soon as possible for their own safety). And another one of my students was still at home, afraid to come to school.

I hardened my face and explained to the girls that we were all going to the office. As with everything in the Academy, they had to take responsibility for their actions, however noble or justified they believed them to be. Regardless of their reasons, the actions they chose were not acceptable or allowable. I told them I respected their impulse to help another Academy kid, but that taking the law into their own hands—especially *violently*—was never going to be okay, in school or the Academy.

I asked them if this was clear, and they nodded yes.

I then pointed to each one of them and estimated the likely disciplinary consequences based on what I witnessed and what I knew about the school's operating codes of conduct. For the puncher, a three-day suspension, maybe more. For the marker-wielder, likely the same. For the others, one-day suspensions for co-planning the attack. I explained that I would not lie to cover up anything I'd seen, and this wasn't about us 'getting our story straight'. More so, I was delivering them to the office so this entire situation could move forward toward a more civil resolution.

I asked again if they understood, and again met with no disagreement or resistance from the girls.

I proposed that I should do all the talking once we got to the office. I would explain all I saw, give my disciplinary recommendations, and provide the full story about their bullied classmate. The girls' part, though, would stay silent until I explained all the essentials to administration. If they didn't want additional consequences, their best move was to not escalate this further once we made it to the office.

Again, nods. They agreed that they understood, and that they could do it.

Finally, I promised that I would request, once we got all the consequences out of the way, that some action be taken to hold the senior bullies accountable and to permanently and satisfactorily move past the situation, and that we activate the school's peer-mediation process to work on an authentic resolution. I told the girls that I would request to be a part of the mediations that ultimately took place, as I knew the parties involved (recall that the assaulted senior bully was a former student of mine[3]). As we still had several months to go in the school year, after all, we were all going to have to find a reasonable peace moving ahead.

Again, they nodded.

Having agreed to all these conditions, they followed me to the office. No resistance, no arguing, no running away. Just five kids that had no regrets about what they did (again, we would have to work on that part) and one teacher who couldn't quite believe how it all was playing out.

When I brought the girls in to Assistant Principal Brian Chance, his disbelief was similar to mine. He watched in stunned silence as I explained the situation and the Academy girls stood quietly behind me. Remember, 15 minutes ago they had smashed and vandalized the face of a popular senior girl. In that time, they had quickly become Osseo Senior's five most-wanted fugitives on all the admins' walkie-talkies. Yet they didn't protest or push back in the least when Mr. Chance began pulling out the suspension and removal paperwork. Even when he opened the floor to them to explain the bullying their classmate had endured, they responded with remarkable composure.

I remember feeling proud of them and their maturity, because they didn't furiously deflect from their own choices by demanding general fairness or 'payback'. Much to the contrary, they spoke their piece as people who completely understood the deal: they had chosen to send a brash message, and they were standing strong behind that message and accepting the consequences.

And, importantly, they trusted that the adults would do their part to make everything right. (Now that these adults had a damn *clue*, that is, and they were right: if we had done a better job picking up signals and intervening, it's doubtful the situation would have come to a head in the first place.) They let me 'turn them in' with complete trust and understanding, and they nodded with acceptance as Mr. Chance explained each necessary consequence. The girls' parents and/or guardians were called to the school, and each was taken home to serve out the assigned consequences.

A week or so later, after all the suspensions were complete and the dust had settled a bit, we went through the mediation as proposed. While the hard feelings weren't eliminated, all parties at least reached a common agreement about how they would act toward one another for the remainder of the year.

Now that you know the full story, here's why we took some *positives* away from our students' choice to assault another student.

First, add it up and let it sink in.

1. Some of the Academy's tougher girls—girls who had no problem using their fists to settle arguments—had organized to preserve the honor of a girl they had nothing in common with previously.

2. As these girls saw it, the lack of previous loyalties with Kelsey was beside the point. The only thing that mattered was their shared membership in the Sophomore Academy. In other words, being in the Academy conferred special status.

3. As they held this in common, the bullied girl was equal to them. *She was worthy of respect and safety within the larger school,* that is, not someone to be looked down on or psychologically tortured, regardless of what had started the bullying to begin with. (As I recall, it all began with shared affection for a senior boy. Pretty typical high-school stuff, in other words.)

4. The victim couldn't stand up for herself and, based on what had transpired over a few weeks, the stupid adults around either couldn't or wouldn't do anything about it.

5. This new community decided to send a message to everyone— the bullies, the senior class, and whoever else in the school

might be watching—in the loudest way they knew: by going after the leader, even if she was a senior cheerleader.

They weren't going to let her get punked like that.

All things considered, we couldn't help but feel at a little positive, as they were signs that they were feeling what we hoped they would feel. Indeed, the Academy students knew they *belonged* within Osseo Senior High, and they were pushing back hard on anyone who attempted to make them feel 'less-than'. It didn't transpire like we teachers wanted it to, of course, but they were indeed plugging into school with chips on their shoulders (which, in all fairness, we absolutely encouraged in light of their competitive nature and desire to be respected). They actively wanted to be full students in the school too, not just 'losers' or 'rejects' who were disrespected by older or more 'popular' students.

In their own way, they were displaying real compassion and taking significant—if *unacceptable*—risks to protect what was important to them. Rather than preserve their individual selves or the other students they hung with, they were standing up for Academy students unlike themselves to ensure that *no one* was made to feel like they didn't belong. The community of fellow Academy students gave them feelings of safety and identification, and they were extending those feelings to each other in the best ways they knew how. While these extensions of safety were no doubt still on the undesirable side (no one should get physically harmed, for goodness's sake), we were all quite moved that the Academy kids were organizing and asserting themselves—and holding one another up—like this.

So, yes, in full, it was all quite encouraging. We had, after all, placed a premium on creating an Academy-wide sense of belonging. What's more, Dr. Bob had expressly hoped we could build this exact sense of belonging within these kids when he shared his nascent vision of the Sophomore Academy with each of us.

It was an aspiration we all shared because, after our years in education, we all came to know this kind of belonging was a crucial grounding or 'root' for students. If it wasn't in place for a student, that student was vulnerable to all kinds of negative choices and habits. When this vital root took hold, though, the chain of positive effects was profound, especially in light of the Sophomore Academy's original mission:

- Regardless of proficiency, kids who felt like they belonged to something kept showing up—a truism that applied in classrooms, athletic teams, music groups, co-curricular clubs, everything;
- Kids who kept showing up usually did the required work and tasks as, simply, it was part of the 'belonging contract'—because they valued belonging, they were willing to pay such costs;
- Kids who reliably showed up and did the work near always earned passing (and better) grades, and were better-prepared for future coursework;
- Kids who earned passing grades and were better-prepared for future coursework didn't drop out or need extra time to graduate.

Again, not exactly rocket science. To make that sense of belonging happen without over-coddling students (e.g. by lowering academic expectations or loosening behavioral standards), however, is harder than it looks.

The negative effects so common in much of the research literature on ability grouping (or *tracking*) are instructive with regard to how difficult this balance can be to find. Many such reports (and especially those so prevalent around the time Dr. Bob was leading Osseo Senior High) condemn tracking and lower-ability-tracked classes in particular, describing them as hindering student growth and 'typically characterized by an exclusive focus on basic skills, low expectations, and the least qualified teachers'.[4]

In other words, it's not so much that tracking is bad, full stop, but that tracked classes tend to fall into bad habits of instruction and expectation. To borrow from the distinguished scholar Sterling A. Brown, who once said that 'kindness can kill as well as cruelty, and it can never take the place of genuine respect':[5] while educators in charge of these classes believe they are extending kindness in the forms of making students feel welcome and accepted for their abilities, they essentially disrespect their students by not pushing them to grow.

From the beginning of the Sophomore Academy, Dr. Bob was adamant that we avoid this imbalance. From the outset, he was explicit that while our school-within-a-school was most certainly cordoning off a certain set of kids—and thus could be considered 'tracking'—it *would not* devolve into the habits that had so damned tracking of any kind across education. He was most clear, and checked us on it often throughout our time together: cultivating a shared sense of belonging and building students' identities as students within Osseo Senior High were our targets, but they were never to come at the expense of properly preparing the Academy kids for the rest of high school. We chose and worked according to a set of messages, policies, and operations we believed would keep these two factors in balance. But it took us a while (and lots and lots of effort and angst, you can be sure) to know if we were succeeding.

In all, the first-year assault incident was a rather noisy and shocking signal that the sense of belonging we wanted Academy students to feel was there. They were feeling it. For the first time, we saw that our students weren't only feeling like they belonged, but also looking out for and holding up classmates whose sense of belonging or respect were threatened.

And this is how, unlikely as it may have sounded, the assault ended up as a validating experience. It was the first real sign that the 'old-school' beliefs we were uniformly enacting (e.g. our tighter management expectations, heightened academic expectations, and continual badgering of Academy students about their behaviors/attitudes/well-being) could raise a sense of pride among at-risk kids and drive the group *closer together.*[6]

* * *

The Academy's sense of community didn't always express itself so explosively, thank goodness. More so, the community expectations were assumed as part of the Academy culture—the way we did things and how we treated one another: 'In here we work hard, we know each other well and trust each other so we can be very honest (and occasionally goof off) with each other. We're not the type to take crap from anyone, and we all—teachers and students—look out for each other.' Simple as that.

We teachers didn't have to say it a whole lot, because it became understood. Even with each successive year of Academy students, we didn't have to explicitly 'train' new kids into getting the deal. We just stayed the course with our policies and messages and each year the culture more or less fell into place—aided, of course, by our growing reputation among the kids and our growing confidence. (While the 'Game of Life' group could be considered an exception, recall that their intra-Academy culture was quite strong. They never resisted getting along among themselves or connecting with teachers, for instance. They were just incredibly slow to pick up the 'in here we work hard' part of our cultural expectations, causing us to take drastic action.)

With that said, it can be hard to pinpoint observable examples of 'positive culture' or 'feelings of community' in the day-to-day of schooling. A lot goes on in classrooms, after all, and few episodes will ever be—again, *thank goodness*—as obviously illustrative of this community spirit as the assault incident. Plus, no matter how you look for it, 'positive culture' is difficult to *see*. In the Academy it was a concept many of us *felt* from day to day, even if we were a little short on specific incidents to illustrate what made us feel it. (This is not the most scientific or objective assertion, I realize.) These factors make it challenging to explain more about the Sophomore Academy's community and culture, as not all illustrations are as obvious as the assault incident.

Luckily, however, the Sophomore Academy alumni had a lot to say on their own feelings of belonging and our shared Academy culture as I interviewed and surveyed them for this book. In those interactions, I found myself struck by how frequently and fervently they spoke about the Academy's community spirit. Indeed, talking to them ten-plus years after their sophomore year, the sense of community and individual belonging were what many of them focused on most when talking about our time together. Repeatedly, alumni described how the Academy felt more like a 'family', a place where students appreciated what the adults expected of them (even if they didn't always show as much outwardly), and a haven where deep and supported relationships with peers formed.

Still, this is not to say that membership in the Sophomore Academy automatically made the diverse members of our classes click into harmony with one another. Some of our kids had pretty rough, fighting histories in junior high, after all, which meant they brought long lists of 'enemies'. Also, our kids were, by virtue of Osseo Senior's central geographic position in the district, coming from all four feeder junior high schools. The bridges between all these students, in other words, were not always the sturdiest, a factor that could've had some fairly deleterious impacts on culture-establishment.

Of all things, the Academy alumni I spoke with said again and again that our structures and demands actually *helped* build and repair these absent or shaky bridges more quickly. (When they were absent or shaky at all, that is—many of our kids came in on good terms already.) According to them, the continual required contact with one-time adversaries helped to smooth out and regulate their relationships and to connect one another to additional peer-level supports.

Tayvon Reynolds, from the Academy's fourth year, outlined this arc of growth and connection particularly instructively in my visit with him.

Describing himself in junior high school as someone 'who didn't react well in certain situations' (he was suspended six times over his junior high years, usually for fighting), he admitted that the Sophomore Academy initially stretched him and his classmates in terms of personalities and relationships. If anything, the only subject they agreed on at the start was how much they hated the Academy. 'In the beginning,' Tayvon said, 'no one liked it. I didn't understand why I had to look at these same people for four classes, plus Advisory, plus *lunch*. It started off really irritating.'

Over time, though, the deep familiarity he mutually built with his Academy peers helped him grow socially. 'By the end,' Tayvon continued, 'it turned out to be really *helpful*. It did for all of us. First, we had to handle conflicts different. You had to get over a problem or learn to avoid it. I mean, if you didn't like somebody that was in there, you were still going to have to see them all day. You just had to get over it together—sit down and talk through it—or avoid it. I had to learn that *fast*, but I did. And people I went in there having problems with, we got over them together. We *had* to.'

Similarly, Tayvon said he felt academic benefits from these deepening relationships. And looking back on it nearly a full decade out, the connections he made in the Academy are people he considers part of his life-long network.

'For class stuff,' he said, 'we all knew who was really good in which subjects, and we'd lean on each other to get help. Haley Moore [one of Tayvon's Academy classmates], she helped me in certain categories, and I helped her in others. We used to love to debate certain things, get competitive like, "Let's see, I bet I can win this."

'It gave me a sense that these are my *people*. Haley, she's still a friend of mine. Micah [McGary] is my best friend to this day. Eleesha [Jundt], same thing. Some of those kids I had problems with early on, I see them to this day and talk with them, ask them about their kids, all that. Even when things weren't going well for me in school, like in senior year, I had Mr. Ruska. He was my people, even if he wasn't one of my teachers anymore. There were teachers and kids I didn't get along with, and Mr. Ruska made it so I could bring work to his room. It really worked for me at the time. I knew I had *people*.'

* * *

I could go for pages more about students who felt similarly about the Sophomore Academy and how it genuinely gave them something to belong to in Osseo Senior High School's large world. I could describe how a student (Kaylynn Murphy, from third year) I interviewed admitted to bombing her first-trimester grades so she could get let into the Academy, or how several students remembered wishing for a Junior Academy as sophomore year wrapped up, and on and on, but it's time to wrap my discussion of the Sophomore Academy itself.

To sum up the previous chapters' discussion of how we worked to get the Sophomore Academy kids *stable* but move them to *able*, I'll say that what we experienced in the Academy threw some doubt on all the negative reviews of ability-grouping/tracking and 'traditional' methods and expectations. Indeed, bringing kids together as we did, tightening managerial operations, and raising academic expectations actually seemed to *strengthen* students' feelings of academic competency and social connection—to the school and to one another.

As first-year Academy student Abdi Mohamed put it in an interview: 'We started doing a lot better in there than we ever were. We kinda learned how to be students for the first time. Do work, get it done, then we started to see the honor rolls. We realized what it took. The first time Davar [McGee, Abdi's classmate] and I had been on honor rolls, we were like, "Yo, let's do this again." It got to the point where people were proud to be part of our Sophomore Academy.'

As well, the Sophomore Academy's genesis, design, and maintenance all made a strong impression on *me* as an educator. I agreed to carry out tasks I was initially opposed to, and I was supported on all sides toward an experiment that ultimately created a great learning environment for students—all in a very classroom-up (as opposed to top-down and regimented) fashion. I'm glad to have been a part of the Sophomore Academy for many reasons, but perhaps most of all because it gave me the opportunity to see how schools can absolutely build improvements like these for themselves. I will re-visit such more specifically in Chapters 15 and 16.

In the next chapter, however, which will close out this section on the years 2004-2008, I will move on from the Sophomore Academy to describe another major improvement initiative built by Dr. Bob during this period: Osseo Senior High's Continuous School Improvement (or 'CSI') team. While the CSI worked on schoolwide, not targeted, improvements, its formation and operation worked according to many of the same principles that allowed the Sophomore Academy to come into being and, ultimately, to thrive within Osseo Senior.

Endnotes

1. For more on the first year group's initial pushback and the types of reflection and regrouping it sent the team of Academy teachers into, see Chapter 6.

2. Note: Out of respect for the people involved in this incident, I will not refer to them by name here. While I did interview and/or survey several of these people for this book, and while they gave me their permission via signed releases, some of the information shared here may be sensitive to the parties involved here—more than seems worth it in regard to the intent of including this episode.

3. Incidentally and unfortunately, the senior bully targeted in this attack by the Sophomore Academy girls had herself been the target of senior bullies when she'd been a sophomore in my class. I had been directly involved in resolving that situation, in fact, by speaking to the bullies and by alerting administration to the ongoing situation. To put it mildly, it was most disappointing to learn that she was on the bullying end of the present dynamic.

4. Heubert, J. and Hauser, R. (1999) *High stakes: Testing for tracking, promoting, and graduation*. Washington, DC: National Academy Press, p. 282. (Though this is not the most recent or thorough analysis of ability grouping's effects, it is included here as an illustration of the type of message available around the time of the Sophomore Academy.)

5. Brown, S., A. (1996) *A Son's Return: Selected Essays of Sterling A. Brown*, edited by Mark A. Sanders. Boston, MA: Northeastern University Press, p. 73.

6. Speaking for myself, this moment greatly relieved my early skepticism. To date in my career, remember, I had been a much more permissive classroom manager than the Academy required me to be, and I had never really had to hold up messages/expectations across a group of teaching teammates. In its very definite way, the assault incident showed me that many of my pre-conceptions about what students needed to feel accepted and respected had been incomplete at best.

Chapter 11

Building the School They Wanted to Work In, Part 1: Finding the Best Way

'Failure is simply the opportunity to begin
again, this time more intelligently.'

– Henry Ford

Now you know about the Sophomore Academy. You know why it was necessary, what kind of infrastructure it required and how Dr. Bob secured it, and who he tabbed to build the Academy and keep it moving. You also know how the Academy worked: the premiums we established to encourage crucial student habits and outlooks, the practices we enacted and revised to keep those premiums alive, and the effects these practices had on the students' academic preparation and the teachers' professional growth.

A legitimate question to ask is: so what?

Because for all the good the Sophomore Academy did, it was pretty limited as school improvements go. Its focus was narrow and its objectives were targeted. In terms of direct impact, we're talking about 50 kids a year in one Minnesota high school. So what can the Academy really teach us?

Quite a lot, as it turns out. About motivating at-risk sophomores, yes. And while that's very important, it may not be particularly relevant to you. Because not every school needs a Sophomore Academy. What every school does need, however, is improvement. What the Academy showed us was that continuous school improvement works best when it is built from within, from the bottom up, starting in the classroom. And through what the Academy accomplished, it provided important groundwork for Dr. Bob's entire culture of collaborative improvement.

Again, the Academy was designed to improve on Osseo Senior's previous approach to reducing dropout/late-graduation statistics, one that was both highly reactive and deeply ineffective. This improvement was a worthy pursuit, of course, but the school needed much more. Its population and politics, as you may remember, were undergoing seismic shifts, creating new student needs and community pressures. If the school didn't shift its practices in similar fashion, it risked being overwhelmed by the challenge. So, inspired by the success of the Sophomore Academy, Dr. Bob widened the scope of his improvement work to develop and implement multiple school-wide shifts in practice. To do that, Dr. Bob followed the same process as he did with the Academy. Namely, he declined to follow the path of least resistance and bring in an outside consultant or adopt a ready-made third-party program. Instead, he chose to draw on the strength of the staff. In this chapter and the next, we'll see how Dr. Bob scaled his collaborative, 'classroom-up' improvement philosophy from one program to an entire school.

Before we dive in, however, let's fast-forward a bit to see what 'walking the talk' on Dr. Bob's school-improvement philosophy ultimately created at Osseo Senior, because some of you may still be asking 'so what?' So, what does it look like when a culture of collaborative improvement is fully established?

It looks downright contagious. After several years spent strengthening the school's overall product with targeted initiatives (like the Sophomore Academy) and school-wide efforts (more on these shortly), Dr. Bob's mission to 'personalize the school-improvement process' caused numerous teachers and departments to propose their *own* improvements. Their ideas ranged widely, bound only by the staff's imagination and, of course, Dr. Bob's rigorous demands for quality and feasibility.

At one end of this spectrum were individual-led ideas. For example, English teacher Heather Casella went to Dr. Bob with proposals for replacing the district-provided (and ineffective, expensive) reading intervention program Read 180 with a remediation program she designed herself, inspired by her own daughter's reading growth at a classical charter school. And at the other end of the improvement spectrum, Dr. Bob entertained team-constructed ideas from entire departments. In the early 2010s, for example, the school's math department approached Dr. Bob with a scheme for shared grading practices and policies they felt would encourage all math students to work harder toward mastery—not just completion—of concepts. Once Dr. Bob approved these teacher-led improvements, he moved into an administrative role as he did with the Sophomore Academy. He wasn't 'monitoring for fidelity', but supporting with ideas (and funds as necessary), and continually overseeing for quality and mission-consistency.

'Bob was almost like this father figure,' Casella told me in an interview. 'He would always listen and was always open to what I thought might work, but it was on me to bring proof of why a change was needed and some kind of plan. When he'd agree it was worth trying, he'd work with me to make it happen—even over a couple of years if that's what it took.'

Incidentally, in addition to the changes she made to Osseo Senior's remedial reading programming, Casella later worked with Dr. Bob on a school-wide routine she called 'Stealing Minutes'. To encourage more reading across the school—and to cut down on visiting, cellphone browsing, and so on—all students were provided with books of choice they could read in instances of unstructured time, and all teachers were provided with messages to encourage students toward their choice books in these times. Since its initial, positive trials at Osseo Senior, Casella has been invited by numerous Minnesota schools to share about Stealing Minutes' philosophies, operations, and impacts.

* * *

As you might imagine, collaborative, classroom-up improvement culture—the kind that can actually improve a school continuously—doesn't happen overnight. It was not the kind of thing Dr. Bob simply dropped into place when he became Osseo Senior's principal in 2001, in other words. To the contrary, it took a great deal of hard work, over several years. And it had to progress through some extremely challenging phases to reach full maturity and effectiveness.

Early in Dr. Bob's principalship, for example, most of his coordinated school-improvement initiatives followed a standard sequence and were closely guided by his administration: first, Dr. Bob and his administrative team identified issues based on various data points; next, they imagined possible solutions to these issues and weighed for feasibility and potential impact; third, they recruited specific teachers to flesh out designs and to execute in accord with the origin vision and mission; and finally, they routinely stayed in touch with the initiative to guide, monitor, and correct as necessary. The Sophomore Academy detailed over the past five chapters stands as a prime example of this method/sequence. These initiatives weren't exactly bottom-up, in other words. But neither were they top-down, mandated by the district. Ten years later, however, the classroom-up approach had taken root. Teachers *themselves* were imagining, designing, proposing, and coordinating improvements, while Dr. Bob and his admin team stepped back to handle quality control and general support.

In between came the Continuous School Improvement team, or the CSI. More than any other school-improvement initiative, the CSI helped move Dr. Bob's school-improvement processes from 'closely guided' to 'earnestly shared'. Indeed, if the CSI had never happened, the collaborative improvement culture might never have come to pass. More than anything, teachers needed proof—and that's a good instinct. To believe they could lead improvements from the classroom up, they needed to see how it would work. They needed the CSI.

Remember, teacher-leadership is the same to education as informal leadership roles are in any other field: in order for people in non-supervisory roles to commit to leading their peers (and to the extra workload and pressure, but often not much extra pay, leadership entails), they first have to *see* what such leadership might look like and what it all might cost them. They want to get a sense of whether their idea will be micromanaged, whether their effort will have the right administrative support, whether they'll actually get to lead on projects they value, and the like.

Also, potential teacher-leaders want the clearest sense of these matters because they're almost certain to endure a bit of 'chosen one' or 'principal's pet' backlash from their colleagues. Ask any teacher who's been tabbed by their principal to help on a school improvement initiative and they'll tell you it's not always a comfortable position. Thick skin is required. (And, by the way, particularly dedicated teachers tend to get selected for these initiatives over and over, which can compound their reputations as 'chosen ones'.)

When jumping up to lead within a school almost always involves no (or very little) extra pay, no possibility of promotion or advancement, lots of extra work, and many of your colleagues suddenly whispering behind your back, it makes sense that teachers would hesitate to become teacher-leaders. They want to know, up front and the best they can, that doing so will be worth all that trouble in the end. And when they don't have any way of knowing what the shared-leadership can and will look like, they are less likely to step up.

And this is what made the CSI a crucial bridge between purely administratively led improvement and genuinely community-shared improvement under Dr. Bob's administration. The CSI team's leadership—and, importantly, Dr. Bob's sharing of the building's leadership decisions and duties—allowed the larger staff at Osseo Senior High to get a clearer impression of what shared leadership looked like under him. Where Dr. Bob's more administratively-imagined-but-teacher-run initiatives (like the Sophomore Academy) operated in ways that the rest of the faculty couldn't really see,[1] the CSI team's contributions were openly visible and accessible.

Part of this visibility and accessibility was a sheer product of Dr. Bob's design. Its members were from all over the school, for one thing, not just the 'Holy Four' academic departments of English, math, science, and social studies. Also, CSI members were regularly seen leading portions of faculty meetings, facilitating small action-planning sessions about improvement priorities during pre-service week, and delivering supplies for various schoolwide efforts, all on matters that had school-wide reach.

So 'chosen ones'? Okay, yeah, if you *must*.

But unlike the stereotypical 'principal's pets', the CSI members weren't just parroting the administrative line. They were also serving and actually *leading*, all in plain sight.

In all, the CSI group's leadership contributions provided a strong bridge between stage one (Dr. Bob and his admin team doing all the improvement thinking) and stage two (Dr. Bob genuinely sharing improvement decisions and its tasks with staff). For teachers who may have been skeptical about Dr. Bob's messages about shared leadership and 'working together to create the type of school we all want to work in', the CSI's visible contributions provided tangible proof that this principal wasn't just handing out administrative lip service.

I've asserted several times that I was lucky to be at Osseo Senior High in the early 2000s, as it gave me a unique chance to learn a lot about school improvement. That theme continues with the story of CSI as yes, Dr. Bob invited me to join CSI when he brought the team together in the fall of 2004. And through my experiences on the team, I can confidently say that it showed me how to effectively consider, organize, and execute school-wide improvement actions.

While my experience in the Sophomore Academy sharpened my classroom practices and philosophies, my time with the CSI team helped me understand school-improvement more broadly. It afforded me a better view of the myriad dynamics and limits that have to be accounted for within schools. It made me see how important it is to set improvement priorities based on sound and compelling rationales. And it gave me a better sense of how, when, and what to broadcast about operational changes—and why.

I wasn't the only one so inspired and instructed by their time on the CSI, either. Several faculty members Dr. Bob tapped to serve on the CSI team went on to take leadership positions within Osseo Senior, the Osseo School District, and elsewhere in the years following their CSI servant-leadership. Though the CSI didn't directly certify the teachers Dr. Bob recruited to participate, the team's over 50% rate of future administrators, education-doctorate-earners, department heads, instructional coaches, and researcher-advisers certainly suggests that the experiences, insights, and inspiration generated within CSI influenced our career trajectories.

Shortly (I promise), I'll provide more specifics about how the CSI team did what it did and why, a few school-wide improvements the CSI team pulled off particularly well, and how the CSI model gave drive to improvements that subsequently sprouted upward from classrooms.

More importantly, I'll revisit the struggles the CSI had to navigate. We were, remember, a doing this Dr. Bob-style, which meant we were operating without strict guiding formulas or playbooks. While today's education leaders spend a lot of time and energy on 'continuous school improvement', Dr. Bob was doing so long before that term became popular. And this meant, naturally, that we had no ready-made processes, templates, or cycles to follow, no district- or state-level support coming to lend a hand, and no consultants available to guide the process.

Based on my considerable experience in the school-improvement space in the years following the CSI, though, I believe we were better off without a lock-step process to follow. Essentially, it forced our team to learn what 'continuous school improvement' *meant* at the same time we were working to *create* it—all while, of course, getting the larger staff in the school to believe and to pitch in.

The initial challenge: Making 'shared decision-making' productive

With that rather gushing prelude in mind, it may be surprising to learn that Dr. Bob's CSI brainstorm all rose from an utterly *failed* attempt at shared leadership.

In an interview, Dr. Bob recalled for me how in the late 1990s and early 2000s, many prominent school-improvement thinkers were commonly pushing a concept called 'shared decision-making'.[2] The Osseo District's superintendent at the time (Dr. Chris Richardson, now retired), versed as he was in the tenets of shared decision-making, required that each district school set up a *site council*. These councils were viewed as promising vehicles for moving school improvement, in that all schools' most crucial stakeholders—teachers, administrators, parents, and students from each school community—would be brought together to collaborate on issues of school improvement.

As far as Dr. Bob was concerned, though, that ideal state never quite materialized. While he could see how the concept could be valuable, and while he accordingly did as he was directed by his district superiors, the site council model didn't produce much actionable payout with regard to the improvements he wanted to see. As early as his first year at Osseo Senior (2000-01), while helming a site council he inherited when he took the job in October, he questioned whether the site council model was worth preserving.

'I'd go to these meetings once a month in what was then the school library,' Dr. Bob said, 'and I could see right away that the people volunteering for a group like this one were really there for one particular reason—something they personally wanted to see happen, not really for the larger common good. And as this tends to go, I started to see some of these people and their agendas taking over the narrative of the meetings. And that, of course, led to fewer and fewer people showing up for future meetings.

'By the time I got to spring of that first year, the meetings were down to me, the faculty rep Jess Stewart [a social studies teacher who is still at Osseo Senior at the time of this writing], and one parent—the one parent, I'm guessing,' he added with a wide grin, 'who had not yet had her issue resolved satisfactorily. She was staying *around*. I think everyone there, though, felt like the meetings were torture by the end of that year.'

At this time, Dr. Bob made a decision to drop the Sisyphus act and 'stop rolling the boulder,' as education thinker Rick Hess puts it in 2015's *Cage-Busting Leadership*. Dr. Bob decided, in other words, that no matter how he might make changes to small parts of the site council model of shared leadership, this model was still *rolling a hill up a mountain*.[3] He knew that if he wanted to arrive at truly useful improvement-related decisions, he was going to have to do as Hess suggests and figure out how to 'flatten, bypass, dynamite, [or] chip away' at the 'mountain' itself.[4]

As the site council came together for its May meeting, Dr. Bob recommended to the few remaining members that they dissolve the site council in its current form and format. In exchange, he promised, he would speak with his bosses at the district about a different way to share the decision-making around school improvement. The council members agreed this was the best course, and Dr. Bob went to Superintendent Richardson and Associate Superintendent Dr. James Boddie to discuss other directions.

To the district-level administrators, Dr. Bob offered, 'If we're going to do this—if we're going to use our time in ways to really help the school improve—let's get a site council forum that can really make that happen. They thought it was worth exploring, and they let me propose a plan. Later, I went back to them with the idea that would eventually become our school's Continuous School Improvement team.'

To his district superiors, Dr. Bob proposed that a cross-disciplinary team of teachers would be best for making effective school-improvement decisions and actions happen. The team he envisioned would feature representatives that cut more widely than usual across the school. The 'Holy Four' academic departments (i.e. English, math, science, and social studies) would be represented, of course, but they would be joined by other teachers from technical/business education, special education, and elsewhere. This team's stated responsibilities would be twofold: improving overall community-building and professional staff-development.

'Instead of trying to think so broadly and not always knowing what the issues were—like the site council did and couldn't really make *work*,' Dr. Bob told me, 'I thought we could contain it a bit: get people thinking specifically about how to improve the overall community of Osseo Senior High, and do what it took to help teachers be the best they could be in their classrooms.

'Also,' he added, 'I didn't want it to be the departmental-chairperson group.[5] I wanted it to be an invitational body of people I thought could be a real creative force within the school: people I'd gotten to know well, and that I knew would be honest about what the school was then, could see what they thought we should become, and who knew how to make one become the other.'

Recognizing that such an approach had potential (and that it could well be more productive than their fairly fizzled site council concept), Dr. Bob's district superiors agreed to let him give it a try—to resume pushing his boulder, that is, just not up shared-decision-making's Site Council Mountain.

All mission + little method = morale boosting (and malcontent)

Having approval to activate what he envisioned as a more productive brand of shared decision-making, Dr. Bob thus recruited his Continuous School Improvement team (CSI-Osseo) over the 2003-04 school year. He did so in much the same way he lobbied the Sophomore Academy team: he made a personal list of the people he thought fit the profile, went to each of them individually, and then told them what he was picturing and why.

Working according to his plan, the 'Holy Four' academic departments were of course represented (myself, English; Michelle Goetz, math; Gerry Zelenak—also of the Sophomore Academy—for social studies; Bill Quan, science). Other departments were included as well, first because they saw students in more specialized settings, but also because they had perspectives that weren't always included in the comprehensive-improvement conversation. Specifically, Dr. Bob invited members from business/tech education (Jill Kellar), counseling (Jackie Trzynka—still another from the Sophomore Academy team), media (Toni Beckler), special education (Cindy Loftsgard), and world languages (Anne-Marie Martin).

Thus fully assembled, the CSI group formally convened for the first time in the fall of 2004.

High as Dr. Bob's hopes may have been for this team after the site council debacle, however, I'll say it plain: we didn't exactly hit the ground sprinting. If anything, we spent a year or so stumbling and weaving around. Some CSI members, even (myself very much included), ended up wondering what they were even doing there.

But again, we didn't have an instruction manual. Echoing a bit of how Dr. Bob set the Sophomore Academy off to work together, the CSI's Michelle Goetz remembered our early times together this way: 'Bob never exactly told us what we were supposed to do. He told us what we were supposed to be working on, then for the most part left us to figure it out.'

Accordingly, we also didn't make many particularly meaningful impacts on the school at large. While we reviewed various school performance data and had several interesting discussions in our meetings, we had very little sense, overall, of how our shared insights and conclusions were supposed to manifest as actions. Much as we were told we were to make decisions and be leaders, we produced more *questions* than decisions in our first year together.

For instance, were we in the CSI to teach the wider staff about all the topics we were talking about together? And if the answer was yes, where should these updates fit among already-scheduled (read: district-mandated, professional-relicensure-required) staff development activities?

Also, what should come of our updates after we'd shared them? Would this CSI group do things like determine and design school policies for more immediate implementation, or were we supposed to be thinking strictly about big-picture, long-term-strategic matters?

And if we were indeed supposed to be shaping current policies, how were we supposed to roll them out to the entire school community? *Could* we, even? As we weren't administrators, we weren't sure what we even had the authority to do.

In short, the CSI spent this early period being little more than a periodic 'State of the School' discussion group for dedicated teachers—a more philosophical, more idealistic, and far less productive version, essentially, of the very administrative and practical Building Leadership Team (or BLT, the department heads Dr. Bob explicitly wanted CSI to complement, not emulate). Where the BLT got together monthly to consider very concrete matters of school operations and emerged with news and updates for departments to put straight to work, the CSI was merely having all kinds of scintillating talks about what schooling was for, how we may or may not have been achieving our ends, what kids' deepest needs were, and so forth. We certainly weren't *deciding* anything.

When it came right down to it, in other words, we spent a year or so accomplishing roughly the same amount as the unproductive site council that had preceded us.

Rather short on ideas about how to enact meaningful improvements—and given uncertain amounts of professional-development infrastructure to operate on—in this early stage, the CSI group thus defaulted to the 'building school community' half of Dr. Bob's original objectives. Many of our conclusions about what could be improved within the school thus came back to low staff morale or 'buy in'. And wanting desperately to do something but unsure of what we *could* do, we effectively became Osseo Senior's *Morale-Building Team*.

This is somewhat excusable, as we had no real processes for analyzing school performance data, digging down to root causes, and using evidence to determine potential solutions. We were going with the observations and lived experiences of ten or so people, and then with majority opinions to start various actions into motion. And following such an 'organic' process, several on the CSI team landed on that school issues—whether we were talking about kids who were failing multiple classes at mid-trimester, kids who weren't passing the Basic Skills Writing Test, kids who were chronically absent, kids who presented repeated behavior challenges, or whatever else—boiled down to, 'If teachers felt more *personally engaged* to the real issues here, we could get them to change their practices and the results would follow.'

Thus gut-directed, we spent a year 'enhancing' staff's professional development days and hours with things like team-building activities: staff socials, school scavenger hunts, that kind of thing.

Yes, *actually*.

Some of us were in no way thrilled with the early direction. I have distinct memories of acting like a disengaged student in the CSI team meetings, usually in tandem with Zelenak, my Academy teammate. Frustrated with our team's focus and/or fuzzy conclusions, Zelenak and I would add difficult wrenches to team discussions or check out altogether. (Shrug, eye-roll, walk away.) On occasion, even, we passed notes to one another trying to evoke giggling fits.

No doubt, the two of us had gotten spoiled into petulance by the Sophomore Academy's planning sessions. There, our team always focused tightly and applicably on kids' struggles and what each teacher needed to do their best job, and never on how to raise one another's morale or spirit, no matter how low either may have sunk. (And believe me, there were many, many times over the course of the Academy—especially in the rocky first year referred to several times throughout this book—when kids' and/or teachers' collective morale/spirit hit damagingly low points. Staying trained on those real issues often took a great deal of discipline.)

In short, there was one major difference between the Sophomore Academy's approach and the CSI approach that we found so frustrating: the Academy approached low morale as a *symptom*, never the *disease*. When morale was low with the Sophomore Academy's kids or adults, or when the climate was tense between Academy kids and adults, we saw it as being low for a reason. In accord, we chose always to focus first on finding and addressing the *reason*, not the *morale*, even if it meant leaving instructional comfort zones to present an organized front.

While doing otherwise and working on lifting spirits might temporarily fix morale issues, we thought, it would only do so superficially, leaving the root reasons for the low morale to remain. In the Sophomore Academy, at least, we knew that if we chose to focus on how to make everyone *feel* better when dynamics got choppy, it would only be a matter of time before the superficially puffed-up positivity wore down and the root issues pushed back to the top. We did not, then, schedule movie days or otherwise empty 'fun days' to release rising pressures within the Academy. Instead, we did our best to locate the real sources of the tensions, then to address those sources directly via various situation-appropriate actions: crafting and repeating new messages, instituting new policies across all Academy classes, scheduling conferences with specific students, and the like.

In the CSI's early period, members like Zelenak and me pushed to see this kind of problem-solving substance work its way into the CSI team's methods and actions. If we just kept organizing scavenger hunts and helping to design each year's staff t-shirts, well...we didn't really view that as doing school improvement at all. If these kinds of tasks were what the CSI was assembled to create, some of us thought, we *deserved* to be scoffed at in the teachers' lounge as Dr. Bob's 'chosen ones'.

...and I, for one, sure as hell hadn't signed up for that.

I had agreed to join the CSI because I sincerely wanted to help lead Osseo Senior High into becoming a better place for its kids and professionals, not to have overly sentimental discussions about the state of our school and to plan donut parties for the staff who had the professional blues. As far as I was concerned (and I know my colleague Gerry Zelenak felt similarly), I wasn't interested in being a part of the CSI for its second year if it looked much like its first.

Endnotes

1.   There was nothing intentionally opaque about the Academy or other more administratively guided initiatives like it. Rather, most of the Sophomore Academy's inner workings were just the kinds of things that happen outside the larger school staff's sightlines. There was no real way for most staff to know how the Academy's classes ran (or how the teachers and students were often fighting each other) from day-to-day, how the Academy's guiding principles were decided, how we were required to regularly meet around students' needs, what we talked about and how we reacted in accord, how the Academy students were selected to begin with, or any of it. To many staff in the school, the Sophomore Academy was just kind of, 'that thing for tough sophomore kids that makes all of our class sizes a little larger but a bit better behaved.' This is fairly typical for any improvement initiatives that operate on their own within a larger school ecosystem. It's not so much that the surrounding staff members are kept out, but more that there's just no particularly good way—and, frankly, no real reason—to let them in.

2.   For samples of the professional literature available during this period and promoting shared decision-making as a promising model for improving schools, see: Glickman, C, D. *Renewing America's Schools: A Guide for School-Based Action.* San Francisco, CA: Jossey-Bass; Hergert, L., F. (1994) 'Profile of an Effective School Site Council', in *The Regional Lab Reports.* Andover, MA: The Regional Laboratory for Educational Improvement of the Northeast and Islands; Malen, B., Ogawa, R. and Krantz, J. (1990) 'Unfulfilled Promises', in *School Administrator*, 42 (2), pp. 30-59.

3.   Hess, F., M. (2013) *Cage-Busting Leadership.* Cambridge, MA: Harvard Education Press.

4. Ibid., p. 4.

5. By 'the department-chairperson group', Dr. Bob is referring to the school's Building Leadership Team or BLT. This standing group of department chairs met regularly to deliberate changes/updates to school-wide policies, logistics, and operations, often issues of compliance coming from the district's central office or the state department of education. Also, the BLT members were responsible for communicating relevant conclusions and information back to their respective departments.

Chapter 12

Building the School They Wanted to Work In, Part 2: More Than a Feeling

'Never tell people how to do things. Tell them what to do and they will surprise you with their ingenuity.'

– General George S. Patton

In 2005-06, the CSI's second school year together, malcontents like me and Zelenak started feeling better pretty quickly.

In the team's earliest meetings that fall, we looked back on our first year's high concentration of community-building activities and agreed: when it came to designing and enabling school improvements or 'contributing to the school we wanted to work in,' we hadn't done much of anything.

We further agreed that we could create more impact and more durable change if we directed our energies toward the other half of Dr. Bob's CSI objectives, namely 'helping teachers be the best they could be in their classrooms', through staff professional development.

Before we could begin thinking about what the staff needed to develop, we first had to think harder about the practices and operations already in place at Osseo Senior High, and not just in general, lived-experience or observational ways. To shape any subsequent professional-development actions, we needed better, more accurate and actionable insights about how kids were performing, attending, and behaving.

To kick this off, we looked more carefully at our school's standardized test data from the previous spring as well as various school-climate indicators like attendance and behavior. Also, we broke all these data sets down by demographics, comparisons to previous years, and other factors, to suggest more specific directions.

Right now, a couple decades after the standardized-testing and accountability explosion of No Child Left Behind, which became law in 2001, of course I realize that reviews of school performance data by school professionals are fairly old hat. Based on my experience in the field, I know that school personnel nearly everywhere are routinely expected to analyze their schools' performance data at the very least, and quite a few in the U.S. have built improvement cycles based on foundations of assessment and other data. Indeed, an entire industry has sprung up to support various facets of these cycles, from assessment to coaching to strategic planning.

Back in the fall of 2005, however, analyzing school data with explicit improvement intentionality wasn't an activity the typical American teacher had much experience with. Dr. Bob threw us into the deep end of the data nonetheless, and he made us join him in an exercise strikingly similar to the one that paved the way for the Sophomore Academy.

Here's how it played out. He wanted us to identify numbers that bothered us, articulate why they were bothersome, and look deeper for what might be causing those numbers. Going through this work, Dr. Bob knew, would be a key to helping us avoid the rather empty path we followed in our first year, when we only considered our gut reactions and lived experiences. Plus, he knew that doing our own homework would serve us well as *leaders*. We were eventually going to have to explain our improvement rationales more widely to staff, after all, and that meant it was in the CSI Team's best interest—and the best interest of our recommended improvements—to know all of this material intimately. It would give us stronger legs to stand on.

Looking back, the process was probably a bit too much for a group of data novices who still had full-time commitments in our classrooms. (CSI only convened for half-days every couple months.) Though I can remember us really getting after the task, we sure weren't able to unearth anything as eye-opening and directly actionable as the sophomore-year credit threshold, which accurately predicted dropouts and late graduates.

We did, however, notice several areas where some additional learning could be done by staff to strengthen their classroom practices with regard to the data sets we studied.

This step forward became a bit of an issue in itself, though, because we ended up with more than ten learning topics for professional development. This volume was problematic for several reasons: it was too many to support with outside learning providers, too many to fit into the school's professional-development schedule, and too many topics that were not relevant to all teachers.

As a result, we needed a way to offer lots of cheap professional-development options in small chunks of time. To do this, the CSI worked with Dr. Bob to organize our own in-house professional-development days. We had Dr. Bob cordon off two afternoons of the year's allotted professional-development days, then we arranged for our PD 'experts' to come from within the halls of Osseo Senior according to our data-informed list of learning needs.

To populate our PD 'programs', we used a number of strategies. We invited certain teachers, based on reputation, to share about promising classroom management techniques. We invited teachers who had attended beneficial trainings elsewhere to share what they learned. And we opened invitations to the wider staff and reviewed proposals. (I submitted one myself and ultimately presented to fellow staff about the importance of background knowledge to reading comprehension. I ended up adapting that very presentation for work I've done with educators all over the world, and even drew from its main participation activity for a demonstration in my book, *Education is Upside-Down*.[1]) Once we secured several periods' worth of multiple teacher-experts on a variety of instructional and managerial topics, we drew up a schedule for the day, and all teachers were able to roam from room to room to see talks and learn from their colleagues.

In all, it was a positive improvement on previous PD structures for a number of reasons: it allowed 'expert' teachers to be recognized and showcased, it identified pockets of strength within the staff for their later reference and counsel (as opposed to a PD expert who comes in for a day and is never seen again), and it offered a great deal more choice and variability for individual teachers' growth needs.

More to the point, this approach scored more than a few wins. The entire staff got exposed to a great deal of relevant content and ideas they could carry directly into their practices, staff who presented felt more like leaders/experts that day and long afterward, and, aside from the costs of substitute teachers to cover the CSI's planning work, *it didn't cost a thing*. (Dr. Bob used discretionary professional-development funds to cover all our meeting costs: classroom substitutes and—for meetings outside the contract day—our hourly rates.)

While the PD days recorded these wins, however, they were far from a perfect school improvement. They did not, for instance, offer much in the way of follow-up. We knew a lot of learning was going on and that a lot of teachers were feeling positive about being tabbed as experts, but we had no real way of knowing if anyone was applying any of their new knowledge, and if they were, whether they were succeeding. And if we couldn't get a feel for how any of the new learning was being used—or, indeed, how effective it was in terms of improving kids' outcomes—we had a tough time calling what we produced actual 'continuous school improvement'.

In sum: while we produced some actions that improved on previous staff-development experiences and generated positive, staff-affirming energy within the school, nothing we did was particularly strategic. We still hadn't taken aim at any improvement objectives in particular as an entire school, and we still didn't know if anything was actually, you know, improving.

(But at least we were done organizing staff socials and scavenger hunts in hopes of making the building *feel* better.)

Making our mission matter

In the summer of 2006, at a meeting Dr. Bob hosted between our second and third years together, the CSI became an actual decision-making and action-coordinating body.

In advance of that session, Dr. Bob directed all of us to be ready to talk about our school's mission: what the (dusty and education-cliché-bloated) school mission statement at the time said, whether or not we considered it descriptive of our current work or the work we wanted to do, and, if not, what we, as leaders in the Osseo Senior High community, thought we should do about it.

While re-writing the school mission statement may seem an empty or purely ceremonial exercise, it was, with regard to the CSI's subsequent work, the exact right step at the exact right time. For a group that had progressed from a meandering mass of morale-building to a more focused, if imperfect, group of professional-learning designers, making us go back to our mission was more *necessary* than appropriate. If we were ever to address any school-wide concerns and truly affect The Way We Do Things at Osseo Senior High in comprehensive ways, we needed to start somewhere definite. And what better place to start than affirming what we wanted to accomplish and why we believed it mattered?

Plus, just as with the Sophomore Academy, the last thing the CSI wanted to do was create improvements that made *us* feel good and had no impact on anyone else. If the improvements we designed weren't improving outcomes for kids, we were failing on our mission as a school. So it made perfect sense to start with that mission itself: first to see if we agreed with the current default version, and second to see if we could re-package and re-present it in ways that effectively framed the comprehensive improvements we wished to create.

To move the mission discussion along and give it structure, a CSI team member (Media Specialist Toni Beckler[2]) suggested we look over a few readings, including *Proposals Relating to the Education of Youth in Pensilvania*, a pamphlet by Benjamin Franklin.[3] Written in 1747 when Franklin was working to establish his state's first formal academy of learning,[4] the *Proposals* shared a lot in common with the CSI in that moment: it sought to build something entirely new, it appealed to possible supporters, and it broke apart and simplified education's very complex venture. We didn't need the entirety of Franklin's point-by-point description (the outline of his envisioned academy's programming, for instance, wasn't directly valuable), but its themes were most helpful in moving us toward a revamped school mission statement.

In particular, we trained our attention on the 'why this academy must exist' spirit and intent of Franklin's *Proposals* and, after much discussion, ultimately distilled three big points to apply to our task, namely that schools exist to:

1. Prepare students academically.
2. Prepare students to function in and among the world outside of school.
3. Allow students to live happier lives.

And when we laid these three big points over the then-operating school mission statement, we saw how badly it needed cleaning.

(I would love to share that messy thing in all its redundant glory, but after much searching I was unfortunately not able to find the original. This is fitting, considering that, while I had worked at Osseo Senior eight years by that point, I never paid any attention to it. I remember well, though, that it was a huge and unwieldy paragraph—printed on faux-academic paper and framed in the office conference room, to boot—and loaded with meaningless mumbo-jumbo like 'preparing life-long learners', 'skills for the 21st century ', and so on. It was exactly the type of school mission statement, in other words, lampooned by cognitive scientist Daniel Willingham in his indispensable *When Can You Trust the Experts: How to Tell Good Science from Bad in Education*.[5])

We scrapped the prior mission statement altogether and landed on this instead:

At Osseo Senior High School, our purpose is to teach ALL students to...

1. *Become successful learners.*
2. *Be responsible citizens.*
3. *Pursue personal fulfillment.*

Not particularly flashy, I realize.

But after having gone back to a U.S. Founding Father who was hoping to set up an academy for training future leaders, then connecting it to our own reasons for being, we decided that 'not-flashy' was the point. Though we could set our sights on all manners of outcomes and innovations and building particular habits of mind and all the rest, it came down to this: schooling, when you think about it, is actually pretty simple. It exists to do those three things, for all kids, period.

So…great. We had some new words on a less pretentious piece of paper. So *what*? As I mentioned, it actually turned out to be much more than ceremonial or cosmetic for the CSI. Indeed, we viewed our revamped mission statement—and its firm, distinct pillars of emphasis to replace the hazy morass of a mission we inherited—as providing much-needed structure for future improvement-planning.

We decided that all our improvement conversations would begin with our new mission's three pillars and *just* these three pillars (read: *not* anecdotes about teachers' collective morale, general notions of how professional development could be improved, or anything similar). For as much as we might want to take on all of educational improvement every single year, the plain fact was that *when everything's a priority, nothing's a priority*. The goal was continuous school improvement, and that had to mean getting better at things a *few* things at a time.

The continuous school improvement cycle we envisioned looked something like this:

- At the beginning of each year, the CSI would be responsible for examining the school's performance with regard to each pillar and target particular areas of emphasis accordingly.
- The CSI would design and/or recommend actions specifically designed to improve outcomes in each category, with suggestions for monitoring/follow-up.
- The CSI would coordinate the rollout of these recommended actions, to include communications outward to the larger staff.

- The CSI would assist these actions' implementation throughout the year in a number of ways: monitoring them for effectiveness, collecting fellow teachers' input, adjusting procedures (and communicating changes), and providing additional learning/ support to staff individually or en masse as necessary.

Taken together, it was a structured, sequential system for growing The Way We Do Things at Osseo Senior High. It would come together methodically, one new shared practice at a time, all aligned directly to our three-pronged mission of teaching students to be prepared academically, to become responsible citizens, and to pursue personal fulfillment.

At last, and after much tinkering, we had designed a model and process for driving continuous improvement.

The real challenge would be putting it to work.

From Dr. Bob's living room to our classrooms

As much still had to be figured out and prepared, we were lucky that the rest of the teachers were still over a month away from coming back for the year. We got down to business.

First, and in accord with the lessons we learned from our first year, the CSI team started everything with school data, reviewing various performance and school-climate statistics. This time, though, we shoved all our conclusions and recommendations through our new mission's three filters to determine our improvement priorities for the year.

By following our new process and examining our data with more purpose and focus, we declared these school-wide priorities in line with our new mission:

- *Becoming successful learners*: Creating stronger readers, school-wide. We were dismayed by our 67% proficiency rate on the previous year's state reading exams, and we wanted to see if we could close the gap on neighboring Maple Grove Senior High's

77%. Plus, as Minnesota's testing schedule was shifting its annual 10th-grade Basic Skills Writing Test into a new annual test (the MCA, or Minnesota Comprehensive Assessment) of reading, we aimed to get in front of the imminent accountability measurement. (It should be noted, too, that in 2006-07, all staff stood to earn modest bonuses if we met certain performance targets under Q Comp, the state's new alternative teacher pay program.[6] This most certainly played a role in our later messaging to staff about operations and rationales. More on that shortly.)

- *Being responsible citizens*: Improving students' preparation for class. We chose this for a rather obvious reason, namely that arriving to class unprepared to learn exerts a number of academic costs for students: they're unable to fully participate, take notes, get assigned work in on time, and so on. In choosing this priority area, however, the CSI also had a building climate/safety issue in mind. Because students were so often arriving to class unprepared (and then had to leave classrooms to go to lockers for supplies), students were sent unsupervised into school hallways more often than staff could possibly keep up with. This naturally led to high numbers of unexcused absences (students who used the locker excuse to roam hallways, in other words) and hallway-based behavior infractions/safety issues. We knew we needed a way to encourage students to arrive to class with what they needed to learn for the day. Excusing them to leave was disrupting their learning and school safety.

- *Pursuing personal fulfillment*: Boosting student participation in the school's extra-curricular and co-curricular activities. This emphasis area emerged in part from my, Trzynka, and Zelenak's and Sophomore Academy-informed perspectives on student belonging (the three of us pushed a *lot* in CSI based on what we witnessed in the Academy) and in part as a response to the data we studied about participation in extra-curricular and co-curricular activities. For while activity rosters were almost never short, we realized that a small percentage of kids were doing virtually everything—with a much larger percentage of kids not participating in any activities at all.

In all the work the CSI had to do to bring the mission from Dr. Bob's living room to Osseo Senior's classrooms, landing on these priorities was, of course, the easy part.

Anyone, after all, can look at reams of data, have conversations and arguments about it, and declare that the rest of the school should focus on improving in certain areas. Making those improvements happen, though, with a staff of more than a hundred, is another matter altogether.

From here, in other words, life was going to get *real* difficult.

For one thing, we had to figure out what we were going to *do*. The priorities we landed on weren't really actions, after all, but more *aspirations*. And while these three targets/aspirations were more definite than anything the CSI had previously proposed, we knew we had to do more than just implore teachers to be more mindful of them and hope for better outcomes by year's end. We needed some actual actions/practices teachers could carry out.

And this, it goes without saying, was going to be exceedingly challenging. What could math teachers or physical education teachers, for instance, do about our declared focus on building stronger readers? Similarly, how could any of us in any discipline get more kids to participate in extra-curricular activities? Tough as those questions were, we had to come up with at least a few proposed answers and specific actions teachers could take. Our fellow teachers would demand them, and they would be right to do so: to give teachers the targets and leave it at that would be like handing a construction crew a picture of a house and saying, 'Build this.' To pull it off, we needed to give teachers the *blueprints*.

Also, once we decided on actions to be carried out across the school, we knew we had to plan for monitoring effectiveness. If we didn't build in processes to track our progress, update staff as we went, and adjust course or provide support as necessary, we knew that the actions we chose would fall from teachers' minds.

Finally (and crucially), the CSI knew it had to find a way to get in front of the pushback that was certain to arise from some of the staff at large. Teachers' plates were full enough to begin with, and we were about to tell them to concentrate even harder on school-wide priorities they had no hand in selecting. No matter how well we prepared, rolling out our improvement ideas was sure to get a little ugly. Still, for our school-wide focus areas to improve, we needed a truly school-wide execution, or as close to one as possible. Anything less wouldn't be a school improvement at all.

Accordingly, the CSI next went from planning strategic foundations (e.g. re-working our school mission, putting that mission to work as our improvement template, setting priorities based on school performance data, and scoping how it would all become operational) to designing our rollout and execution. And just as we learned from Dr. Bob, the most important piece at this stage was securing the staff's willingness through sturdy relationships.

As we didn't have the time to walk the building and have the one-to-one conversations that were critical to Dr. Bob's leadership, we thought carefully about how to authentically engage and involve staff en masse.

Former CSI member Jill Kellar (then a business education teacher who now works in school administration for a neighboring district) recalled it this way: 'At that point we knew the school's cauldron and places that were really hot. To get the ideas we wanted to percolate in there—to see the things we wanted to see happening—we needed to build a sense that all this was a *we* thing, not an *I'm-telling-you* thing. Nothing else would have worked.'

Making school improvement a *we* thing

As a critical first step in gaining the staff's buy-in and participation, the CSI team roughed out samples of school-wide actions that could be carried out to meet our mission-aligned aspirations. The intent was not to *prescribe* these actions, but to have some recommendations for the staff to react to, build upon, reject, or adopt. I'll share more about how we engaged staff on these choices shortly. Here's what we came up with (again, aligned to the new mission pillars):

- *Becoming successful learners*: To strengthen student readers, we proposed READvisory, a weekly routine of school-wide reading based loosely on the Independent Reading Project I used in my own classes (plus the researchers and models I consulted to design it[7]). The rough plan included a number of logistical considerations, including changes to our master schedule (e.g. adding one instance of Advisory, a weekly academic check-in and 'homeroom', every week dedicated to the reading initiative—hence the name READvisory) and how the CSI would handle distribution of reading materials and protocols to each classroom. To track progress, teachers were expected to note which students were or weren't reading during each READvisory period, and they were provided with protocols for connecting with students about what they were reading. These running records of READvisory's operations would inform subsequent policies and supports.

- *Being responsible citizens*: To help students come to class prepared, we put forward a school-wide action adapted from the Sophomore Academy. Namely, we proposed that the entire building stop issuing locker passes. We knew it was a bit extreme and 'tough-love', but CSI teachers like me and Zelenak had seen it do wonders in our Academy classrooms. We saw that after a few weeks of being firm on and respectful with our expectations, students rose to the bar we set, ceased pushing back, and came to class with what they needed day in and day out. Plus, we knew first-hand that it could all work if teachers were consistent in their operations and messaging. And the two of us, you may remember, were the Academy teachers who were most resistant about such a policy in the first place. (For a more thorough refresher on this Academy policy—which also, incidentally, did not excuse students to use bathrooms during class time—and how it went over, see Chapter 7.) At the very least, the CSI figured, it was worth suggesting to the staff as a possible starting point toward this aspiration. As a potential monitoring mechanism, the CSI first deemed 'to class on time with writing utensil and writing surface' (i.e. notebook, loose paper, and so on) as our baseline of preparedness. Next, we brainstormed that we could check our progress on this baseline by conducting periodic, school-wide, random materials checks. These materials checks would take place during random periods throughout the trimester, simply via the school intercom. When announced, the expectation was that students in all classes would hold up their writing utensil in one hand and their writing surface in the other, then teachers would count up numbers prepared and numbers unprepared, and report the figures to CSI's Toni Beckler via email. Beckler would be responsible for compiling all reported rates and for keeping a running tally of our 'students prepared for class' percentages. Also, to keep tabs on our 'shadow objectives' of creating safer hallways and improving the number of minutes all students spent in their learning environments, we chose to follow our progress on those scores via school climate data as the year progressed.

- *Pursuing personal fulfillment*: To boost student participation in the school's extra-curricular and co-curricular activities, we proposed instituting a school activity fair once per trimester. This fair would take place in a main gathering area (like the school gym or cafeteria), and students representing each activity/club would work with faculty advisers to present their activity/club and recruit new participants. If accepted by the staff, this improvement action would also require in-school time for students to be excused so they could browse the fair. To track our success with this initiative, the CSI would simply collect mid-trimester data from all advisers about their current numbers of student participants and compare them to the previous year's figures (which we had from our late-summer data study).

Next, the CSI team outlined a series of steps for rolling it all out to the larger teaching staff. We genuinely sought to make our pillar-aligned improvement process the '*we* thing' Jill Kellar described so well, and that would involve much more than telling and justifying. To get the fullest investment possible from staff, we had to genuinely involve and engage them in the practical discussion.

As we wanted our improvement actions, policies, and practices to be in full motion early into the 2006-07 school year, we leveraged our preservice week (i.e. the week before students arrive for the year, which is typically used for teachers to receive some school-required professional learning, prepare their classrooms, and so on) as a deliberation and launching point. We asked Dr. Bob to block off as many hours as he could spare in that week, which was a tall order as preservice time typically includes various district requirements, departmental meetings, and teachers' individual classroom preparation, so it was prime real estate. He was ultimately able to dedicate time scattered over the course of three days.

During these periods (which totaled six hours altogether, leaving CSI members to huddle during classroom-prep times and lunch breaks to make sure all phases could build on one another), the CSI scheduled content and activities to accomplish the following:

- Introduce our new school mission and its guiding rationales.
- Propose mission-corresponding actions, their rationales, and preliminary ideas about logistics/operations.
- Allow teacher workgroups (which teachers elected according to personal interests) to discuss CSI's proposed actions and/or to propose preliminary alternatives.
- Conduct a large-staff discussion about concerns and questions raised in small workgroups; introduce suggestions of alternative actions brainstormed in workgroups.
- Coordinate a full staff vote to decide on school-wide improvement actions.
- Share results of staff vote, next steps, and shared agreements.

All the CSI members assumed various roles within this process's pieces: leading full-staff presentations, facilitating small-group discussions, counting votes, and so on. It was a fast-moving and occasionally difficult few days, but by the time preservice week ended we had decided, with authentic input from the full staff, which actions we were going to link arms on and commit to carrying out together.

Fortunately, the improvement actions roughed out and put forward by the CSI team were accepted by the staff at large as our common focal points for the year. Others were suggested and put up for vote by the staff via our engagement process, too. But the initial actions put forth by the CSI were ultimately selected.

In the 'next steps' staff meeting that capped this engagement process, CSI promised that the selected improvement policies and process would be refined according to input received in the small-group discussions before official rollout.

For instance, after READvisory was approved, I was charged with finalizing its operations and presenting it to staff by our next staff meeting. (Incidentally, after the teacher workgroups I was joined on this by Leslie Schmeisser, a great English teacher who brought valuable ideas to the mix and ultimately co-presented with me.) Other CSI members were subsequently tasked with assembling and distributing classroom materials for the READvisory initiative. The idea, though, was to have our new school-wide improvement actions fully up and running as early in the school year as possible. (The only exception was the no-locker-pass policy, which all teachers were expected to announce on the first day kids arrived. Taking locker passes away isn't the sort of thing to do few weeks into school—unless, of course, a full-on student revolt is what you're after.)

I won't pretend that all the thought, hustle, and listening the CSI put in caused the staff to stand up and cheer. In fact, the staff's approval of our processes, the actions we chose together, and even CSI's *existence* was nowhere near unanimous.[8] And really, we didn't expect it to be. However, no matter how you cut it, there was no way anyone could say staff input was 'disregarded' or that they were 'blindsided' by our improvement plans.

No question, the CSI made school improvement a '*we* thing'.

For those few who remained dead-set on resisting these decisions (and there are almost always a few), we had one condition, that which turned out to be critical for maintaining our momentum. As CSI member Michelle Goetz recalled in an interview, 'Politically, we didn't try to get everyone to *agree*. That's never going to happen—and it probably shouldn't, as people deserve to hang on to their reasons.

'After we had the vote, though, we just asked everyone in the big group, whether they agreed or not, to not actively *sabotage* any of it. Don't badmouth it in the lounge, don't talk about it in the parking lot, all that. You don't have to agree, but you're not allowed to sabotage. Take it up with Bob if you have a real problem, but don't stir the pot and try to bring others down. It really helped things become successful.'

CSI member Jill Kellar concurred, saying that the 'no-sabotage' request steered staff members away from arguing against the mission-focused actions, and toward making them work for themselves. 'It created almost like an underground support system,' Kellar said, 'with teachers helping kids more and teachers sharing ideas with each other. Staff might not have agreed with the policies, but they still followed them. They pushed themselves on how to better support students *within* the policies, not around them. I knew teachers who didn't agree with the no-locker thing, but they created storage spaces for kids' materials to make sure kids were prepared for their classes. And that's what we wanted all along—kids being prepared, and not wandering hallways. After a while, kids saw it too. They saw us looking out for them.'

* * *

While it took a while for the CSI to arrive at this streamlined mission and annual process for constructing school-wide improvement actions, Osseo Senior High School used this process in 2006-07 and 2007-08 to great effect. Student results and the general school climate pitched upward in this period (which I'll share a bit more about in this book's final section), and the professional culture ultimately became one that, as I noted earlier, generated and coordinated various improvements on its own.

And, it must be noted, *the school didn't spend anything beyond its allotted professional development funds. This is important.*

The CSI's improvement process simply broke the school's needs into parts that were easier to see. Accordingly, specific actions could be designed to address these needs, specific monitoring procedures could be outlined to track progress, and the improvement actions could become fully integrated, one pillar at a time, to The Way We Do Things at Osseo Senior High.

Plus, by genuinely engaging staff, the CSI encouraged wider staff investment, participation, and general *belief* in the actions themselves. We never insisted on full *consensus* for these processes before moving forward, of course, as this is likely impossible when so many adult human beings are involved. To borrow from Dr. Martin Luther King, Jr., the CSI's leadership definitely did all it could to *mold* consensus.[9] And thanks to good old-fashioned peer-to-peer loyalty, the initiatives CSI created and executed generally had a lot more of education's ever-elusive 'buy-in' built into them than ones Dr. Bob or the district rolled out unilaterally.

As a bonus, all parts of the CSI effort registered as a show of good faith between the school administration and its teaching staff. In all it said: 'The input and ideas of teachers are welcome here, even if we have to compromise on a few things to keep making progress as a whole.' This opened the door for teachers and even entire departments to come forward with their own improvement ideas in the years to follow.

The CSI team went on to produce some impressive results in the Osseo Senior High School community and beyond. Where the Sophomore Academy leveraged teachers to attack an issue related to the school's graduation rates between 2004 and 2008, the CSI ran concurrently as a promising model for designing and coordinating school improvements— and, crucially, for building, distributing, and perpetuating leadership capacity within the school.

Unfortunately, both initiatives effectively came to an end at the end of the 2007-08 school year. Due to shifts in budgets and the ramping-up of the Osseo Area School District's centralized improvement strategies, these promising school-improvement initiatives imagined by Dr. Bob were eclipsed. While the effects echoed positively through Osseo Senior High School for years afterward, the school found itself less and less able to control its own improvement by the early 2010s.

In the next chapter, which kicks off this book's final section, I'll discuss more about where Osseo Senior High School went from here: how the ability to create improvements from the classroom up disappeared bit by bit, what kinds of improvements were impressed on the school instead, and how the school has fared in the years since. To follow, the next section will conclude with school-improvement lessons from this critical and transformational period at Osseo Senior High School, as well as some recommendations about how to move forward in the current school-improvement climate.

Endnotes

1. Kalenze, E. (2014) *Education Is Upside-Down: Reframing Reform to Focus on the Right Problems.* Lanham, MD: Rowman & Littlefield, pp. 57-59.

2. At the time of this writing, Beckler works in school administration. In 2013, she was named Outstanding Assistant Principal by the Minnesota Department of Education, and I personally consider her one of the best education thinkers I have ever been around.

3. Franklin, B. (1931) *Proposals Relating to the Education of Youth in Pensilvania.* Public Domain. Available at: https://archive.org/details/ProposalsRelatingToTheEducationOfYouthInPensilvaniaBenjamin Franklin/page/n29

4. The academy springing from this proposal, by the way, would eventually go on to become the renowned University of Pennsylvania.

5. Willingham, D., T. (2012) *When Can You Trust the Experts?* San Francisco, CA: Jossey-Bass, pp. 115-116.

6. Office of Governor Tim Pawlenty (1 June 2006) 'Governor Pawlenty Announces Osseo School District to Implement Q Comp'. Available at: https://www.leg.state.mn.us/docs/2010/other/101583/www.governor.state.mn.us/mediacenter/pressreleases/2006/PROD007630.html

7. When I was building my classroom's Independent Reading Project, my goals were multiple: To create something more accountable and rigorous than the wasteful—but at the time ubiquitous—Drop Everything and Read (DEAR) routines, to continually have students taking on more background knowledge (inspired by various cognitive scientific research I had learned about through the work of E. D. Hirsch—see note 6, Chapter 8), and, perhaps too obviously, to cultivate the various benefits a sheer increase in volume of reading can produce. On this final point, I was

guided in particular by the work of developmental psychologists Anne Cunningham and Keith Stanovich. For good introductions to their work, see: Cunningham, A. and Stanovich, K. (1998) 'What Reading Does for the Mind', in *American Educator* and (2003) 'Reading Can Make You Smarter', in *Principal*, 83 (2), pp. 34-39. When considering the rationales for and logistics of bringing these kinds of reading routines school-wide, models like this one from California's Florin High School in the early 2000s, were helpful: Wiener, J. (24 February 2005) 'Cultivating a Culture of Literacy', Sacaramento, CA: Sacramento Bee.

8. The CSI would chuckle for months, for example, over how I got beaten up in one of the small work groups. A particularly surly fellow teacher came at me in that session, saying, 'Who *are* you, anyway?! I've never even *seen* you in my part of the building!' If it hadn't been for my Academy mate Kelly Klecker backing me up there, in fact, I'm not sure if I would have made it out alive.

9. King, M., L. (November 1967) 'Domestic Impact of the War', Speech given to the National Labor Leadership Assembly for Peace. In the final line of this speech, Dr. King said, 'Ultimately, a genuine leader is not a searcher for consensus but a molder of consensus.'

Part Three

Post-2008: Disruption, Lessons & What Schools Can Do

'Progress is man's ability to complicate simplicity.'
– Thor Heyerdahl

Over the Sophomore Academy's four years, it wasn't out of the ordinary for Dr. Bob to join the team for our weekly student-support meetings. Often unannounced, he would sit in as we talked about All Things Academy over our lunches of leftovers or cafeteria specials.

(Incidentally, we most often met in my classroom. Not for its ambience, as my décor was usually limited to a half-dozen posters of things I liked: musicians like the Replacements and Miles Davis, sports heroes like Muhammad Ali and my beloved Packers, clever movie-promo sendups by The Simpsons, that kind of thing. Rather, we met in my room because I run late. I just do. After a short time working together, basically, the team just figured it was more efficient for everyone to grab their food and come to me.)

We never felt we had to sit up extra-straight or speak in edu-jargon or put on airs when he Dr. Bob sat in. He didn't bring that kind of energy. The principal was most definitely *there*, but his work was always focused on helping kids and teachers do their best work. It's how Dr. Bob lived. He'd jump in, but it wasn't about guiding or *monitoring*. More so, he would subtly interrogate our process: he wanted to know which Academy kids were struggling, and in which classes and why; he asked questions to better understand situations and our responses; he offered ideas or approaches we hadn't considered, and he even intervened if we thought it could help. Plus, as he's genuinely a big 'relationships' guy (and yes, it's not lip service), he often jumped right in with us to crack wise and get caught up on everyone's personal and family life.

With a few months to go in the 2007-08 school year, though, Dr. Bob joined one of these meetings with his 'Administrator' hat pulled down tight. He scheduled and confirmed his appearance in advance, even, and explicitly requested we give him some time. Something was definitely *up*.

When we got to the meeting, Dr. Bob announced that, due to state education funding shortfalls, substantial cuts would be coming to Osseo

Senior's budget next year. He didn't have all the details, but he could say with good certainty that many of the flexibilities he negotiated in the schedule—the idiosyncratic adjustments that made the Sophomore Academy work, that is—would be gone. 'Now I'm not saying you have to fold up shop,' he said. 'In fact, I'd love if you'd keep it going. With the financial situation we're facing, though, you might have to make some tough choices.'

Then Dr. Bob got more specific. He laid out a few possibilities for us (again, final budget and enrollment numbers were still several weeks away) so the team could begin mulling the Academy's future. He presented considerations like the following (accompanied by some of the Academy team's initial processing):

- **Post-cut consideration #1, larger academy class sizes:** As the budget cuts would likely reduce teachers from all or most of the school's departments, the Academy class sizes were sure to exceed the 25-student threshold we set back in the spring of 2004. Basically, we were stretching limits as it was. If sections were taken out of the schedule due to staffing cuts, maintaining small class sizes for the Academy would mean sending average class sizes everywhere else far above any reasonable limit. While no one in the Academy team was averse to large class sizes as a rule (I always kinda liked them), the idea of having sections with 30 or more Academy kids made us nervous. Considering the intensity and variability of the typical Academy students' needs (to say nothing about how those needs reacted with one another when combined), cramming too many into one space seemed to be inviting disaster. At best, it would be difficult to give the less assertive kids the support and feedback they needed; at worst, the Academy's more volatile peaks—and yes, there were always a few every year—might turn our classrooms *unsafe*.

- **Post-cut consideration #1a, number of total academy students:** If Academy sections were to balloon to 30 or so students to maintain balance across our departments, this would impact how many students we could serve in the Academy each year. Here, we would have to choose: go down to one packed-out Academy section and serve fewer kids in total (from 45-50 per year to more like 30), or take advantage of the higher per-class numbers and serve even *more* (two packed sections, say, or a total of 60 or more students). One seemed not enough to be worth it. The other seemed like it could only end in tears.

- **Post-cut consideration #2, loss of common planning time:** Dr. Bob said it was possible that, with fewer teachers in the overall master schedule, the flexibility might not be there to maintain our shared prep period. If we wanted to meet regularly about our Academy kids and how we might help them, in other words (a crucial piece of the Academy's just-in-time responsiveness to students' needs and issues), we would have to do it on our own time. And as before- and after-school times were always dicey due to our various planning/grading, extra-curricular, and family commitments, the team knew it would likely lead to a lot of canceled meetings or hurried, unproductive complaining sessions.

- **Post-cut consideration #3, loss of consecutive class configuration:** We also stood to lose our back-to-back class meetings, where students would go directly from my room to Zelenak's, from Ruska's to Klecker's, and vice versa. While this may seem like a minor issue, these mass-transitions were critical. We learned that after an 'off' class period (e.g. in which a shouting match broke out between two kids, half the Academy bombed the same science test and were surly about it, or some individual was made to feel very embarrassed and went into full

276

shutdown mode), a simple 30-second phone call to the group's next teacher was great for providing context, information, and cautions about the entire class culture and mood. Being able to communicate whole-class and individual-student issues in close to real time allowed us to defuse more landmines than any of us could count over our four years, and it was something we never could've done if our kids had scattered to a dozen or more classes at the bell. As an important (if implicit) side benefit, communicating among ourselves this way always sent a clear message to the Academy kids that we were working together to look out for them. It would be very hard to do without.

The more we talked it through, the more the list of possible changes—and, in turn, our list of reservations about those changes—grew. (Recall how I talked about master scheduling and its importance to all school operations and improvements back in Chapter 3? I'm hoping this only underlines those points.)

Dr. Bob didn't pressure us to make a decision in that moment, thank goodness. His big ask was that we communicate any agreements to him within the next couple weeks, as he needed to know what the Sophomore Academy—if there was to still *be* a Sophomore Academy, of course—would look like for master scheduling and staffing purposes.

We all mulled it a while, but the decision to dissolve the Academy altogether came together remarkably easily. Our team didn't see any reason to keep the Sophomore Academy going if it was going to be compromised in any of the ways under discussion. There wouldn't be any point.

There was heartbreak, of course, but no great ceremony or last-gasp attempts at rescuing the Academy. We didn't protest at the school board, write angry letters to newspapers, or rush around applying for grant funding to save jobs. We skipped our spring rituals of contacting junior highs and sifting through suggested candidates, and we got on with our professional lives. (More accurately: Klecker, Ruska, Trzynka, and Zelenak got on with things. I left classroom teaching in 2008 and began work in educational leadership, research, and writing.)

Interestingly, not long after we communicated our decision to Dr. Bob, the Osseo district found a way to stave off most of the forecasted and drastic labor layoff. Many teachers' jobs across the district were saved, thanks to a state grant of close to $1 million for expanding Advanced Placement (AP) programming in the 2008-09 school year.[1]

While the grant and subsequent AP expansion rescued a lot of jobs, though, no retroactive play could be made to preserve the Sophomore Academy. The grant's funds were earmarked specifically for AP teacher training and, where necessary, hiring additional staff to provide the new AP classes.

So while it wasn't the original force exerting pressure, the grant-powered expansion of AP ultimately pushed the Sophomore Academy (in its intended, optimal form) out of Osseo Senior. The original force was the forecasted budget shortfall, of course, which would have reduced staff and removed scheduling flexibilities. Grant dollars prevented this and kept our staff intact, but the schedule flexibility required to make the Sophomore Academy work wasn't going to be there. The retained staff resources were dedicated to expanding access to AP across the school, even in exotic AP subjects like French, studio art, and psychology.[2] (Yes, the AP grant saved jobs *everywhere* that year.) Supporting a group of credit-risky sophomores so they could stay on track to graduate, even if it cost next to nothing in operating dollars? A priority?

Not so much.

* * *

It may sound like it, but let me assure you I'm not running through this episode to air my resentment. (Really, I'm over it. Took a while, but I'm good.)

More so, I bring this sequence up because it is highly instructive, particularly with regard to what happened in the district and our school after the Sophomore Academy years. For indeed, this exact progression—expanding an unproven improvement initiative (Advanced Placement programming[3]) in multiple district schools and using up all the resources necessary for planning, executing, and refining school-built improvements (Sophomore Academy)—became a pattern in the Osseo district moving throughout the 2010s. The chapter ahead will explore a few examples of these centrally driven improvements, as well as the effects they had on student achievement, professional climate, and community satisfaction.

As I visit those examples, however, please keep in mind that while I'm putting the Osseo Area Schools District in the spotlight, that's only because it's the district I know the best. My intent is not to expose or criticize the district. That's not what this book is about.

When it comes right down to it, in fact, this book isn't about Osseo Senior High, Dr. Bob, the CSI, or even the Sophomore Academy.

Rather, it's about how hard it is to get school improvement right *anywhere, even if you succeed*. I mean, when it comes to the Academy and even broader efforts like the CSI, we nailed it. We did what we set out to do. These initiatives show what school improvement can look like when districts trust leaders, leaders empower teachers, and teachers collaborate (and, of course, work their butts off) to make school better for kids.

It worked. And yet it didn't last. Why?

To answer that question, we need to take a much closer look at how much *harder* continuous school improvement is today and how we got here. For though Dr. Bob and his staff did a lot of things right, big changes affected the entire school (and the entire district) as the 2010s came to pass. As was the case across U.S. education during this period, waves of district-imagined and -required improvements rolling into

Osseo Senior High picked up in number and intensity, and they eroded the priorities and actions—and, indeed, the entire *identity*—the school had worked so hard to build.

To reiterate, as I share Osseo Senior High's fate, please know that I do so intending to shine a light on the tendencies I see again and again in my ongoing work in and study of the education field. I'm *not* trying to make the Osseo Area School District look bad. The decisions the Osseo Area Schools central offices made may not seem particularly wise, but they weren't the only district making the same confounding choices. They are part of a much bigger story—one we have to understand in order to start making more effective improvement decisions across the enterprise.

That story is one you may already know. If you work in or follow education, I'm guessing several of the examples I'll share will sound hauntingly familiar to you.

If they do, and if you have been frustrated by similar tales of bureaucratic woe, I hope it gives you some comfort to know this: it's not just your school, it's *everyone's*. And the reasons why it turned out this way have very deep roots. It's not just power-hungry tyrants or a loose cannon suddenly taking control of your district office. All the initiative-shoving, data-diving, individual-growth-planning, SWOT-analyzing, and autonomy-sacrificing you've come to hate didn't materialize out of nowhere. It was decades in the making. (While it's impossible to locate an exact starting point, it's fair to say that the top-down philosophy running amok today traces back formally to the U.S. government's 'A Nation At Risk' report in 1983. While the report didn't immediately ramrod reforms into schools nationwide, its assertion that 'the educational foundations of our society are presently being eroded by a rising tide of mediocrity that threatens our very future as a nation and as a people' most certainly put the entire education enterprise on notice.[4])

This situation intensified when the Accountability Era kicked off, namely with the passage of the No Child Left Behind (NCLB) Act in 2001. With NCLB (and its accompanying slew of federally incentivized innovations[5]) humming a decade after its inception, more and more top-down influence pressed down on individual schools. Much of American education rolled out centrally ordered (and evidence-weak—more on that shortly) improvements, leaving less and less room for schools to grow their own improvements. Rather than determine and work on the best actions for their unique sites, school leaders were instead relegated to *coordinating* district offices' 'innovative' and non-negotiable improvement processes. All over the U.S., principals were suddenly charged with overseeing matters like the following, effectively reengineering how they spent their time:

- Evaluating and coaching teachers via systems of observation, conferencing, and reporting, usually according to standardized effectiveness criteria handed down from districts (or, in some cases, state departments of education).
- Coordinating benchmark testing resources and facilitating data-review protocols in order to standardize teachers' collaborative learning/planning.
- Bringing more educational technology online in schools, which required entirely new administrative procedures and considerable professional learning time, not to mention significant hardware (especially in older facilities that required substantial upgrades to make new technology usable).

Where districts' central offices had always been at most a nuisance to principals and teachers, in other words, they've become much more aggressive and directive in the Accountability Era. Billions of dollars are spent on measurement and evaluation. Schools' achievement results and ratings are front-page news. More school-choice options are channeling families out of traditional public schools, taking millions of dollars away from those schools' budgets. In response, the typical district's course of action is to show how *transformational* and *disruptive*[6] they can be, in every sense of those words.

Every sense, that is, except the ones *that are supported by evidence.* From the school level all the way to the federal level, education's decision-makers tend toward the innovative and promising over what is actually *proven.* For all the research that's been done in recent years about the connection between strong curriculum and student achievement,[7] for example, it's still shockingly rare to hear about districts or schools going 'all in' on the best curricula possible for their specific population's needs. (Test it out for yourself. Watch your local newspaper for a few weeks, and note how often education coverage mentions the verified effectiveness of improvements currently flowing through the local schools. My guess is you'll read many more stories about various *cool practices:*[8] exciting experiments the hometown schools are trying with things like yoga breaks, restorative-justice discipline, or technology expansions. Alas, the improvements that actually work are never quite sexy or bold enough to attract the same degree of attention.)

In short, district leaders' actions in our time (and indeed, many before it[9]) seem to say: 'There's not any proof this Cool New Thing will fix what we need to fix, but admit it, it's very *new,* and unquestionably *cool.* And we're so dang urgent about getting better at all this that we'll push everything else away to make these kinds of bold transformations work. Whether it delivers the intended results or not, no one will be able to say we weren't *trying.* Now please—*please!*—don't send your kids to a charter school!'

In this paradigm, leaving decisions up to individual school leaders (a level of trust the Osseo district once extended to Dr. Bob, as you may recall) is no longer an option. Districts are more worried about creating positive impressions far and wide than they are about creating sound practices locally, and this has essentially neutralized the effect of site-level leaders.

As we close in on 2020, school leaders generally have even less authority to understand their sites and design appropriate actions. Schools' decision-making about everything from professional development to discipline policies have been shoved aside by central office mandates (and superior wisdom, of course), which are often guided by recommendations from third-party vendors, consultants, and 'fidelity checklists'.

(Note: While I could take a detour here to explore how these outside organizations are influencing—read: *interfering with*—American school improvement in the Accountability Era, that topic requires an entire book to itself. It's a book I'm interested in researching and writing, but first things first. Do stay tuned.)

I've said repeatedly that I've been fortunate to be in the right place at the right time, over and over again during the past two decades. My particular path has afforded a unique view of trends in education. The same is true for shifts in leadership philosophy. I've been at the mercy of these shifts as a front-line practitioner. In my ten years outside the classroom, I've gotten to see how centrally adopted improvements take shape from the administrative side and, of course, the many ways they impact all of schools' operations.

As I draw from these professional experiences and my study of the field, please know (again) that the following is presented to demonstrate two points: how educational leadership is now done across much of the U.S., and how the already challenging job of continuous school improvement has become incredibly constrained and difficult.

Endnotes

1. Draper, N. (11 November 2008) 'Osseo Schools Set Higher Bar for Students.' Minneapolis, MN: Star Tribune.

2. Ibid.

3. For how it increases historically undeserved students' access to challenging coursework and potential college credit, the expansion of Advanced Placement programming is widely accepted—and, accordingly, politically and public-relationally popular—as an effective equity-building strategy. While there is little question that offering AP courses give an overall boost to the rigor of a school's catalog (and that these boosts are generally good things), studies of this strategy have repeatedly shown mixed results at best. Associations between AP course completion and genuine college readiness are very loose, the quality of AP courses across schools has become highly variable as programming has expanded, and scores on the AP tests have declined nationally, just to name three concerning patterns in the research. For more, start with these studies: Kolluri, S. (2018) 'Advanced Placement: The Dual Challenge of Equal Access and Effectiveness' in *Review of Educational Research*, 88(5), pp. 671–711; Hallett, R., E. and Venegas, K., M. (2011) 'Is Increased Access Enough? Advanced Placement Courses, Quality, and Success in Low-Income Urban Schools', in *Journal for the Education of the Gifted*, 34 (3), pp. 468–487.

4. Kamenetz, A. (29 April 2018) 'What 'A Nation At Risk' Got Wrong, And Right, About U.S. Schools.' NPR. Available at: www.npr.org/sections/ed/2018/04/29/604986823/what-a-nation-at-risk-got-wrong-and-right-about-u-s-schools

5. Within 15 years of NCLB's passage, the U.S. government threw hefty sums at various education-serving entities to build and provide innovations that would, as I put it in *Education is Upside-Down*, 'lubricate the mechanisms of private-sector-inspired reform: better statewide data systems for improving student measurement, improved assessments to increase accuracy of student measurement, [and] strengthened systems of teacher-evaluation and hiring to improve teaching and leadership forces.' For more on the two largest grant programs powering these innovations, Race to the Top and i3 (the Investing In Innovation Fund), see: U.S. Department of Education (2009) 'Race to the Top Program Executive Summary'. Available at: http://www2.ed.gov/programs/racetothetop/executive-summary.pdf, and U.S. Department of Education. (2013) 'Investing in Innovation Fund (i3)'. Available at: http://www2.ed.gov/programs/innovation/index.html

6. Education has been fairly overrun in the past decade or so by reformers—and, importantly, *businesspeople*—seeking to 'disrupt' longstanding operations toward better results. By educational 'disruption', futurists

like Clayton Christensen, Tony Wagner, Sir Ken Robinson, and Michael Horn typically mean finding ways to fully personalize education: Getting students precisely what they would like to learn, all in the ways they would most prefer to learn it, apparently because it will do more to create more innovators (if not, of course, people who are actually educated or prepared to learn the way the world will actually ask them to). For a sample of this thinking, see: Wagner, T. (14 August 2012) 'Graduating All Students Innovation-Ready'. Education Week. Available at: www.edweek.org/ew/articles/2012/08/14/01wagner.h32.html. For a more detailed version, see: Christensen, C., M. (2008) *Disrupting Class: How Disruptive Innovation Will Change the Way the World Learns*. New York, NY: McGraw-Hill—the education-business volume that essentially showed the private sector how to most perfectly storm education's beaches.

7. Though much work has been done about the importance of well-sequenced, knowledge-rich curriculum to effective teaching and learning in recent years, resources like these may be instructive as starting points. They range in theme—from studying curricular quality to just how the presence of common curricular resources effects student achievement—and are suggested here to show how thoroughly education researchers and some education leaders have begun to explore the relationship between curriculum and results. See: Boser, U., Chingos, M. and Straus, C. (October 2015) 'The Hidden Value of Curriculum Reform: Do States and Districts Receive the Most Bang for Their Curriculum Buck?' Center For American Progress. Available at: https://cdn.americanprogress.org/wp-content/uploads/2015/10/06111518/CurriculumMatters-report.pdf; Chiefs for Change (10 August 2017) 'Hiding In Plain Sight: Leveraging Curriculum to Improve Student Learning'. Available at: http://chiefsforchange.org/policy-paper/4830/; Jackson, K. and Makarin, A. (3 August 2018) 'Can Online Off-the-Shelf Lessons Improve Student Outcomes? Evidence from a Field Experiment', in *American Economic Journal: Economic Policy*, 10 (3). Available at: https://www.aeaweb.org/articles?id=10.1257/pol.20170211; Koedel, C., Li, D., Hardaway, T., Wrabel, S., L. and Polikoff, M., S. (2016) 'Mathematics Curriculum Effects on Student Achievement in California', Columbia, MO: University of Missouri. Available at: https://economics.missouri.edu/paper/wp-16-12; Steiner, D. (2017) 'Curriculum Research: What We Know and Where We Need to Go'. StandardsWork. Available at: http://edpolicy.education.jhu.edu/wordpress/wp-content/uploads/2017/04/sw-curriculum-research-report-fnl.pdf. For a useful summary piece on this wave of research interest, see the Manhattan Institute's Charles Sahm in USA Today: Sahm, C. (4 January 2017) 'A Compelling Case for Curriculum'. US News & World Report. Available at: https://www.usnews.com/opinion/knowledge-bank/articles/2017-01-04/data-builds-a-

compelling-case-for-taking-curriculum-seriously-in-education? src=usn_
fb&fbclid=IwAR2RmDfNuY0qYr3cB5JocGblWWERRnEQLmO7z29IW
yzKXcQQ2yzMHIZIPpw

8. See Chapter 8 of my book *Education is Upside-Down.*

9. While several great histories of education reform and improvement are available, two are particularly instructive about this tendency throughout American education's history. See Ravitch, D. (2001) *Left Back: A Century of Battles Over School Reform.* New York, NY: Simon & Schuster; Tyack, D and Cuban, L. (1995) *Tinkering Toward Utopia: A Century of Public School Reform.* Cambridge, MA: Harvard University Press.

Chapter 13

The District Knew Best

'The fact that an opinion has been widely held
is no evidence whatever that it is not utterly
absurd; indeed in view of the silliness of the
majority of mankind, a widely spread belief
is more likely to be foolish than sensible.'

– Bertrand Russell

For Osseo Senior High and all schools in the Osseo Area School District, there wasn't a clear *point in time* when everything changed. No formal announcement was made, such as, 'Effective July 1, 2009, Osseo's district offices will be making the improvement decisions for each school. After that date, principals' improvement visions will be null and void, and all professional-development time will be filled in according to our priorities.' That's not how it worked. The reality was much more subtle—and insidious.

More so, the district leadership's centralized improvement philosophy expressed itself one initiative at a time. It emerged in the same period as the Sophomore Academy, ironically. Recall, for instance, how the district standardized expectations about teachers' collaboration time (and frustrated me intensely). You may also remember that in 2007, the district imposed the most comprehensive school improvement imaginable upon Park Center Senior High, Osseo's in-district neighbor to the east, fully restructuring the school as the district's sole International Baccalaureate (IB) high school.[1]

In other words, there's no question: Osseo Area School District didn't start imposing massive improvement initiatives all at once. By the end of the 2010s, it was already on an upward trend.

'We became obsolete'

At some point, district aggression reached a pitch where Dr. Bob and his staff weren't able to maintain the improvement structures they worked so hard to establish over the previous five years.

When I asked Dr. Bob about when the district's leadership-philosophical shift started to impact Osseo Senior, he couldn't pinpoint any particular event or turning point. The district offices began rolling out larger required improvements across the district in the early 2010s, he said, but much of the collaborative, classroom-up improvement culture he created at Osseo Senior continued undaunted.

'It was tough sometimes but we managed it,' Dr. Bob told me in another one of our pizza-joint interviews. 'We usually found a way to incorporate changes the district was bringing in so we could stay true to who we were. We still had the mission CSI drew up, and I put that in front of staff during pre-service week every year. We still planned what we wanted to improve according to that mission, and we still had teachers coming forward with things they wanted to do better in their classrooms and in their departments. We were fine for a while there, even after the Academy was gone.'

And looking at the school's state standardized test scores from this mid-2000s to early 2010s period[2] Dr. Bob's assessment seems right on. It wasn't just a case, in other words, of the school organizing to 'do cool things': Osseo Senior was putting site-relevant improvements into motion and recording notable growth in student achievement.

The pattern of 10th grade reading scores between 2006[3] and 2012 shown in *Figure 1*, for example, shows a school stumbling to stay in line with—and even dipping below—state averages. Historically, this checks out: the first two years in the graph, after all, correspond with the CSI's two aimless years (first as a morale-building exercise, then as a kitchen-sink PD provider). In 2008 and beyond, though, it looks as though the school-wide improvement actions built in year by year via CSI's leadership (i.e. actions like READvisory, school-wide requirements and policies to boost student preparedness, initiatives to build students' senses of belonging) might be having an impact. Aside from the anomalous 'hiccup' logged in 2011, the school's reading scores jump up to, then surpass, the state's average proficiency rates each year.

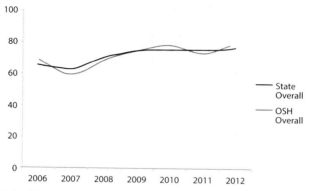

Figure 1 *Proficiency rates on Minnesota Comprehensive Assessment (MCA) in reading (grade 10), 2006-2012.*

While Osseo Senior's percentages-proficient on the state's 11th grade math test remain below the state's proficiency rates over this period, an upward trend like that of the reading scores can be observed after slightly descending rates from 2006-2008. After the bumpy and downward 2006-2008 stretch (in which, remember, Osseo Senior was still finding its improvement groove), the school's juniors began to pass the state math test at higher and higher rates. These rates didn't reach and exceed the state's average rates as with reading, but their year-to-year growth rate most certainly keeps pace.

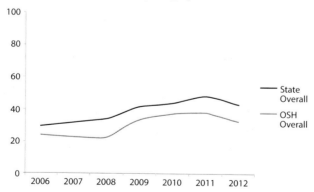

Figure 2 *Proficiency rates on Minnesota Comprehensive Assessment (MCA) in math (grade 11), 2006-2012.*

Moving a few years into the 2010s, though, the trends changed. Dr. Bob said his school-based systems of practice and policy improvement had 'less and less room to move.' The faculty leadership group CSI, for example, which acted as a nucleus for the school's data-driven, mission-directed, and staff-created improvement actions, ultimately ended up where the Sophomore Academy had at the end of 2008: squeezed out by district-determined priorities.

'Something like CSI, we just became obsolete,' Dr. Bob told me. 'There was no need to continue it, because we couldn't work on our own changes. Central office became much more assertive with the staff-development expectations, mostly tied to the performance-pay system [the Alternative Teacher Professional Pay System, or ATPPS, the district's version of Minnesota's Quality Teacher Compensation—or Q Comp—program[4]]. The district created new positions and placed them in buildings, professional-learning committees were formed within buildings by directive, and PD came through the instructional coaches based on district vision and goals.'

By the early 2010s, the priorities and initiatives coming from the district's central office were occupying virtually all available school-improvement resources—not just at Osseo Senior High, but everywhere across the district.

Transformational system change, indeed

The district's vision and goals after this early-2010s hinge point were definite and decidedly *disruptive*. According to district leadership, the overarching strategy was to 'create transformational system change to ensure equitable student achievement',[5] and this meant large-scale efforts that swept across all schools. The district had clear ideas about what needed transforming, and they ordered these ideas up for everyone. These large improvement initiatives cost millions to roll out and, just as Dr. Bob alluded to when he said district intervention had made Osseo

Senior's CSI obsolete, they overshadowed individual sites' improvement visions and processes.

Three major improvement initiatives in particular exemplify the Osseo district's 'transformational system change' in the early 2010s: the district-wide adoption of standards-based grading practices, a digital learning plan that included outfitting thousands of district students with iPads, and standardized behavior practices informed by racial-equity-focused professional development. (As I stated earlier: if you currently work in or follow American education, these 'transformational' initiatives may look quite familiar to you. They and others like them are being rolled out across the country with great frequency.)

While none of these initiatives had strong enough evidence to justify their adoption, all of them had large impacts on schools' operations, required high costs to enable, and kicked up considerable animus from the district's practitioners and parents. Worse (and as I'll share in the next chapter), the combination of all three ultimately didn't do much to move student achievement. Indeed, when viewed in light of all the money, time, and angst spent to bring these initiatives to life, they accomplished *tragically* little in terms of student outcomes.

Revised grading practices

On their way to 'ensuring equitable student achievement' in the early 2010s, Osseo's central office leaders placed a high priority on revising grading practices across the district. Beginning in the 2011-12 school year, district schools were to move toward a system of 'standards-based instruction and grading' to drive greater and more consistent student mastery.

According to the district's assessment through 2010, grading practices across their schools were inconsistent and unreliable. District leaders found that, on average, the grades teachers ultimately assigned did not accurately reflect students' mastery of standards, did not allow teachers to give effective feedback toward students' growth, and restricted students' access to more advanced learning opportunities.[6]

District leaders followed this assessment by bringing a new grading system online—one that would ensure students' course grades were based primarily on students' masteries of state-specified learning standards. The idea was to make grades more accurate representations of what each student knew and were able to do with regard to the state's learning standards, and this meant getting rid of all the 'noise' that traditional percentage-based letter grades can include: scores on daily assignments, participation points for practice test completion and discussions, and the like.

Think of it like the SAT. The score one earns on the SAT doesn't automatically decline if the test-taker didn't do any preparation, nor does it automatically go up if the test-taker did a lot. The performance is what counts. Similarly, the Osseo district's new standards-based grading system sought to move mastery-demonstrating performances to the fore. That way, kids and families would know all along how well they were performing with regard to the state's academic standards.

In short, if you can get a B in your English class, you'd damn well better pass the state's end-of-year reading test. If one happens and the other doesn't, something's out of whack. One of the main objectives of standards-based grading is to bring these two sides into alignment.

The new grading system specified a number of processes and principles for district teachers to follow. All coursework was to be divided clearly into formative tasks and summative tasks, for instance, with rubrics for each task that would gauge students' level of mastery on a 0-to-4-point scale. Also, homework and other practice activities (e.g. *formative tasks*) were to have only minimal effects on final grade calculations. As well, greater flexibility was to be allowed with assignment due dates and the number of times students could retake assessments.[7]

On its face, this strategy seems sensible. It prioritizes mastery of standards, *period*, not mastery of standards *by a certain date*.

The theory goes like this: if Brayden needs five tries on a summative assessment to show that he has reached a certain set of learning standards, then so be it. Let him keep re-taking tests or revising essays until he shows that he truly knows the content or that he is truly proficient in the skill. Just because he hasn't turned something in doesn't mean he should get a zero or, worse, fail the class and fall behind on credits. He hasn't formally demonstrated mastery of the standard yet, but that doesn't mean he's failed at doing so *forever*. As he's still coming along (that's how humans work), his grades shouldn't permanently punish his rate of progress. He shouldn't get shunted off into remedial classes, for instance, where the work won't ever push him beyond his current capabilities, or be denied graduation. Perhaps all he needs is a little more time, like even one or two more practice sessions, to make a concept 'click'—or get to a point, at least, that's acceptably high for him to move forward.

Again, the main point is that Brayden knows content or can perform skills to formally expressed standards. Too many Braydens have been able to pass through school without reaching those standards, grading reformers say, and these Braydens have been able to camouflage what they weren't mastering by gaining points for work habits or extra credit. (And absolutely, the reformers have a decent point. There are indeed way, way too many Braydens out there.)

According to these grading reformers[8] (who are currently tearing up the professional-development circuit, by the way, often framing themselves as promoters of *ethical* grading practices and asserting that assigning zeros for incomplete work is 'grading malpractice' that *harms* children[9]), truly standards-aligned grading practices like these aren't just beneficial for reducing the number of mastery-obscuring Braydens. Reformers also promise that practices like these will eventually produce much larger numbers of students who have verifiably mastered the required learning, and those larger numbers will in turn generate substantial bumps in schools' year-end test results across all student subgroups.

That's right, in addition to being the 'ethical', '*right* thing to do' by kids (it's a masterpiece of framing, honestly), standards-based grading is the key to producing higher test scores—which is the holy grail for 'transformational' district administrators.

Unfortunately, these same reformers can't point to evidence of school systems where standards-based grading practices transformed legions of Braydens—where test scores went through the roof, and the Braydens emerged markedly better prepared for life after K-12—but many education leaders forge ahead undeterred. The ideals and values that standards-based grading appeals to, apparently, are far more powerful than proof.

As that goes, however, proof of standards-based grading may take a long time to accumulate. In reality, the theoretical appeals and ideals of standards-based grading are wildly over-simplified.

The Osseo Area School District got to learn about these over-simplifications first-hand, and it was a painful process. When the standards-based practices were brought online, a first (and rather crucial) oversimplification had to be dealt with: namely, students don't always respond like the grading reformers promise they will when given additional flexibility to master material.

When I talked to several Osseo Senior High teachers who worked to implement the standards-based grading requirements, they regularly told me how students gamed the new grading system. Some would arrive unprepared, then request retakes before even making their first attempt. Others would arrive to an assessment unprepared, sit for it long enough to see what was being tested, hastily complete their first attempt, immediately request a retake, and then prepare accordingly and perform satisfactorily on the next attempt. (You have to hand it to them, right? This is where the real innovation is happening.)

(Note: While we can celebrate that the students in these examples got to know the material via the processes' flexibilities, accepting this behavior probably doesn't send the right message about preparation within a timeframe—an *institutional virtue* I believe schools should absolutely help students understand, appreciate, and strengthen. Many job interviews are one-shot deals, for example. Tax day is always April 15, houses with broken furnaces get very cold very quickly if the issue isn't addressed, and most workplaces have deadlines. To pretend otherwise—and many of the grading reformers very much do—is, flatly, more than a little confounding. To borrow from an idea I've covered elsewhere: this theory runs counter to what motivates people and what the world will expect, making standards-based grading a prime example of *upside-down* educational thinking.[10])

Still other students, knowing that the 'formative' assignments only figured minimally into their overall course grades, would engage very little, if at all, with this work. (Why do it if it doesn't count?) Some would even wait until the very end of the trimester (when final grades were calculated and reported) to hand in hastily done essays and projects that teachers had built up and supported bit-by-bit over several class meetings.

The concerns about how students approached—and manipulated—the standards-based grading policies escalated so much, in fact, that some teachers I spoke with quickly became cynical about the initiative's promise. Some jokingly (and exasperatedly) renamed standards-based grading, or 'SBG,' as '*story*-based grading.' As in, 'Okay, so you want me to give you a retake or an extension. What's your *story*?'

Additionally, teachers I spoke with told me repeatedly about how some students, faced with the prospect of improving on material they didn't get the first time around, simply weren't willing to put in the energy to master previous content while simultaneously keeping up with new material. They would fail the original assessment, then accept that they failed and keep moving. No matter how teachers would regale them about their opportunities to improve a course grade, or about how they were missing an opportunity to learn more via retakes and/or revisions, this set of students would simply accept their failing score. (In other words: many students looked at all the rubrics and formative/summative lingo and multiple opportunities and made the exact same choice as they would have under a traditional percentage-based grading system. The idea seems less like one kids appreciate and maximize, and more like one adults fall in love with.)

Still, teachers did what they could within the new system to encourage habits in students that would ultimately help them learn (even if the new system wasn't particularly cooperative). Mary Jo Skinner, my one-time colleague in Osseo Senior High's English department, explained how the early implementation of standards-based grading— and students' resulting habits—put the teachers into a bit of a scramble. 'It was a challenge to get kids to do the work that would help them learn,' she said. 'As a department team, we knew we had to abide by the policy, but sometimes we had to massage things a little bit to get kids to do the work. We'd put in incentives, but we couldn't call them that—rules like that all formative work had to be complete to be eligible to retake a summative task. We'd write up proposals of our adjusted policies and bring them to Dr. Bob, and he'd sign off if it looked okay, and met all the requirements of the new policy. But we definitely had to get creative.'

Managing the students' approach to the new grading system, however, was just the beginning. The longer the standards-based grading system was in place, *everyone* began having issues with it. Osseo Senior alumni, returning to the school while on break from their first year in college, frequently complained to their former teachers and counselors that the school's standards-based policies hadn't prepared them well for post-secondary institutions' extremely time-bound, one-and-done expectations. Also, teachers' workloads—especially near the end of grading periods, when panicked students turned in piles of previously undone or sloppy work to improve their grades—spiraled out of control, and teachers mobilized in response. (A group of district teachers even took their case to the Osseo Area school board in January of 2013, testifying—and presenting more than 750 letters from aligned colleagues—about how the new requirements were impacting their jobs.[11]) *Parents* even joined the anti-SBG chorus, railing at school board meetings and in Facebook forums.[12]

Despite the popularity of standards-based grading reforms and the consultants who recommend them, frustrations like these are not uncommon. They have piled up over and over in U.S. education in recent years, all without a corresponding bump in student achievement. Forty-eight states have adopted policies to promote 'competency-based' education to varying degrees (the state of Maine actually tried to implement similar practices statewide, only to roll them back in 2018 due to massive complications and a paucity of positive results), but there remains little evidence that proficiency-based education has improved the effectiveness or equity of student learning.[13]

Still, the standards-based grading reform effort lumbers on in the Osseo Area School District even today. Envisioned increases in standards-mastering students haven't materialized yet, despite six years of full implementation. (Again: I'll share some illustrative results in the next chapter.) What remains constant is the unhappiness of students, teachers, and parents. Still, the district's leadership stands firm. They are so convinced that these grading practices are an essential 'transformational system change' that they continue tweaking policies, procedures, and professional development in hopes of someday getting the desired results.

Digital learning plan

The central office's grading policies in the early 2010s were joined by another 'transformational system change to ensure equitable student achievement' in the 2014-15 school year, a comprehensive digital learning plan. (*Shudder.*) The plan was to roll it out over the next three to five years, with an end goal of helping 'teachers transform instruction from a focus on content delivery...to more engaged, personalized and self-directed learning by students.'[14]

In practical terms, the district gave schools a number of considerations to incorporate into their operations during the plan's launch phase. A learning management system (Schoology) was brought online for educators to create and share resources with students, colleagues, and parents, and iPads were distributed to thousands of students and teachers.[15] Accordingly, significant training was necessary to get schools' staffers up to speed on the new technologies' functionalities and potential applications. Also (and importantly), schools had to dedicate significant time to how they were going to manage students' use of the new iPads. Putting so much expensive, communication-accelerating technology into the hands of students, after all, meant that several new policies, from acceptable use to damaged-device replacement, would have to be thought through, established, communicated, and carried out.

Taken together, it was a huge amount of work to launch these digital-learning enhancements across the district. It was an especially large price to pay for an improvement strategy that hasn't yet produced much in the way of measurable results. No matter: Osseo's central-office leadership used all the typical ed-tech tropes and promises to puff up its digital learning plan. They asserted that expanding digital learning resources would personalize instruction, empower students' voices and choices, and generally prepare students for the digital age by helping them become better collaborators and critical thinkers. Importantly, there's not much proof that the moves they were making would—or even *could*—produce anything of the sort.[16]

In the years since the Osseo district announced the rollout of this digital learning plan, in fact, stories of educational technology producing verified positive results have been much harder to find than stories of decision-makers in education pumping the brakes on ed tech. Some of these stories show how the field is only now becoming more prudent after the initial (and explosive, and confounding) excitement over 1:1 iPad initiatives,[17] while others—like Los Angeles Unified School District's lawsuit-riddled, $1.3-billion meltdown[18]—show how ugly things can get when prudence is an afterthought.

The Osseo district's digital learning plan has seen its share of administrative headaches. Through the 2016-17 school year, for example, the district was more than $300,000 short on iPad replacement and repair costs billed to families, moving the district to re-think their managerial policies.[19] As well, progress surveys of Osseo district students, teachers, and parents have shown conflicting views about the value of new technology and the thinnest possible connections between new technologies and student performance.[20] (As promised, I'll take a look at some metrics in the next chapter to see if this improvement initiative transformed student results as envisioned.)

In all, however, the administrative headaches and fuzzy data haven't caused the district's central office to waver on their digital learning plan as a 'transformational system change'. Just as with standards-based grading, which produced considerably more blowback, the district leadership has managed to keep its digital-learning initiative moving forward through the time of this writing.

Standardized behavior protocols, informed by equity-based professional development

For yet another 'transformational system change' that would 'ensure equitable student achievement', the Osseo district leadership enacted a multi-tiered approach to focus on schools' behavior and discipline practices and policies.

Since the early 2010s, the Osseo district has sought to improve these practices and policies by providing both substantial practice-level guidance and practitioner-level training, all aiming to achieve two goals: to make schools safe places for all to learn, and to cut the number of out-of-school suspensions, particularly for populations that are suspended disproportionately often. This has meant taking concurrent steps to shape both day-to-day discipline practices and the dispositions—the underlying racial biases, that is—of its teaching professionals.

On the practice-level tier, the Osseo district's schools were trained in and expected to implement various pre-packaged practices intended to improve student behavior. For instance, the district used the popular Positive Behavioral Interventions and Supports (PBIS) framework to institute preferred practices and to establish common language and expectations among teachers and administrators. The PBIS framework has seen its appeal grow widely in recent years, likely for how its preventive (as opposed to punitive) philosophy aligns with schools' urgent desire to lower suspension numbers. Ostensibly, PBIS concentrates less on defining and punishing misbehavior, and more on stopping misbehavior before it happens—a stoppage that is made possible by controlling the unruly tendencies that *lead* to misbehavior.[21] According to a FAQ on PBIS's website, this preventive approach equips teachers to 'explicitly [prompt, model, practice, and encourage] positive expected social skills across settings and individuals' toward making 'school climates more positive, learning environments safer, and student-educator relationships more trusting and respectful'.[22]

In addition to the PBIS-guided practices, the Responsibility-Centered Discipline program's 'Give 'em Five' philosophy and technique[23] was trained, expected, and monitored in some facilities across the district, including at Osseo Senior. When they described how these techniques and expectations fit into the day-to-day of schooling, and especially into the handling of disciplinary incidents, several of the teachers I spoke with shared that incident-related conversations with administrators became less about understanding what had transpired (as with the

Sophomore Academy's infamous assault incident) and more about what the teacher may or may not have done correctly. 'I'd send a kid to the office, which I never really do, but y'know, it happens sometimes,' said Osseo Senior High social studies teacher Gerry Zelenak (who you may remember as the Sophomore Academy's single best relationships-building teacher). 'And we'd get to the conversation with admin, and right away the question was, "Well, did you give 'em five?" It gave us all a procedure, but I think I'd always handled that fairly and with respect in the past. All our professional judgment was taken out of it. Then usually the student was right back in class.'

On the practitioner-level tier, meanwhile, the district ordered up large amounts of cultural competence training, presumably because the disproportionality of discipline infractions was rooted in teachers' implicit racial biases.

Specifically, teachers from across the district were required to attend professional development sessions provided by the San Francisco-based Pacific Education Group (PEG), an organization that engages 'in sustained partnerships with educational organizations to transform beliefs, behaviors, and results so people of all races can achieve at their highest levels and live their most empowered and powerful lives'.[24] In these trainings, which PEG has dubbed 'Courageous Conversations', educators are taught to examine their own classroom practices and behavioral expectations in light of Critical Race Theory. While the Osseo Area district saw PEG training as a transformational missing piece for its professionals, educators elsewhere haven't always been as enthusiastic about PEG's potential. In a 2015 opinion piece in the St. Paul (MN) Pioneer Press, for example, St. Paul Public Schools teacher Aaron Benner summed up PEG's philosophies in schools as he saw them, and asserted that they were actually damaging to African American children and to education at large. Benner, himself an African American, accused PEG's stance and message of lowering expectations for African American students—of portraying them as powerless to do anything but underachieve and misbehave within the inherently racist, discriminatory school system.

In the messages of PEG, Benner said, African American students 'are victims of white school policies that make it difficult or impossible for them to learn', and that they should not be held to any kind of standard. He also went on to describe how the PEG-driven school he worked in looked in terms of personnel, policies, and procedures, certainly suggesting an environment that definitely did not seem suitable for student *safety*, much less learning.[25]

The Osseo Area School District's two-tiered strategy (i.e. tightening up how discipline is done and building teachers' awareness of matters like white privilege and their own implicit racial biases) and its attendant frustrations have seen great growth across U.S. education in recent years, thanks in part to a now-infamous 'Dear Colleague' letter from the Obama-era Department of Education in January of 2014.[26]

While the letter gave 'guidance' on how to comply with federal law when it comes to school discipline, the actions many education leaders took across the country in its wake created what some considered unsafe school environments. In district after district, unruly students continued to circulate in schools without consequence, leading significant percentages of teachers to report that their schools have become more violent and that they don't feel supported by their administrations in matters of school/classroom discipline.[27] (Interestingly, in a very recent development, a federal commission led by Betsy DeVos, President Trump's Education Secretary, recommended in December of 2018 to rescind the Obama-era guidance, citing in part that 'students are afraid because violent students were going unpunished'. It's a story worth watching, not least of all for the commission's recommendations around *arming school personnel*.[28] Stay tuned.)

In Benner's district of St. Paul, in fact, the situation quickly deteriorated. Students and teachers were physically harmed,[29] teachers criticizing the approach on social media faced backlash from Black Lives Matter,[30] and the teachers union threatened to strike over working conditions.[31] The situation became so untenable that the St. Paul School Board took a substantial loss to put out the fires in 2016. They fired Superintendent Valeria Silva with more than two years to go on her contract, paying her a severance of more than $750,000.[32]

National and local results aside, how has this approach to addressing the Obama-era 'Dear Colleague' letter and disproportionate discipline referrals/punishments gone for the Osseo Area School District and Osseo Senior High?

The good news, of course, is that nothing close to the St. Paul wildfire has broken out. Aside from an uptick in the 2016-17 school year,[33] suspensions have been down over the past few years, which should be seen as a positive. (Note: As principals have been directed to keep suspensions down, these statistics can be misleading. Ultimately it is difficult to determine if the lower suspensions are an authentic result of the new discipline policies, or if principals are just doing what they were told to do by their central office superiors. Lower suspension numbers, after all, don't necessarily mean that schools are more productive learning environments—or even safer for students. As St. Paul Public Schools' unraveling should tell us: on their own, lower suspension numbers should not necessarily be seen as a victory.

Here's the bad news: the district as a whole has begun to wonder if the money it's investing in its partnership with PEG is really worth it. In 2017, the school board moved to sever its five-year relationship with PEG, saying that the group's insights and contributions were not returning results commensurate with the district's investment.[34]

Additionally, several of the Osseo Senior High teachers I spoke with described a school environment divided by differences and short on consequences for students behaving in patently unacceptable ways. Just as Zelenak described above, students who disrupt class or break other school norms often face little recourse, while teachers are presumed to be at fault for the behavior breakdowns that occur. In turn, numerous teachers told me the school environment under the Osseo district's 'transformational' discipline policies generally lacks the mutual respect necessary for productive learning and healthy relationship-building.

The really bad news was that the 'transformational system changes' to discipline policies cost Osseo Senior High (and the Osseo Area School District as a whole) greatly when they became something of a 'last straw' for Dr. Bob. He decided to retire and leave Osseo Senior at the end of the 2014-15 school year, a little earlier than he originally planned. While he made the change for many reasons—he's never one to stomp away from a tough situation—Dr. Bob shared with me that the district's new discipline policies were definitely in his decision-making mix.

'I could work with a lot of the things coming in from the district in those last years,' Dr. Bob said, 'but when they started to get more directive with how I'd have to do behaviors, I couldn't see how it would work. I'd built up a lot of trust with teachers because they knew that if they were fair with kids, I'd be fair with them when it came to how breakdowns were to be handled. Also, I just think the safety of a building and the mutual respect is key to everything else. I'd always had an umbrella of behavior expectations, and I always had good people to oversee them.

'But under the new expectations,' Dr. Bob continued, leaning across the table toward me for effect, 'if some kid in the heat of the moment now said, "*Fuck YOU, Kalenze!*" the district guideline said I couldn't necessarily stand behind the teacher. Even though, y'know, that kind of behavior should never be seen as acceptable—never, from *anyone*. I wasn't sure it was sending the right message to kids about what would be acceptable in school, or acceptable anywhere. It wasn't helping kids understand the world. Also, I really didn't think I could get through to kids by reading off some sign posted on the wall, "Do you understand how you've violated Rule #4 here?" [referring to the explicit behavior expectations and postings from the aforementioned PBIS Framework].

'And, most of all, I just wasn't sure if I could keep up the kind of trust I needed to run a building if that wasn't in place. If this was going to be the new way of doing things, I just wasn't the right guy to try it.'

* * *

With all of these actions, there's no doubt that the Osseo Area School District made good on their organizational objective of creating 'transformational system change' in the 2010s. Leaving aside for a moment any discussion of whether the changes they enacted were the right ones, the district leadership of this period absolutely deserves respect. Rolling out such huge and costly—and sometimes controversial—initiatives into nearly 30 large, diverse schools that serve families from eight distinct metro-area communities is by no means an easy task. Pulling it all off takes some *serious* leadership chops. (In 2014, the Minnesota Association of School Administrators agreed: that year, they named Osseo's Kate Maguire their Superintendent of the Year.)

The question remains: was all this effort, expense, and controversy worthwhile? Did the district leaders' 'transformational system change' in the 2010s create the 'equitable student achievement' it set out to ensure? While the district leaders clearly set out to *disrupt* matters across its schools, in other words, did they disrupt anything more than the district's operations and attitudes? Did results move in meaningful ways—or at least in ways meaningful enough to justify all the tumult? If the percentage of Osseo Area School District's students who were soundly prepared for the world indeed rose over time, you could make the argument that the district leaders did indeed know best—that the transformational system changes they engineered were the right ones at the right times for the right children, no matter what the literature, the teachers, or even the community, had to say about it.

To get a better handle on the answers to these questions, the next chapter will dive in to the actual results. Some empirical outputs from across the district system will be explored, of course, but first we need to see how the district office's various 'transformational system changes' impacted the professional culture at Osseo Senior High, the heart of this case study.

Endnotes

1. While the decision to make Park Center an International Baccalaureate World School was as much an attempt to shift the district's enrollment balance, as it was to elevate the quality of programming, the anticipated shift never materialized. Then and now, Park Center still serves far more poor students and has far greater racial/ethnic diversity than either of the other two district high schools, Osseo Senior and Maple Grove Senior.

2. A note on the data used in this chapter: since leaving classroom teaching I have done a lot of work in school improvement, which has meant considerable amounts of data study and research. Accordingly, I know well that state reading and math scores are not the best or the only measurements of school quality. Also, I know well that score reports like the ones I'm including here leave out lots of important information: they don't tell us how students in all demographic categories did, they don't tell us about the students' proficiency levels prior to these measurements, and all the rest. In the aggregate, though, they do present effective illustrations of how improvements being made within the school (like those detailed in this book's first two sections) were impacting student results. Imperfect as they may be, they are included here to give empirical depth to the qualitative evidence provided by students and educators throughout this book, and not to go into full data-wonk mode and take every piece of available data apart. Again, this is not that kind of book. As this chapter proceeds, I will dive more deeply into certain data points as necessary, in accord with the argument at hand. Finally—and purely practically—as I'm not an employee of the district, my analysis is constrained a bit by the performance data I was able to access, i.e. public information from the Minnesota Department of Education's accountability website, the State Report Card (see https://rc.education.state.mn.us).

3. 2006 was the first year this reading test was required for Minnesota sophomores. Prior to that, sophomores' English Language Arts accountability measurement was the Basic Skills Writing Test.

4. Enacted in 2005, Minnesota's Q Comp program offers moneys to districts for building and operating various systems of professional improvement. Under the program, districts design and collectively bargain plans for meeting the program components, and teachers are individually incentivized for satisfactorily meeting a number of locally determined, state-approved, professional improvement benchmarks. (For more on the Q Comp program, see the Minnesota Department of Education website: https://education.mn.gov/MDE/dse/qc/.) However, while roughly half of Minnesota's students are learning in districts that participate in Q Comp, the program has generated about the same results as other tries at teacher performance pay—weak ones, that is, especially with regard to the amount of dollars and time dedicated to it. In a 2015 op-ed for Minneapolis's Star Tribune, retired teacher Steve Watson said that, for how little Q Comp had shifted results and for all it ultimately cost professionals, the program should be seen as a 'giant step backward for our educators and… students.' (Watson, S. [15 June 2015] 'The State of Minnesota's Q Comp Program, Ten Years In.' Minneapolis, MN: Star Tribune.) For more on the general failure of performance pay programs for teachers, see Chapter 4 of Dylan Wiliam's fine 2018 book, *Creating the Schools Our Children Need: Why What We're Doing Now Won't Help Much (And What We Can Do Instead)*, West Palm Beach, FL: Learning Sciences International.

5. This statement comes from a presentation delivered to the Minnesota School Boards Association by Osseo district leaders (including district superintendent Kate Maguire) in January 2014. Titled 'Strategic Continuous Improvement: Aligning Instructional Reform & Financial Processes', the presentation recounts processes leaders used to roll out (and adjust) one major instructional reform and substantially revise budget processes in the district. The slide deck for this presentation can be viewed online at the Minnesota School Boards Association website: http://www.mnmsba. org/Portals/0/PDFs/LC2014Handouts/Thursday/QROsseo%20MSBA%20 Jan%202014.pdf

6. Ibid., slide 16.

7. The high-level summary of principles here is based on several resources I consulted to understand how early iterations of Osseo's standards-based grading system's rationales, operations, and requirements. It was a bit of a challenge, as the early years of its implementation (spanning 2011-2014) included multiple phases, re-thinks, and revisions. Indeed: it is to this time

of writing still very much a work in progress. Particularly helpful sources were interviews with Kelly Skare-Klecker, Eric Ruska, Gerry Zelenak, Heather Casella, and Mary Jo Skinner, as well as the previously cited 'Strategic Continuous Improvement: Aligning Instructional Reform & Financial Processes' presentation by Osseo district leaders to the Minnesota School Boards Association (see online at www.mnmsba.org/Portals/0/ PDFs/LC2014Handouts/Thursday/QROsseo%20MSBA%20Jan%202014. pdf), a letter to parents sent out by district schools in August of 2011 to inform of changes to grading process (see online at schools.district279.org/ zw/images/stories/ZW/doc/Communications/sbgparentletter.pdf), and also see: Erlien, W. (18 October 2012) 'Year 2: Standards Based Grading in the Osseo School District.' Patch. Available at: patch.com/minnesota/ maplegrove/year-2-standards-based-grading-in-the-osseo-school-district

8. Some particularly big names at the time of this writing would be Thomas Guskey, Rick Wormeli and Ken O'Connor. For more on them, see their consulting-business websites at https://tguskey.com/about-tom/, https:// www.rickwormeli.com/about, and https://www.oconnorgrading.com/ about/, respectively. Though often considered experts who come with actual, valuable solutions, they are more so innovators and wonderers— challengers of conventional educational wisdom who routinely lead educators to new interesting new possibilities, but who leave the work of actually executing on those possibilities up to educators themselves. The renowned cognitive scientist Dan Willingham, in discussing educationist Alfie Kohn, brilliantly referred to figures like these as education's 'honeyguides' (see Willingham, D. [2 February 2009] 'Alfie Kohn Is Bad for You and Dangerous For Your Children.' *Encyclopædia Britannica*. Available at: blogs.britannica.com/2009/02/alfie-kohn-is-bad-for-you-and-dangerous-for-your-children/).

9. An adapted excerpt from Wormeli's 2018 book, *Fair Isn't Always Equal*: Wormeli, R. (9 April 2018) 'Fair Isn't Always Equal – 3 Grading Malpractices' MiddleWeb. Available at: www.middleweb.com/37435/fair-isnt-always-equal-3-grading-malpractices/

10. Kalenze, E. (2014) *Education Is Upside down: Reframing Reform to Focus on the Right Problems*. Lanham, MD: Rowman & Littlefield.

11. This presentation to the school board was captured remarkably well by a local-access cable station, CCX Media. View on YouTube: CCX Media. (23 January 2013) 'Teachers Speak out against Standards Based Grading at Osseo Schools.' YouTube. Available at: www.youtube.com/ watch?v=H7hjys2GMGw

12. See: Osseo Maple Grove Standards Based Grading (SBG) Conversations: https://www.facebook.com/Osseo-Maple-Grove-Standards-Based-Grading-SBG-conversations-216352325134330/

13. Barnum, M. (19 October 2018) 'Maine Went All in on Proficiency Based Learning - Then Rolled It Back.' Chalkbeat. Available at: www.chalkbeat.org/posts/us/2018/10/18/maine-went-all-in-on-proficiency-based-learning-then-rolled-it-back-what-does-that-mean-for-the-rest-of-the-country/

14. #DL4A. (No date) '#DL4A In Osseo'. Available at: sites.google.com/apps.district279.org/dl4a

15. No author. (28 August 2014) 'Osseo Schools: Back-to-School Changes Include Implementing Digital Learning, All Day Kindergarten and More.' Osseo, MN: Sun Post.

16. Escueta, M., *et al.* (2017) 'Education Technology: An Evidence-Based Review', in *National Bureau of Economic Research*, pp. 13–15.

17. See: Herman, M. (20 June 2018) 'Districts Learn Lessons on 1-to-1 From Others' Missteps.' Education Week. Available at: www.edweek.org/ew/articles/2015/06/11/districts-learn-lessons-on-1-to-1-from-watching.html. For a more Twin Cities-regional angle, see: Koumpilova, M. (14 June 2014) 'St. Paul Schools Plan IPad's Role – and Heed Cautionary Tales.' Pioneer Press. Available at: https://www.twincities.com/2014/06/14/st-paul-schools-plan-ipads-role-and-heed-cautionary-tales/

18. See: Kamenetz, A. (30 September 2013) 'The inside Story on LA Schools' IPad Rollout: "a Colossal Disaster."' Hechinger Report. Available at: digital.hechingerreport.org/content/the-inside-story-on-la-schools-ipad-rollout-a-colossal-disaster_914/. Also, for follow-up stories about the continuing fallout, see: Blume, H. (25 September 2015) 'L.A. Unified to Get $6.4 Million in Settlement over IPad Software.' Los Angeles Times. Available at: www.latimes.com/local/lanow/la-me-ln-la-unified-ipad-settlement-20150925-story.html

19. Miller, K. (25 August 2017) 'Osseo Area Schools Considers New IPad Management Strategies.' Osseo, MN: Sun Post.

20. Miller, K. (11 May 2017) 'Digital Learning to Increase Student Choice in Osseo Area Schools, District Says.' Osseo, MN: Sun Post.

21. Raghavendran, B. (2 May 2016) 'Osseo Schools Head off Misbehavior before It Starts.' Minneapolis, MN: Star Tribune.

22. PBIS. (29 June 2018) 'PBIS FAQs'. PBIS. Available at: www.pbis.org/school/swpbis-for-beginners/pbis-faqs

23. RCD. (No date) 'Give Em Five'. Responsibility-Centered Discipline. Available at: www.givemfive.com/give-em-five/

24. Courageous Conversation (No date) 'Courageous Conversations About Race' Courageous Conversation. Available at: courageousconversation. com/about/

25. Benner, A. (2 October 2015) 'St. Paul Schools: Close the Gap? Yes. But Not like This.' Pioneer Press. Available at: https://www.twincities. com/2015/10/02/aaron-benner-st-paul-schools-close-the-gap-yes-but-not-like-this/

26. Lhamon, C., E. and Samuels, J. (26 September 2018) 'Joint "Dear Colleague" Letter'. U.S. Department of Education (ED). Available at: www2.ed.gov/ about/offices/list/ocr/letters/colleague-201401-title-vi.html

27. Eden, M. (2 April 2018) 'Eden: Teachers Nationwide Say Obama's Discipline 'Reform' Put Them in Danger. So Why Are the Unions Fighting DeVos on Repeal?' The 74. Available at: www.the74million.org/article/eden-teachers-nationwide-say-obamas-discipline-reform-put-them-in-danger-so-why-are-the-unions-fighting-devos-on-repeal/

28. Kamenetz, A. (18 December 2018) 'DeVos To Rescind Obama-Era Guidance On School Discipline'. NPR. Available at: www.npr. org/2018/12/18/675556455/devos-to-rescind-obama-era-guidance-on-school-discipline

29. Du, S. (27 May 2015) 'Distrust and Disorder: A Racial Equity Policy Summons Chaos in the St. Paul Schools.' City Pages. Available at: http:// www.citypages.com/news/distrust-and-disorder-a-racial-equity-policy-summons-chaos-in-the-st-paul-schools-7394479

30. Olson, T. (4 May 2017) 'Theo Olson: Did I Really Morph into a Racist? Of Course Not'. Pioneer Press. Available at: https://www.twincities. com/2017/05/04/theo-olson-did-i-really-morph-into-a-racist-of-course-not/

31. Walsh, J. (10 December 2015) 'St. Paul Teachers Threaten Strike over School Violence.' Star Tribune. Available at: http://www.startribune.com/ silva-to-address-questions-of-teacher-safety-and-union-s-request-for-mediation/361318431/

32. Superville, D., R. (23 June 2016) 'St. Paul, Minn., Superintendent Ousted by School Board.' Education Week. Available at: blogs.edweek.org/edweek/ District_Dossier/2016/06/st_paul_minn_superintendent_fired_by_board. html

33. Miller, K. (11 October 2017) 'Suspension Counts Slightly up in 2017 at Osseo Area Schools.' Osseo, MN: Sun Post

34. Dupuy, B. (6 April 2017) 'Osseo Schools Cutting Ties with PEG Diversity Consultant.' Star Tribune. Available at: http://www.startribune.com/osseo-schools-cutting-ties-with-peg-diversity-consultant/418584173/

Chapter 14

A Productive Disruption?

'You don't get any medal for trying something, you get medals for results.'

– Bill Parcells

A s should be evident, the district's 'transformational' policies and practices definitely kicked up their fair share of discussion and dust. From break rooms to classrooms to Facebook forums to school board meetings, lots of unhappy opinions have been aired throughout the Osseo Area School District in the past decade.

Even worse, these policies and practices consumed considerable amounts of schools' professional-development, administrative, and even staffing resources. And as we saw with bottom-up initiatives like the Sophomore Academy and the CSI, the time and energy spent on district-mandated initiatives ultimately didn't leave much room for individual school sites to execute their own improvement actions.

So in addition to requiring improvements that on-the-ground staff frequently disagreed with, the district's ideas crowded out several improvement concepts and actions local staff held in high regard: opportunities to lead school-wide changes, administrative support to improve practices in individual classrooms and across departments, and unique situations in which to grow professionally and help kids in need. (The types of initiatives, basically, I've spent much of this book rhapsodizing about—initiatives I feel very fortunate to have experienced, and that made a real difference with kids.)

As you can probably guess, losing the school-driven solutions to make room for the district's dubiously justified and work-heavy initiatives took a toll on the professional culture at Osseo Senior High. In some cases, they caused enough damage to necessitate serious repairs.

Impact on professional culture

In my interviews with Osseo Senior High teachers, I repeatedly heard that losing bottom-up improvements eroded the overall professional culture. Over time, teachers went from feeling that their input was not valued to suspecting district leadership did not trust them, period.

Even years after the CSI was dissolved, for example, teachers like former-CSI member Michelle Goetz said she periodically hears from colleagues who look back on the CSI's leadership as something truly unique, and on Dr. Bob's shared-leadership model as one they wish they could resurrect.

'People will still talk to me about the CSI every now and then,' Goetz told me. 'Even people who were kind of against it back when it was going on. They'll say that it might've made them feel a little jealous at the time, to not be picked by Bob to be in on school decisions or whatever, but that they see now how they were really in on the process, even if they weren't officially on the CSI team. They knew they had access to all of us, and the whole staff voted on everything. It was like we were all part of *making our school*. With the way things are now, people really get what it's like to have no say.'

Mary Jo Skinner, my one-time colleague in the English department, met me for burgers in the summer of 2018 with her husband Todd (an educator in a nearby suburban district), and she built upon Goetz's idea. She said that for her, the biggest challenge in recent years at Osseo Senior has been the loss of professional autonomy. She was quick, however, to qualify her statement.

'When I say losing the autonomy was hard,' Skinner told me, 'I don't mean that we were doing whatever we wanted before that. We never asked for that. Our department had guidelines and expectations, and Bob did too, about things like student behavior and all that. I more mean that all these new required ways of doing things—grading, behavior consequences, how we met as a team, all of it—kept coming in and in and in.'

And as time went on, Skinner said, it seemed that more and more matters were being taken away from teachers altogether. It was almost as if the district were attempting to fix what they considered to be broken by replacing each teacher's individual judgment—which changes a great deal depending on the material, the student, and numerous other variables—with standardized, context-free practices, habits, and beliefs. And in some cases, she said, this began to interfere with the most fundamental aspects of how teachers did their jobs.

'It got to be mandatory that every student got lots of chances—and different kinds of chances—to prove they knew the material, and we were required to figure out how that could happen. It was hard because in English, I'm doing things like helping kids learn how to write a paper. The only way to do that, really, is to have the kids go through writing a paper.

'Overall,' she said, 'it got to feel like we weren't trusted to do the right thing. That if any student got an F in a teacher's class, no matter how that student had worked or behaved, it was the teacher actively failing the student—like, *making* them get that F.'

At this point of her account, Skinner's husband Todd added, 'It finally got to the point, really, that the job was killing her,' he said. 'We decided it probably wasn't best for our family for Mary Jo to go on like she was.'

For Skinner, waning 'autonomy' was not simply a matter of 'losing the ability to do my own thing.' *That* kind of autonomy—being a 'lone ranger'—was not something she ever wanted. She belonged to a department that liked working as a team, collaborating on practices and policies and uniformly observing the standards they set together. Skinner's use of 'autonomy' conveyed something even more basic. Namely, she wanted to be respected as a professional who could make effective decisions for her classroom's students. As this decision-making power began to be stripped away, Skinner and others felt like the district didn't *trust* its teachers to teach.

(Incidentally, starting in the fall of 2018, Skinner took a leave of absence from teaching and is strongly considering retirement. In the past five years, the school has seen several other early retirements and outright defections from the school and even from education altogether.

At a time when schools nationwide are struggling to retain teachers, this is simply a shame.)

Not everyone I spoke with felt the same sense of disempowerment and disenfranchisement, of course. Another former colleague of mine from the English department, Joe Booher, is a wisecracking Iraq war vet who is without a doubt one of the most generous people I've ever known. He told me over a beer in the summer of 2018 that he had just finished one of his most satisfying years of teaching ever. He acknowledged that the school definitely experienced some turbulence in recent years (more on that shortly), but said that, by the 2017-18 school year, school operations were running much more smoothly, and that things were feeling more settled among staff and students.

Also, I heard from multiple sources that several other teachers within Osseo Senior believe the district is on the right track, especially with its explicit focus on racial equity. And of these, a number have stepped forward as real champions of the district's policies and PEG's messages, both among their peers and in their work with students. While this has caused some division among staff and some difficult bumps in the road, some of the staff I spoke with believed these bumps were blown out of proportion due to timing.

More specifically, *everything* got tough when Dr. Bob was transitioning out of Osseo Senior High's principalship at the end of 2015. As if it wasn't hard enough for the incoming administration that a majority of the school's staff had been hired by—and only ever worked for—Dr. Bob, the new administrative team was taking over right when Osseo Senior added an entire 9th grade class to become a 9-12 high school. This meant increasing the student population by several hundred new kids, re-arranging the school physically to accommodate more kids and classrooms, incorporating dozens of new teachers from the surrounding junior high schools, re-working schedules for everything from classes to lunches, and much, much more.

Much of the more difficult equity-related work was ramping up at the same time, adding to the pressure of the moment—and, to be fair, may have caused more drastic and dramatic effects as a result.

In short, there's no doubt that the last decade of 'transformational system change' is being felt at the practitioner level. Operations are changing, and strong opinions are flying around about the sensibility and value of these new initiatives. These opinions are important to examine, as they provide insights that can be helpful for future course-corrections and improvement directions.

We should never lose sight, though, of the real proof that a school or district is doing its job well: whether or not kids are getting verifiably smarter and more prepared for the world. It's the 'ensuring equitable student achievement' piece of the district's bold organizational objective, that is—and, at bottom, the primary promise all schools make.[1]

Accordingly, I'll next explore whether all the actions and reactions of the 'transformational system change' years have indeed created 'equitable student achievement' at Osseo Senior High and across the Osseo Area School District. I'll use the schools' standardized test scores for this illustration, with full knowledge of their limitations. (To revisit my rationale, please see note 2 in the previous chapter.)

Also, I'll keep my analysis brief. There are many, *many* statistics I could possibly review (and even more ways to cut, package, and drill further into those data sets), but I'll exhibit some restraint. The idea here, after all, is to see if 'transformational system change' did what it said it would do. And for that, we need to start with the students.

Student achievement

To begin—and because this story revolves around Osseo Senior High School—let's look at how the district's sweeping initiatives affected achievement overall and within a few specific student populations. From there—and to get a better read on how well the district is meeting its educational equity goals—I'll zoom out to look at the performance of the district's high schools.[2] Finally, I'll zoom out even further to see how the transformational system change has affected results across the district as a whole.

Osseo Senior High School

In particular, let's look at reading and math scores from 2012-2018, or where *Figure 1* and *Figure 2* from Chapter 13 left off. In those graphs, you'll see that the school achieved positive trends in both subject areas around 2008-09, suggesting that the school-wide improvement culture Dr. Bob built was having a positive impact on student achievement.

Picking this line up in 2012, the first year of the district's standards-based grading initiative, and following it through to the most recent recorded scores in 2018, there's little evidence that the transformational changes were making much of a difference. (*Figure 3*)

After the first initial drop between 2012 and 2013 (which coincided with Minnesota changing its tests to align with the national Common Core literacy standards—a move that reset the ceiling for schools statewide), Osseo Senior's results on the 10th grade reading test hover right around the state average—just like they did from 2006-2012.

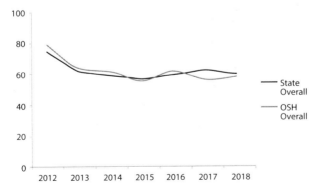

Figure 3 *Proficiency rates—state overall and Osseo Senior High School overall—on Minnesota Comprehensive Assessment (MCA) in reading (grade 10), 2012-2018.*

Similarly, looking at the school's 11th grade math scores from this same period with regard to state averages, it's hard to discern any kind of 'transformational system change' (*Figure 4*). In fact, from 2014 to 2018, the percentages of Osseo Senior students proficient on the state math exam in 11th grade fell further and further below state-wide averages.

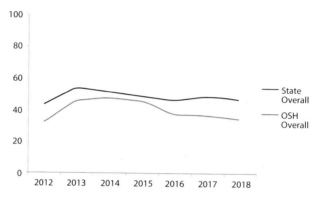

Figure 4 *Proficiency rates—state overall and Osseo Senior High School overall—on Minnesota Comprehensive Assessment (MCA) in math (grade 11), 2012-2018.*

* * *

If we break these scores apart into demographic groups to see if greater equity of outcomes was achieved (per the district's organizational objective), the results are even more interesting.

(Note: Figures 5 and 6 look at three groups—white students, African American students, and students that qualifying for free/reduced lunch—because they represent the three largest subgroups within Osseo Senior High.[3])

After all subgroups take their Common Core 'hit' on the state reading test of 2013, for example (*Figure 5*), the performance of African American and free/reduced lunch students trend upward slightly beginning in 2016, roughly mirroring the shape of state averages over time. The percentages-proficient of African American and free/reduced lunch-qualifying students each make notable jumps after 2015, but a consistently upward trajectory has not yet been achieved. The percentage of white students proficient in reading, meanwhile, moves in fits and starts, but a trend line through this time span shows an overall pattern of decline. Achievement gaps in reading are narrowing, in other words, but not exactly in ways many schools or districts would prefer to see.

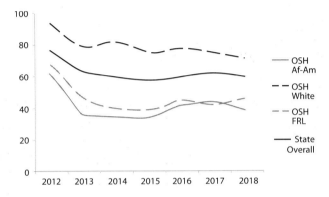

Figure 5 *Proficiency rates—state overall and select Osseo Senior High School demographic groups—on Minnesota Comprehensive Assessment (MCA) in reading (grade 10), 2012-2018.*

In math, meanwhile (*Figure 6*), Osseo Senior High's 11th graders in the 'transformational system change' years haven't exactly seen a transformation of results. After the low point of 2012 (again, the first year of an adjusted state test—note the course-correcting 'bump' across all samples between 2012 and 2013), all groups have stayed relatively flat from year to year—with the exception of white students, who have fallen well below the 60% proficient threshold from 2016 to 2018.

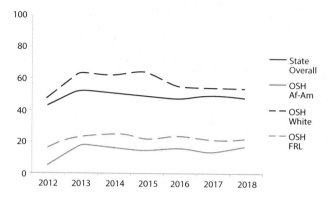

Figure 6 *Proficiency rates—state overall and select Osseo Senior High School demographic groups—on Minnesota Comprehensive Assessment (MCA) in math (grade 11), 2012-2018.*

High schools: Osseo Area School District

As it's possible that the mixed results could be caused by poor execution of the district's transformational system changes at Osseo Senior High alone, let's see how the same demographic groups have performed across the district's three high schools combined.[4] *Figures 7* and *8* will plot these for reading and math, respectively.

On the state reading test (*Figure 7*), a similar pattern to Osseo Senior can be observed, but with all highlighted subgroups declining over time (even from the 2013 Common Core reset). The only group with a non-negative net gain over that span is the free/reduced lunch group, who scored 38.6% proficient in 2012 and 38.6% proficient in 2018—for a net gain of zero.

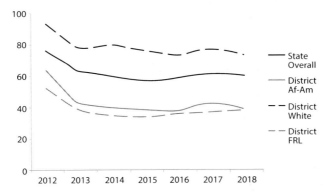

Figure 7 *Proficiency rates—state overall and select Osseo Area School District demographic groups—on Minnesota Comprehensive Assessment (MCA) in reading (grade 10), 2012-2018.*

On the math test over the 'transformational system change' years, we see more of the same: some up and down years, but trend lines that are largely flat across students from all three district high schools. From an equitable-outcomes standpoint, though, this graph should be a bit concerning. The only subgroup to make any significant jumps is the white students, and they make two of note: a series between 2012 and 2014, then another rally after flattening and slumping in 2015 and 2016, respectively.

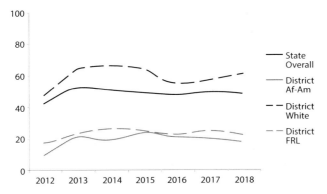

Figure 8 *Proficiency rates—state overall and select Osseo Area School District demographic groups—on Minnesota Comprehensive Assessment (MCA) in math (grade 11), 2012-2018.*

All schools: Osseo Area School District

The 'transformational system change', however, was enacted district-wide, not just at high schools. As that was the case, let's see how all grades in all schools measure up against state averages-proficient. It could well be, after all, that results have been shifting in notably positive ways elsewhere across the district.

On the state reading test across the district (*Figure 9*), performance (after the 2013 drop) remained almost perfectly flat in the 'transformational system change' years, essentially mirroring—if falling a bit below—state averages.

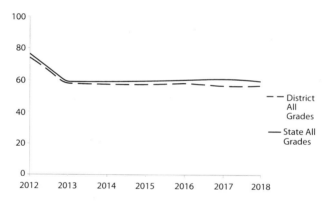

Figure 9 *Proficiency rates—state overall and all Osseo Area School District students—on Minnesota Comprehensive Assessment (MCA) in reading, 2012-2018.*

In math, more of the same. Though some slight rises and falls in percentages-proficient are recorded, the district has stayed parallel to or slightly below state averages. Again, it's hard to see that any of the 'transformational system change' efforts have delivered any of their intended results.

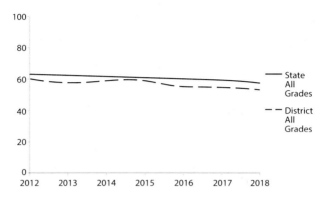

Figure 10 *Proficiency rates—state overall and all Osseo Area School District students—on Minnesota Comprehensive Assessment (MCA) in math, 2012-2018.*

While graphs like these could go on and on, and while we could open up all kinds of other success indicators, the point would remain the same. Student achievement is not more equitable. The system has not transformed.

Conclusion: A productive disruption?

At the end of the last chapter, I posed a series of questions:

- Did the Osseo district leaders' 'transformational system change' in the 2010s create the 'equitable student achievement' it set out to ensure?

- While the district leaders clearly set out to *disrupt* matters across its schools, did they disrupt anything more than the district's operations and attitudes?

- Did results move in meaningful ways, or at least ways meaningful enough to justify all the tumult?

Based on the accounts and statistics shown here, the answer to all three questions would be 'no'.

For all of central office's decade of disruption, the 'transformational system changes' have not yet spurred the 'equitable student achievement' aspired to by district leadership. Worse, in fact, some subgroups' rates-proficient have declined.

No doubt, many ambitious initiatives have been put into motion across the district. Sometimes, these initiatives had to elbow their way past locally grown improvements—like the Sophomore Academy and CSI—to keep moving ahead. In that sense, the transformation was real.

Just not in terms of student results.

Because *so* many variables are in play in these schools (and, indeed, in all of education), it's hard to know why this would be the case. Successful implementation isn't the issue. It definitely appears that teachers are doing as expected with these initiatives. What seems more likely is that the central office's calculus is off in some way.

Maybe, for instance, they misjudged what was lacking from the capacity and dedication of their teaching force. Or maybe the initiatives they chose to enact were not ones that could create the desired 'equitable student achievement' in the district's student population. Or maybe it's a case of flawed implementation strategy: the initiatives they chose were correct, but each one lost a little power (and perhaps even contradicted one another) when they were stacked on top of each other.

Wherever the miscalculations occurred, however, the initiatives imposed by district leadership have had major effects on the health of their organization.

First and most obviously, the strategy upset the system at the site level. According to my research and public reports, many practitioners feel powerless, overworked, underestimated, and even disrespected. Rather than feeling that they are 'building the school they wanted to work in', as they once did under Dr. Bob, it seems more like staff have begrudgingly adopted the mindset of, 'Just tell me what I have to do, and I'll do it.' Or worse, as in 2013 when teachers pushed back on the school board about standards-based grading, the district's teachers are experiencing outright frustration. Even *worse*, some are leaving the school—or the education profession—altogether.

Let's not forget: as the district's imposed improvement initiatives were likely very costly, they must have had a huge impact on the district's long-term financial health.

While it's hard to know exactly *how* costly these combined initiatives were (public records do not include line-item specificity), it doesn't take an accounting genius to know that outfitting thousands of students with iPads—as happened under the district's digital-learning plan—costs millions of dollars. And that's before factoring in related costs, such as the staff time required to manage such an initiative, the professional-development time necessary to train teachers in incorporating the technology into instruction, technical facilities upgrades, and so on.

Similarly, we already know from an earlier example that the Pacific Education Group (PEG) was deemed too expensive at its 2016-2017 allotment of $152,000 and the relationship with PEG ended. This partnership lasted five years, so it is safe to assume that the total cost of the engagement is close to one million dollars.[5] To put it plainly, they spent a million dollars and have very little, if anything, to show for it. That's not, as they say, a good ROI.

Another important consideration in the financial-health discussion—and one I wish more decision-makers would take into account—is the funding necessary to train an entire district's worth of people on any initiative. Think about it this way: one hour of training—with 30 schools employing, for example, 50 teachers each (keeping in mind that each of Osseo's high schools employ more than twice this number), all of whom are working at a professional rate of $25/hour—costs the district $37,500.

Need an hour to tell all the teachers about the new emergency allergic-reaction procedures so the schools can be up to safety code? That'll be $37,500.

Need an hour to discuss the new data-entry system?

That'll be $37,500.

Need 10 hours total of PD time over the next year to make sure all district teachers learn a new standards-based grading system and how to re-work their assessments accordingly?

Well, that'll be *$375,000.*

(And yes, including third-party experts or consultants goes *on top of that.*)

In short, it's safe to assume that rolling out transformational initiatives across the district cost several million dollars, even if we'll never know how much they really cost.

And at those rates, you really shouldn't settle for anything less than a *damn transformation.*

Even worse than the raw financial cost, though, is the fact that every dollar and every hour the district spent on these initiatives were dollars and hours they can't get back to spend on more appropriate, evidence-supported initiatives. All of that money and all of that time are just *gone.*

This trade-off is called *opportunity cost,* and it may ultimately be more damaging to education-organizational health and effectiveness than any financial expenditures. Only so many resources are available to train staff, after all. And because there's no way to get these resources back once they're spent, and no way to retroactively give students the gains they didn't make over any span of ineffectiveness, it is crucial that leaders choose improvement initiatives wisely.

More specifically, 'choosing wisely' means selecting initiatives that the available evidence suggests will address the actual needs of learners and professionals. Anything else wastes money and time and kids' potential, and it does so *irreversibly.* Think of all the time, money, and angst spent on the teacher observation/evaluation boom of the past decade. New departments and positions were created; fleets of observers and/or coaches were trained and mobilized; teachers were given preobservation/observation/post-observation instructions, many times replete with paperwork and meetings with observers/coaches; observers were trained to achieve greater inter-rater reliability; data systems were implemented to capture all the information; and on and *on*, for years.

But what did the evidence at the time suggest? Well, that's easy. Better accountability systems had never been proven to be The Answer. Not anywhere, at any time. Still, the entire education field was so convinced of their promise and so excited by their (unproven) possibilities that they spared no expense to make them happen.

As it turned out, the lack of evidence supporting massive teacher-evaluation efforts was entirely predictive of its failure. After all that effort and cost, student achievement across the field didn't make anywhere near what could be considered commensurate leaps upward. And *transform*? As *if*.

Even if we now turn our attention to evidence-backed actions like curriculum improvement (see Part 3 introduction, note 7), that doesn't help the decade's worth of kids who were in the seats while we were all playing ring-around-the-rubric. Those specific kids will never see the benefits of our improved vision, now that we've seen the error of our ways.

This irretrievability—this permanent opportunity cost—is not discussed enough, perhaps because it's so difficult to quantify and 'hold'. I'd wager, though, that it's the most damaging part of every failed initiative in education, from Osseo Area School District's attempts at 'transformational system change' all the way up to the Gates Foundation's $575 million attempt (and failure[6]) to improve the U.S.'s teaching force through value-added modeling. Standards-based grading rules don't apply. We don't get multiple chances to teach kids. It's very important that we use our opportunities wisely, and going with our gut—or with what vendors and education futurists insist is true, without evidence—isn't particularly wise.

So... a productive disruption? One where the student results outweigh the costs? One that was markedly better than the processes and cultures it replaced? No, the Osseo district has not achieved that. Not even close.

* * *

In my introduction to Part Three, I mentioned that the issues I'm sharing about the Osseo Area School District and Osseo Senior High School are in no way meant to excoriate the Osseo Area District or to hold them up as a particularly massive failure. They are a case study, selected for magnification here because I was lucky enough to have a front row seat.

Fascinating as this case study is, however, it is nowhere near unique. Through my work with and study of schools and districts around the U.S., I know well that the model of 'transformational system change' Osseo is attempting to pull off is much more the rule than the exception. And honestly, I've done work with some U.S. districts that have been making these same errors for much longer than the Osseo Area district and are *much* worse off.

Simply, a lot of education professionals currently believe that comprehensive, centrally driven, top-down change is the best way they can improve, and *fast*. I've touched on some of the reasons behind that belief and where all the urgency is coming from—a level of urgency that only seems to be accelerating, well past the point of rationality—but fully exploring these reasons is not my main concern.

More so, this book is intended to help education professionals understand the current milieu, nod knowingly in its general direction, then work out how to help kids within it (or in spite of it). And along the way, of course, this book is also intended to help education professionals work out how they can help the people working in schools and ensure the schools' continual success. (The kids, though, come first. That's always the deal.) This is why Part Two provided a narrative tour of how we did exactly that at Osseo Senior High, back before 'transformational system change' came in like a steamroller.

The next two chapters will conclude this book by focusing on these intentions. Ultimately, I hope you can use them in your own classroom practice, departmental organization, or continuous school improvement. It's not a step-by-step guide. Considering how much schools differ in terms of their operating structures, writing one would be just as presumptuous—and bordering on disrespectful—as any top-down initiative. Rather, I'll wrap up like my mentor Dr. Bob did with school improvement: with key principles, not a playbook.

This wrap-up will happen in two stages. First, Chapter 15 will sum up key features of the collaborative school-improvement culture led by Dr. Bob at Osseo Senior High. Then, informed by perspectives gained from that experience—because in hindsight there is a lot we could've done better—and my time in (and study of) school improvement since, Chapter 16 will outline a corresponding set of continuous school improvement recommendations for the field.

Endnotes

1. A public service note, from all of evidence-supported educational improvement: please remember this, reader. The next time you hear of a study reporting an initiative's effectiveness via criteria like teachers' or students' satisfaction or personal beliefs about their own growth (and yes, they are most certainly out there), be sure to ask for more. Satisfaction, harsh as it might sound to say, is not the end goal of schooling. Preparation—moving kids from *stable to able*—is. If someone is trying to tell you a particular PD offering is wonderful because '87% of teachers reported feeling more confident about...' or that a particular math-intervention software is worth the expense because '79% of students said they believed they were better at math after using it', it's not good enough. Demand more proof.

2. The scores of high school students are effective to review for two other reasons as well. First, these students are the closest of all the system's tested students to the world after K-12, so their indices give us some insights into percentages of college- and career-readiness; if only 25% of a school's sophomores are scoring as proficient on the state reading test while 50% of students at the state level do, the district system is behind, basically, on rates of producing kids who are 'ready' for the next steps of their post-

school lives. Second, the students tested in these cohorts have had the longest amounts of exposure to the district-wide improvement initiatives. In theory, if more long-term benefits were to accrue from multiple years of things like standards-based grading, increases in digital learning, and equity-focused disciplinary practices, the scores for each successive group should rise and rise.

3. According to most recent demographic information on the Minnesota Department of Education's *Report Card* (https://rc.education.state. mn.us/#mySchool/), white students constitute 38% of Osseo Senior's population, and African-American students 33%. Of special populations at Osseo Senior High, 48% of Osseo Senior students qualify for free/reduced lunch.

4. Similar to the Osseo Senior-specific graphs, the three subgroups here represent the Osseo Area School District's three largest subgroups: white (43% of all enrolled students), African American (25%), and eligible for free/reduced lunch (43%). Data from Minnesota Department of Education *Report Card*, https://rc.education.state.mn.us/#mySchool/

5. Dupuy, B. (2017) 'Osseo Schools Cutting Ties with PEG Diversity Consultant'. *Star Tribune.*

6. In addition to wasting loads of opportunity, the Bill and Melinda Gates Foundation's Intensive Partnerships for Effective Teaching initiative cost well over a half a billion dollars and didn't do much at all in terms of student achievement (see: Stecher, B., M., Holtzman, D., J., Garet, M., S., Hamilton, L., S., Engberg, J., Steiner, E., D., Robyn, A., Baird, M., D., Gutierrez, I., A., Peet, E., D., Reyes, I., B., Fronberg, K., Weinberger, G., Hunter, G., P. and Chambers, J. [2018] Improving Teaching Effectiveness: Final Report: The Intensive Partnerships for Effective Teaching Through 2015–2016. Santa Monica, CA: RAND Corporation. Available at: https://www.rand. org/pubs/research_reports/RR2242.html). Even worse, mathematicians like Cathy O'Neil levied that its use of data was irresponsible and called, in an opinion piece for Bloomberg, for the Gates Foundation to publicly recognize the harm they'd done (see: O'Neil, C. [27 June 2018] 'Here's How Not to Improve Public Schools: The Gates Foundation's Big-Data Experiment Wasn't Just a Failure. It Did Real Harm.' Bloomberg. Available at: www.bloomberg.com/opinion/articles/2018-06-27/here-s-how-not-to-improve-public-schools).

Chapter 15

A School Improvement Culture to Learn From

'The reality is that the only way change
comes is when you lead by example.'

– Anne Wojcicki

A merican education has undergone nearly two decades of increased accountability—in the form of standardized testing, teacher evaluation, and school ratings—combined with transformational system change, like the centrally imposed, top-down improvement actions that swept through the Osseo Area Schools. These efforts have not produced the leaps in student achievement many reformers believed they would. They have essentially remade much of America's education system for the foreseeable future, but, as the Thomas B. Fordham Institute's Mike Petrilli put it in a November 2018 piece (fittingly called 'The End of Education Policy'), it is now time for reformers to 'finish what we started...to usher in a Golden Age of Educational Practice.'[1]

Perhaps sensing the limitations of accountability and system-wide 'disruption', some leaders in education have recently turned their attention to the concept of *continuous school improvement*. Anthony Bryk and the Carnegie Foundation for the Advancement of Teaching, for example, are taking lessons from improvement science to help districts and schools tighten up their improvement routines. (Bryk and his group also produce content, like 2015's *Learning to Improve: How America's Schools Can Get Better at Getting Better*.[2]) The Bill and Melinda Gates Foundation obviously sees promise here as well, jumping in to sponsor content about continuous improvement in trade publications like *Education Week*[3] as well as funding schools and partner organizations' school-improvement networks to accelerate the spread of promising practices.[4]

Accordingly, all the new interest in improvement science has PDSA cycles spinning and all kinds of 'disciplined inquiry' happening in schools and districts nationwide. ('PDSA' stands for 'Plan-Do-Study-Act', and is, like the term 'disciplined inquiry', a regular player in Bryk's work.) Genuinely remarkable improvements, however—as in, 'we implemented, we monitored, we changed, and kids' learning improved verifiably and dramatically'—are still a long way off. This is likely due to several factors.

First and rather obviously, applying improvement-science principles and habits to education is still very new. We're likely to struggle with it a while. Frankly, we don't tend to read the fine print real well. Typically, our field becomes quickly enamored with promising ideas presented on the conference circuit (such as the recent explosions of growth mindset interventions or personalized learning, but you can probably think of a dozen other examples), then rushes back to their schools and starts practicing them before fully *understanding* them, much less how these ideas can be effectively integrated into classroom practice and school operations. It's just our habit, and it's been this way for a long time, from differentiated instruction to interactive whiteboards to character report cards that grade kids on 'zest' and 'grit'. (I don't want to veer too far off-track here, so I'll refrain from further discussion. I've written about this on my blog, though, so feel free to take a look.[5])

We're likely experiencing the same dynamic with continuous school improvement. Even Mark Elgart, the CEO of AdvancED (a school accreditation group that has studied continuous improvement and that regularly works with schools on matters of strategic improvement), said to *Education Week* in February of 2018: 'The problem with continuous improvement,' Elgart said, 'is it's becoming a buzzword— it's in virtually everybody's ESSA plan [the federal Every Student Succeeds Act required states to submit detailed implementation plans], but they haven't unpacked what it is.'[6]

It's also important to remember that many of improvement science's most proven methods and models were road-tested in business, not education. And if education's (failed) Accountability Era taught anyone anything, I sure hope it's that the education enterprise is absolutely *not* the same as the business world. Education is guided by completely different norms, objectives, social and legal contracts, schedules, and stakeholders, and these fundamental differences will always make it extremely challenging to graft business-oriented principles onto the education sector, to put it very mildly. Your instinct may be to dismiss this. You may be thinking, 'All of education would work better if we just ran it more like a business—we've just got to get schools and teachers planning and executing like *businesses*'. If you are, well, enjoy the ride. It doesn't ever end well. (Again, I'll stop here and refer you to my previous work for a more thorough investigation of the differences. In particular, see Chapter 7 of my book *Education is Upside-Down*.[7])

Another reason continuous improvement practices are still 'stuck' when it comes to moving student outcomes is the lack of a crucial *learning* element. This is especially important to educational improvement, as so much of the field is guided by flawed notions of how young people effectively learn, develop, and prepare for life after their K-12 education. This can make selecting the appropriate intervention or adjustment to operations next to impossible. A team can do the best root-cause analysis imaginable, for example ('root-cause analyses' being a regular feature of improvement science), but if the team's knowledge of effective interventions is limited, or if their beliefs about 'best practices' are misguided and/or unshakeable, they are doomed to throw the wrong solution at the correct problem.

Take it from me, as I've done a lot of improvement work with schools nationwide, from New York to Minnesota to California. And far too many times, I've seen school leaders choose completely misguided solutions based on solid root cause analysis. Here's a quick illustration:

- As part of continuous-improvement planning, an elementary school's leadership team reviews school data and accordingly decides to prioritize literacy study. (We're on the right track so far.)
- The leadership team collaborates on a detailed 'five-whys' root-cause analysis exercise,[8] ultimately arriving at this root cause (in italics): 'Our reading results are poor because *far too few of our kids read at grade level by the end of grade three*'. (Still looking good.)

- After some discussion about the best improvement strategy to address this cause, the leadership team decides to look for and schedule more artists-in-residence to build students' engagement to reading. (Wait, what?)
- The school spends the year fumbling the artists-in-residence: thousands of dollars are paid out, no one in the school is quite sure how the artists are supposed to fit with the school's programming, and connections to reading are practically non-existent. The school's reading scores for the year don't just flatten, they dip. *Again.* Reflecting on these results, the leadership team collectively scratches heads, confused about why it didn't work. They blame the dip in reading test scores on poor implementation, pledge to do much better next year, and decide to go with artists-in-residence yet again. (How about: no.)

I wish I was kidding, but this example comes directly from an actual decision-making process I witnessed. And trust me, there's a *lot* more where that came from. (Please know, too, that I tried to talk them out of it every time. At the end of the day, though, it was their building, their teachers, and their kids.)

The point is that the school leaders simply didn't have the knowledge to choose an appropriate strategy. Where strategies like—I don't know, just spitballin' here—*requiring a stronger emphasis on phonics in their grades K-3 literacy instruction or researching and implementing an early grades curriculum that has strong phonics resources* would have been effective, evidence-supported options, the practitioners didn't even consider them. They were trained to believe kids' engagement to (and mindsets about) reading were more important to reading ability than *decoding*. (Yes, this is actually how most American teachers are trained—an unfortunate reality that is, thank goodness, finally being brought to light.[9]) They never seriously entertained the phonics-related options. In the eyes of these instructional leaders, phonics-based strategies wouldn't make reading *joyful like it is supposed to be*, will actually work against *building the students' love of reading*, and all the rest, and so they didn't stand a chance of being selected.

Quick reflection point for leaders:

If you're a school principal or district-level administrator—a superintendent, associate superintendent, director of curriculum and instruction—and you aren't soundly versed in these matters, are you sure you belong in instructional leadership? It's a tough question, but one I think all kids and all teachers under you would appreciate you answering honestly. It's all crucial material for you to know with regard to planning continuous improvement, of course, but almost more so with regard to how you grow effective instruction among the professionals in your purview. All those efficient check-in routines and coaching sessions and whatnot won't amount to much, after all, if you aren't leading on principles that are truly based in how people learn and what young people need to succeed beyond K-12. As you are so central in determining which qualities and habits are the most important for your frontline staff to develop and daily demonstrate, I urge you to look closely at your own expertise with evidence-supported practices.

Thanks in advance for reflecting on this.

Unfortunately, examples like this can run amok in all academic disciplines, grade levels, and types of student needs. When it comes to knowing what kids really need to learn and succeed, we are a poorly trained profession, period. This is not education's *fault* (indeed, it's mainly the fault of schools of educations; again, that's a discussion for a different book[10]), but it's definitely their *problem*.

Without a more explicit learning element that urges educators to effectively research appropriate solutions before making any change to operations (a guardrail that many business-born improvement processes lack), these same tendencies will be create problems when it comes to applying improvement science to education. For in education it's not just the operations that are off. Nor is it always the case that practitioners have full and diverse instructional knowledge, and they just need to start making better choices. In some cases, we have to go all the way back to the beginning and *learn about* the best options. (And in the process, of course, get folks to let go of the upside-down choices, which can be a very hard sell.)

With all these factors in mind, the near future will be an interesting case study. Continuous improvement processes can definitely be powerful for schools, especially schools not led by someone with improvement philosophies as strong as Dr. Bob's. The processes available provide structures for leaders who may not possess Dr. Bob's fully realized vision, and that's a good thing overall. Some crucial holes still exist. But I hope the improvement-science folks recognize them and figure out how to address them very soon.

To sum up: there are probably quite a few education leaders who've read *Learning To Improve*, or seen the Carnegie folks talking about improvement science at a conference. I *hope* there are, anyway, as it holds a great deal of promise. If you are one of these leaders, though, and you're thinking that the one thing you need to kick off wildly successful continuous improvement in your district is a squad of Six Sigma Black Belts working with your Instructional Leadership Teams, I'd urge you to pause before ringing them up. Here's why: *You may be able to build continuous school improvement—and build it better—completely on your own.*

* * *

That brings us back to the continuous school improvement work of Osseo Senior High under Dr. Bob's leadership in the early 2000s.

Long before the term 'continuous school improvement' was a buzzword—before all the books and models and planning templates and fishbone diagrams—Dr. Bob and his staff made some pretty interesting choices to keep their school improving continuously. This book's middle section looked closely at how some of them actually *worked*. The remainder of this chapter, though, will explore some practices the school did particularly well without all the formal improvement-science structures and guidance available today.

> **A note before I continue:** Very little in this summary may strike you as particularly revolutionary from a leadership or effective-schooling standpoint. Some of this story may seem eye-rollingly obvious. If you like your instructional-leadership advice served up with lots of 'flywheels', 'hedgehogs', or 'right-people-right-seats' maxims, in other words, you may be a little disappointed.
> But frankly, simplicity and sincerity are the point.

Think about it. Under Dr. Bob, Osseo Senior High was practicing effective continuous improvement well before continuous improvement was cool, and the school logged some pretty damn good accomplishments. If we use the district's 'transformational system changes' as our bar, anyway, Osseo Senior under Dr. Bob chose and implemented improvement actions every bit as effectively, and earned better student results, all without the myriad innovative improvement processes and facilitation you would expect from a similar effort today.

There were no gimmicky or faddish solutions. Nothing the school did was packaged or over-managed. Leaders—from Dr. Bob to his co-administrators to the teachers he tapped to lead various initiatives—relied instead on reliable leadership virtues like thoughtful self-analysis, relationship-building, consistency, and hustle. And instructionally/managerially, these school leaders consistently focused on education's fundamentals much more than exciting or innovative frontiers. Virtues like these may not seem particularly sexy, and they certainly don't promise quick fixes or 'turnarounds'. What they do, though, is *produce*.

Having been a teacher under Dr. Bob before the days of 'transformational system change'—and, of course, having led this kind of work in many schools since—I can confirm that these simple, sincere virtues were the key to making school improvement just *work* at Osseo Senior. In the main, they helped the school's professionals feel recognized and valued, not just that they were 'doing a job'. Also, the structures created by Dr. Bob and his various improvement initiatives ensured the pros working within them had the support and development they needed to execute on the preferred practices. Best of all, it was remarkably effective.

And as a bonus? Everyone can do what Dr. Bob and his leaders did.

On that note, my hope in this chapter and the next is not to provide a *playbook of actions*, but rather a *set of key principles* leaders can build around as they embark on their own continuous improvement efforts. For brevity's sake these principles will be presented in 'top five' format, but they aren't in any particular order of importance. They are all are *equally* important.

In this chapter I'll explore those five key features of continuous school improvement, focusing on what the school did well to build a strong culture of learning. In the next chapter, I'll build on these summaries with five recommendations about continuous school improvement that education professionals can implement today, even within our current 'transformational system change' milieu.

Five continuous improvement successes at Osseo Senior High

1. Set limited number of priority 'pillars', designed specific action for each.

2. Committed to *molding* consensus, not *holding out* for consensus.
3. Focused improvements on schooling's 'blocking and tackling'.
4. Fundamentally believed in students, set expectations accordingly.
5. Got genuinely personal.

1. Set limited number of priority 'pillars', designed specific action for each

Throughout section two, which discussed the continuous improvement culture of Osseo Senior before it was crowded out by the district's 'transformational system change', you may have noticed that all specific improvement actions began from clear organizational priorities and premiums. For example:

- Dr. Bob's priority was solving his school's stubborn historical dropout statistics, which led him to research the credit-earning histories of past dropouts, which ultimately created the Sophomore Academy.

- Knowing the habits of their students and which habits they wanted these students to practice more actively, the Sophomore Academy team placed a high premium on in-class time. They then worked together to design expectations and policies to uphold across all Academy classes.

- The CSI, after spending a couple years floundering without strong guiding priorities, took time to establish a firm three-pillared school mission. Each pillar formed the center of a specific school-wide improvement action per year. (Which were then monitored and improved upon throughout each year and ultimately incorporated permanently.)

- Individual teachers like Heather Casella set a priority to provide higher-quality instruction for her remedial reading students than the district-provided Read 180 programming.

She crafted an alternate program—which included heavy amounts of independent reading—and pitched it to Dr. Bob for his approval and support.

Again, 'setting priorities' is not revolutionary. It is, however, *essential* to every step of continuous improvement that follows: the selection of appropriate adjustments/interventions, the learning and communication of revised expectations, the monitoring for effectiveness (and, of course, the subsequent adjustments, plus the learning and communication out), and the ability of practitioners to execute multiple improvement strategy simultaneously.

Plain and simple, if you make everything a priority, *nothing will be a priority*. See continuous improvement as a long game, and be comfortable working on a few improvement priorities (and their attendant actions, of course) at a time. Perfect them, integrate them into 'the way we do things around here', and move on to the next set of priorities and actions.

2. Committed to *molding* consensus, not *holding out* for consensus

I haven't said anything like this yet, but I have to be honest: when the Sophomore Academy team first came together to design our school-within-a-school, there was one thing I couldn't stand about my new teammates.

Namely, they infuriated me with how *right* they could be about positions that were the opposite of mine. It drove me *nuts*. I had my ways of doing things, I had my reasons for doing them that way, and all those things went pretty dang well in general. Team or no team, I was never real into the idea of fundamentally changing my practices. (Plus, I've never been real good at admitting when I'm wrong.)

When we reached an impasse about which practices to make uniform across our Academy and why, my opposing colleagues (usually Kelly

Klecker and Eric Ruska, as you may remember from Chapter 5) just had a way of making so much *sense*. They wouldn't directly attempt to change my mind, and they certainly wouldn't work out compromises with me, like, 'We'll all do it this way, but Kalenze can do it his way.' They simply *framed* the proposed shared practices in terms of why we all agreed to sign on to this project in the first place (appealing to my personal values of helping at-risk kids) and how teamwork was going to be crucial for the Academy (appealing to my personal values of putting the team over the individual—hopelessly, I am an offensive lineman until I die). And looking at our differences that way, I saw how right my colleagues were—and that my resistance was more about being hard-headed than anything else.

(So yeah, they made me nuts at the time. I know now—and I have for a long time—that they also made me a lot *better*.)

At bottom, on certain crucial issues throughout our time together, the Sophomore Academy team did not hold out for team consensus or *buy-in*. With respect to one another's preferences and feelings, we didn't have time to wait for everyone to come around. The kids, after all, were in the seats.

Instead, we took to heart Dr. Martin Luther King's famous reminder, 'A genuine leader is not a searcher for consensus but a molder of consensus' (see Chapter 12), and sought to mold the group consensus as necessary to keep moving ahead. By not getting mired in the 'building buy-in' phase, we were able to agree on—and get to applying— practices and policies much more quickly, which helped us figure out how we could continuously improve on them. Once they were actually in motion, we could make adjustments all together or, when one of us was struggling, pick one another up individually with suggestions and other support (like defending one another to the Academy kids).

Where the very close-knit Sophomore Academy group was able to influence one another through appealing to individuals' values (i.e.

framing) and subsequent support, a large-scale improvement group like the CSI had to work a bit differently. There's no way to do with an entire staff what we could within the four teachers of the Academy. Much as we may have wanted to, there was just no way our team of a dozen or so could individually counsel more than a hundred staff members spread over a dozen departments into full acceptance and functional agreement.

The CSI team did, however, always make time to think through how to mold the consensus of the entire staff. We talked about the kinds of pushback we were likely to receive, and we considered the counter-messages and counter-actions we could present to best demonstrate our good faith. We did our homework to make sure we were organized and thorough when presenting rationales for new improvement initiatives. We facilitated brainstorm-and-voting processes for selecting improvement actions to communicate that full staff engagement was important to our collective success. We had Dr. Bob meet individually with the most stubborn and vocal holdouts (usually two or three people) to put them on 'no-sabotage' notice (see Chapter 12). We learned to go on the offensive the hard way, as you may recall. Our entire first year together—which was effectively dedicated to 'buy-in' alone—was a giant waste of everyone's time (see Chapter 11).

In short, Dr. Bob's continuous school improvement efforts reached their apex when we stopped waiting for staff consensus or trying to cajole people into it. Now to be clear, we did not steamroll anyone. That's what the district's (not-so-) 'transformational system change' did. Rather, the school community under Dr. Bob refused to let 'building buy-in' or 'achieving consensus' become an obstacle to 'making progress'. They did what was necessary to mold consensus, and they kept improvements moving ahead. And as a result, school-designed initiatives didn't get hung up in the design phase, and school-wide results kept up with and outpaced state averages. Importantly, teachers looking back on these methods miss feeling like they were part of the school-improvement process (see Chapter 14).

It takes some thought and it can certainly be hard to do. But molding consensus matters.

3. Focused improvements on schooling's 'blocking and tackling'

Speaking of the things that matter, you may have noticed that all of the bottom-up improvements detailed earlier don't have particularly 'innovative' or 'disruptive' character.

Given the task of continuously improving, in other words, Osseo Senior's staff didn't worry themselves much about adopting untested but intuitively appealing solutions. Indeed, you would've been hard-pressed to see the staff leaders at this time pushing for greatly expanded access to instructional technology, school-wide commitments to more project-based learning activities, opening up spates of engaging electives, or anything of this kind.

Rather, the staff first broke down effective schooling into what they considered its most essential parts, then got down to figuring out how to improve those parts the best they could. To borrow from billionaire entrepreneur Naveen Jain in a 2012 article for *Inc.* magazine: in the period covered by this book, Osseo Senior built very effective continuous improvement by strengthening the school's 'blocking and tackling'.[11]

In the Sophomore Academy, for instance, the team asked themselves how they could shape student *attitudes* about education to better motivate them. They deemed minutes of learning time as precious, and they built policies and expectations to protect those minutes and make them as productive as possible. They built routines for checking on kids' progress, met regularly to make sure kids weren't falling through the cracks, and they designed actions accordingly.

Note also all the 'innovative' things we *didn't* do: no 'Mindfulness Mondays' with yoga sessions to make our occasionally volatile students more relaxed, no restorative circles to resolve conflicts, no students in charge of selecting their own curricula, or anything like that. In Jain's football metaphor, all of these 'innovations' would be exotic plays to call. But the more pressing issue was that our Academy students needed better fundamentals. They needed to become sharper, more reliable 'blockers and tacklers' in the game of school.

The CSI team followed a similar philosophy. They created a three-pillared mission that described schooling's purposes in the most basic terms: academic preparation, ability to be productive citizens, and personal fulfillment. They then worked with the larger staff to figure out actions that would make sure kids were reading more, that the school was encouraging responsible personal habits, and that kids were finding places to belong within the school, respectively.

From classroom improvement levels, teachers like Heather Casella (whom we visited in Chapter 11) designed and proposed programmatic improvements to *reduce* dependence on technology. Watching how her remedial reading students were floundering (and on the verge of hating to read) when they were subject to the district-required remedial reading software Read 180, she crafted an entirely new program. She saw that the innovative technological 'solution' was hindering kids' progress, and went back to the 'blocking and tackling' of building reading ability: she infused elements of choice and accountability into her programming, and subsequently watched her struggling readers— many who were English-language learners—become energized like never before. (Heather went on to expand her program into a professional-development resource called Reader's Choice Works. She has trained several schools and districts around the state in the program's philosophies and methods, and some have seen some impressive results. How's that for cultivating leadership?)

Having a firm handle on schooling's most fundamental elements meant so much to someone like Dr. Bob, in fact, that the prospect of having it compromised or scripted by the district turned out to be unbearable. As you may remember, the district's revised policies and procedures on handling student behaviors ended up being a major factor in his decision to retire early. He knew that for a school to run successfully, it had to be run with consistency, fairness, and compassion. ('If the behaviors and respect aren't in place in a school,' Dr. Bob's told me more times than I can count, 'nothing else you do will even matter. It will all fall apart if people don't feel safe.') For him, student behavior was such a fundamental, 'blocking and tackling'-type issue that it couldn't be left to outside micromanagement.

As should be clear, Osseo Senior's staff placed high premiums on doing the 'blocking and tackling' of schooling well. By focusing continuously on how they could do the best job possible on behavior/safety expectations and follow-up, academic programming, and building students' habits and outlooks, they achieved as much, if not more, than the district's innovative 'transformational system change'.

4. Fundamentally believed in students, set expectations accordingly

Just as Osseo Senior believed continuous school improvement happened best when it focused on the fundamental 'blocking and tackling' levels of schooling, they also fundamentally believed in their *students*.

The staff respected their students' capacity and aspirations and, in areas that students were still developing, their potential and resilience. This didn't mean, though, that the staff was committed to platitudes like 'having high expectations' or 'believing these kids can learn'. Indeed, they set expectations and policies they knew kids could rise to, and they dedicated time to working out how they could both respectfully justify their expectations and support kids to reach those expectations when help was needed. To borrow a term I used a lot when describing the work of the Sophomore Academy, the improvements we planned at

Osseo Senior in this time were all about moving kids from *stable* to *able*. That meant pushing kids to push themselves, plain and simple.

This can be seen throughout several of the improvement initiatives. From the Sophomore Academy's restrictions on leaving classrooms and 'Game of Life' simulation/self-reflection/resolution to the CSI's Activity Fair and beyond, Osseo Senior's improvements often started with the question, 'Based on what we see here, what do our *kids* need to strengthen in order to better prepare them for life after high school?'

From the answer to *that* question, they designed according expectations, messages, support plans, consequences, and professional learning. Once all the professional pieces were in place, they were able to explicitly ramp up expectations of students.

The point here is to remember that 'having high expectations' of the kids wasn't just 'setting a higher bar and making kids deal with it'. When the various school improvers at Osseo Senior High—from the Sophomore Academy team and the CSI to individual teachers—raised expectations on students explicitly, they also did a lot of back-end work: how practices should adjust, what kinds of messages to reinforce, and which methods would work best for monitoring progress.

And within this fully formed *culture* of raised expectations— *surprise!*—kids rose to the challenge and learned what they could accomplish. (For a refresher on some kids' perspectives on this assertion, see some of their quotes throughout. Remember Bionca Brown: 'It made me change a lot. I feel like I made it to the top and now I realize that I have to do what I gotta do...This is not the streets and outside, it's school.' Or Siera Walton: 'I learned about myself that when I want something I will work towards it...I also learned that if I work hard enough it all will pay off.' Or Abdi Mohamed: 'We started doing a lot better in there than we ever were. We kinda learned how to be students for the first time. Do work, get it done, then we started to see the honor rolls. We realized what it took.')

The Osseo Area School District's 'transformational system change', on the other hand, took a categorically different approach. It was created exclusively to address qualities district leaders perceived as 'broken' in their *school-level practitioners*.

When they studied grading practices and found them to be inconsistent and unreliable, for example, changes were ordered to standardize the whole system for all; teachers got heavier workloads (new processes, managing retakes and late work), while students were given multiple chances and extensions, with little regard for how much (or how little) effort they put in to learn the material initially. When students were disciplined disproportionately by race, district leaders identified teachers' implicit racial biases as the obvious culprit, and diversity trainers were dispatched to ameliorate those biases. Relatedly, standardized behavior-response protocols were established to remove school-level professionals' individual judgment from the disciplinary mix.

In short, the district's new policies and initiatives gave very little responsibility or accountability to students. They raised expectations significantly for teachers, but expected the same—less, probably—of the kids. And in education (and as our effective school-improvers always held dear when they planned their actions), this lopsided approach misses at least half of every improvement opportunity.

As I put it in Chapter 7 of *Education Is Upside-Down*, the whole learning and growth enterprise for students works much like a health-club membership. The goal for the health-club member is some kind transformation, and that requires the person who is transforming to put in the effort. Yes, the club needs the right equipment and personal trainers need to know what they're doing. But that's only half of it. If the member never shows up to work out, or doesn't break a sweat during their sessions, it's first and foremost *their* fault if their muscles don't grow, their weight stays the same, and their health doesn't improve over the course of their membership. (And they wouldn't have a leg to stand on if they demanded their money back.) To sum up (and greatly oversimplify) loads of research on how learning happens and how expertise is built: to grow, students have to leave their personal comfort zones and exert deliberate effort.

To put it another way: those who look at the problem of transformation and only seek to address one side of the equation while absolving the individual student of responsibility are sure to be frustrated quite quickly with the resulting situation. Both sides of this arrangement are vitally important. *Both* sides share responsibility for making the transformation happen.

Worse, there are often dire side-effects of assigning all responsibility to the institution. Disenfranchising practitioners will surely become a real factor. If you assume the people working for the institution are incompetent, deeply flawed, and patently unable to make their own decisions or exercise their professional judgment, then heap loads of new work and expectations on them to neutralize these flaws, you're going to alienate your staff. As you may recall, the Osseo district's attempts at 'transformational system change' created a groundswell of alienation. Teachers talked about losing autonomy, then quickly moved to losing *trust*, and it went downhill from there.

In all, it's to the credit of the school-improvers at Osseo Senior that they designed adult-level improvements *around* the kid-level improvements they needed to see, and not solely on their own practices in a kind of professional quarantine. Effective schooling absolutely needs to consider both teachers and students, and preferably in the 'desired student habit > outlook > mindset > professional practice' direction, not the other way around. The results—and the health of the school—absolutely depend on it.

5. Got genuinely personal

While this final success of Osseo Senior High's pre-'transformational system change' improvement culture may look a little squishy or sentimental at first glance, it's absolutely true: initiatives worked well under Dr. Bob because he consistently emphasized—and *personally modeled*—strong interpersonal relationships. In all my conversations with him, it's something he always came back to as the one factor that made everything else *go*.[12]

And as I've revisited Dr. Bob's leadership, I must concur: every step of these improvement processes was built on a foundation of strong relationships. Sometimes it was Dr. Bob walking the school to lobby influential teachers, one by one, about the schedule shifts he needed to enable the Sophomore Academy. Elsewhere, the CSI engaged the full staff through small work groups and let them in on selecting the best mission-aligned actions. In other cases, Dr. Bob required the Sophomore Academy team to meet face-to-face weekly during a shared prep period, a requirement that was both strategic from a student-support standpoint and wildly effective for building our personal and professional bonds. As he filled out the Sophomore Academy team, Dr. Bob didn't just appoint Kelly Klecker or start pitching his idea from the get-go; he got to know her over a period of *months* to see if she was right for the initiative he had in mind.

Contrast all of this to the Accountability Era's capacity-development through highly structured professional growth plans, progress-monitoring, tightly scheduled and protocol-driven visits with instructional coaches, and so on. The difference is rather stark. While it's true that these structures help leaders interface with staff more regularly and (at least in theory) more productively, they seem cold and bureaucratic, lacking the imagination and humanity that was so crucial to Dr. Bob's success. I can say this: as a teacher and leader in that school, I was never motivated to work harder or adjust my practices by a spreadsheet or instructional coach; but I would have done anything for Dr. Bob and my colleagues.

Important note: This is *not* to say, 'Structures are dehumanizing! A good relationship culture focuses on people and throws out its structures.' Not in the least. Schools that adopt pure people-over-structure mentalities can, in fact, quickly end up with the CSI's empty year of 'morale-building', and I'd *never* recommend that.

The trick is finding the proper balance. Recall the CSI's small-to-large-group decision-making process, for example, or the Sophomore Academy's meeting routines, and the emphasis on structure should be evident. Genuine relationships were built, and professionals were brought together so they could reach solutions, but always in a coordinated, deliberate fashion that fully aligned with the school's strategic objectives. The school got genuinely personal on several different levels, but they always did so in service of the bigger goals.

In this very positive and productive improvement culture, relationships weren't the destination. They were fuel for the journey. When improvement initiatives run low on this fuel—or attempt to use a synthetic substitute—they are sure to sputter.

* * *

The next chapter will build on these five successes, bringing us to a close with specific recommendations for how schools can work on continuous improvement. In hindsight, we didn't get *everything* right. (Nobody could, and nobody does.) Knowing what we know now, I'm quite sure we would do a lot of it differently. And in light of the current educational-improvement environment and its attendant pressures, any improvement effort needs to account for some additional environmental considerations.

Endnotes

1. Petrilli, M., J. (14 November 2018) 'The End of Education Policy'. Thomas B Fordham Institute. Available at: edexcellence.net/articles/the-end-of-education-policy

2. Bryk, A., S., *et al.* (2015) *Learning to Improve: How America's Schools Can Get Better at Getting Better.* Cambridge, MA: Harvard Education Press.

3. No author. (21 November 2018) 'An Inside Look at School Improvement (Perspectives)'. Education Week. Available at: www.edweek.org/ew/collections/commentary-continuous-improvement/index.html

4. No author. (2018) 'Networks for School Improvement'. Bill and Melinda Gates Foundation. Available at: k12education.gatesfoundation.org/what-we-do/networks-for-school-improvement/

5. For a general piece on this tendency, see Kalenze, E. (1 March 2016) 'Do Not Go Stupid into That Pumping Blood'. A Total Ed Case. Available at: erickalenze.wordpress.com/2016/03/01/do-not-go-stupid-into-that-pumping-blood/. For a discussion of how this tendency of the education enterprise is being applied to personalized learning, see: Kalenze, E. (9 August 2017) 'Do Not Go Stupid into That Personalized Learning Blood: Part 1, Mind the Evidence'. A Total Ed Case. Available at: erickalenze.wordpress.com/2017/08/09/do-not-go-stupid-into-that-personalized-learning-blood-part-1-mind-the-evidence/

6. Sparks, S., D. (20 June 2018) 'A Primer on Continuous School Improvement'. *Education Week.* Available at: www.edweek.org/ew/articles/2018/02/07/a-primer-on-continuous-school-improvement.html

7. Kalenze, E. (2014) *Education Is Upside-Down: Reframing Reform to Focus on the Right Problems.* Lanham, MD: Rowman & Littlefield, pp. 108–117.

8. The 'five whys' method of determining root causes dates back to the 1930s, when Toyota Industries founder Sakichi Toyoda first used it. It is one of a number of root-cause analysis protocols used by improvement science facilitators.

9. Hanford, E. (10 September 2018) 'Why Aren't Kids Being Taught to Read?'. American Public Media. Available at: www.apmreports.org/story/2018/09/10/hard-words-why-american-kids-arent-being-taught-to-read

10. Kalenze, E. (2014) *Education Is Upside-Down: Reframing Reform to Focus on the Right Problems.* Lanham, MD: Rowman & Littlefield, pp 143-148.

11. Jain, N. (13 August 2012) '10 Secrets of Becoming a Successful Entrepreneur'. Inc. Available at: www.inc.com/naveen-jain/10-secrets-of-becoming-a-successful-entrepreneur.html

12. Note: I could go down a rabbit hole here to share more about recent research in the area of relationships and their effects in education, in workplaces, and in general child-development. For one example of this research, see Roehlkepartain, E., et al. (2017) *Relationships First: Creating Connections That Help Young People Thrive.* Search Institute, Available at: http://page.search-institute.org/relationships-first-020217a

Full disclosure: *I've worked with Search Institute on bringing their research insights about relationships and student motivation to school's practices for the past few years. I will refrain, however, just as I have for the other four of these top-five successes. The idea is to keep the focus on what Dr. Bob and his school did well—again, well before most playbooks on the research-verified importance of relationships and effective relationships' various elements had been written.*

Chapter 16

Building Your Own Continuous School Improvement

'Continuous improvement is better than delayed perfection.'

– Mark Twain

In the years since I was fortunate enough to learn about continuous school improvement first-hand—and about effective instruction *through* the process of school improvement—I have worked with several U.S. schools on continuous-improvement planning and execution. I've done this work as an in-district support resource and as an outside adviser in a wide range of settings to meet a wide range of improvement objectives. This decade of experience has allowed me to witness school improvement trends, challenges, and potential from several informative angles.

Thanks to my field experience, I've gotten an up-close look at what school leaders worry about as they plan and manage continuous improvement, what kinds of roles district leadership play, how outside providers interact with and influence these processes, and how all of these forces push and pull on one another. No doubt, it can get messy. But it's a struggle that includes so many of the questions I believe American education must have better answers for,[1] so I find it both endlessly fascinating and absolutely essential. (Flat out: it's work I *love* to do.)

I might not say it outright when I'm on the job, but I'm always drawing heavily from my time at Osseo Senior. In particular, I draw from the five successes. Whenever possible, I steer schools toward them, so they can make each one come to life in their own way. It doesn't always work, of course. Some of the improvements I suggest don't always look like the ones they have in mind.[2] When they prefer to stick with more innovative or accountability-based visions of improvement, I don't hold it against them. To the contrary, I totally get it.

I was offering my insights as an external, third-party adviser/ supporter/consultant after all, never as a superior school leaders had to report to. And from my non-supervisory vantage point, I understand it's next to impossible to convince a district or school leader to focus on the 'blocking and tackling' fundamentals if they have an 'innovation-first' mindset. Doing so goes completely against the grain in our field. It's as if this tendency—to favor the shiny, untested, and intuitively pleasing possibility over the boring but reliable reality—is hard-wired into the enterprise. (In fact, we have a long history of doing exactly that.[3]) And so, because my suggestions lacked supervisory weight, they were rarely strong enough to jolt leaders out of their default mode, to say the least.

Because of this power dynamic, the onus is on education's upper-level administrators to themselves improve at fostering the most effective and evidence-backed school-improvement actions and instructional practices. Take it from me, administrators, the principals working under you are following your lead and respecting your guidelines. Even someone like the inimitable Dr. Bob wasn't a rogue leader, working outside the lines to build improvement his way. While he took a different approach than the standard district models suggested, every initiative he tried was carefully planned, then proposed to—and approved by—his superiors before going into effect.

District-level leaders, I'm looking at you. Your school-level leaders are 'going by the book.' So please make sure you have the soundest 'book' possible. (Hint: You may want to take a look at some of the points below and in the previous chapter to see how they might apply to your own leadership.)

Another reason why school leaders hesitate to adopt the improvement principles I evangelize is because doing so ultimately means some of the biggest, most complicated systems in a school will have to change. And make no mistake, adjusting these systems—from ongoing professional-development structures and master scheduling to things like lunch-supervision duties—is incredibly hard and frustrating work. It takes a lot of forethought, planning, communication, continuous management, and exhausting politicking.

To be more specific: when a principal passes on my suggestion to redo the school's entire master schedule in order to give the sixth-grade team more shared prep time and let them 'get genuinely personal' (from

Chapter 15), I completely understand the hesitance. While *I* might think the prep time could take the team's collaboration to the next level, it's *the principal* who will be accountable, not me, to all of the upset students, angry teachers, and confused parents who come calling to complain about the new schedule.

Leading a school from day to day is tough enough as it is. Making significant changes mid-year or even over a single summer, no matter how important they are to creating real improvement, can be too scary to consider.

Again, I totally get it.

Still, I always figure it's worth a shot. It was only by taking those risks, after all, that I got to see so many idealized elements of continuous school improvement come to life and work in concert: definite improvement aspirations determined according to school data, tangible improvement actions imagined and adopted across the school reasonably and thoroughly, creative solutions to real school issues sparking all throughout the school, and progress continually monitored and applied forward toward improving operations. Even better, my risk-taking allowed me to see these processes produce the *desired outputs*: the school community's professionals feeling respected and empowered, teachers growing their instructional and leadership capacities, and student achievement rising steadily.

As such, I figure I'll be carrying what I learned at Osseo Senior into as many schools as I can. I am well aware that emulating these actions and operations may be a bridge too far (and indeed may not be a good fit, as everything works somewhere and nothing works everywhere, as we'll see shortly), but the basic improvement principles can help every school as they build their own continuous improvement processes.

* * *

With all that in mind, it's time to set aside Osseo Senior High and start turning those specific experiences—and my own diverse field experience and study—into general recommendations about continuous school improvement.

Remember: while initiatives like the Sophomore Academy, the CSI, and various other bottom-up improvements Dr. Bob supported turned out well, nearly all of them had to find their way through trial and error, often learning the most important lessons the hard way. Each initiative had a clear destination in mind, but none of them really knew how to get there. To the contrary, the roads had to be *built along the way*. (Think back to how the first year of Sophomore Academy students overwhelmed us, or the entire year CSI spent building staff morale, and you can see we had our share of false starts and outright fails.) And while I can't speak for everyone involved, I would do a lot of this work differently if I had the chance to do it all again.

The recommendations here will be made with Osseo Senior's experience in mind, in hopes that leaders and practitioners can build better roads more efficiently. If my school-improvement advisory experiences have taught me anything, it's that the most vital considerations often don't get enough attention from the outset. And once you start building a road in the wrong direction, the journey quickly becomes bumpy, difficult, or even impossible.

To reiterate, though, I won't tell you exactly which actions to take. I'll do my best to hold off urging you to start your own Sophomore Academy, to schedule weekly academic monitoring exams, to ban cellphones in classrooms, to completely revise your (*ahem*) grading practices, to use a certain agenda format for your Instructional Leadership Team meetings, or whatever else. While I have some strong opinions about these tactics, the choice isn't mine to make. It's yours. Without knowing the reality inside your building—its actual needs based on student data, its staff composition, its history of improvement—making specific recommendations would be presumptuous if not disrespectful. That's top-down improvement at its worst.

I can, however, draw from my experience at Osseo Senior High, my ongoing field study, and my multifaceted advisory work to offer five critical points all education leaders would be wise to consider as they embark on any serious continuous school improvement effort. While the five successes weren't listed in order of importance, the five recommendations are ranked. It's still not a step-by-step guide. But my experience has shown me time and again that the order in which schools approach these recommendations matters quite a bit.

* * *

Before I launch into the recommendations, however, I have one quick request: do a quick Google search on the term 'school improvement plan'. (If you're extra curious, add the name of a nearby school or district.) You should be able to find an example fairly quickly, as plans like these—which may be called 'school performance plans', 'comprehensive school improvement plans', or some combination of these types of terms—are pretty typical across American education. Once they're approved by a district and/or state, the final plans are often available on school websites.

This is especially instructive if you haven't seen one of these plans before. Even if you work in education, you may never have seen one—even for the school you work in. You really should, just so you know how a comprehensive school-improvement plan typically organizes itself.

Got one? Good. Now take a quick look through it.

When you do, you'll likely see that the plan includes all kinds of information about where the school wants to focus improvement resources and why. You'll see several points of achievement data describing the school's current state (and justifying the focus areas), plus elements like performance goals for the coming year(s), strategies the school will prioritize in the year(s) ahead, and so forth. All this is fine. Strategic thinking is important.[4]

In my school-improvement work with schools, however, it's about *here*—when the strategic planning phase wraps up, that is—that I see big issues cropping up. (Some issues do emerge in the planning itself, to be sure, particularly when schools select improvement strategies—more on that in a bit.) The following five recommendations are based on the issues I see most commonly, both as schools develop improvement plans and implement improvement actions.

Five continuous school improvement recommendations

1. Reflect thoroughly and assess your school honestly.
2. Learn to be good learners: Build research into improvement processes.
3. Rethink 'PD': Make it continual and collaborative, and make the time.
4. Figure out if your improvements are working.
5. Let teachers lead (no, *really*: let teachers lead).

1. Reflect thoroughly and assess your school honestly

Given education's current achievement- and accountability-conscious culture, I'm quite sure I don't have to sell you on the importance of knowing your school's data. At this stage, it's more an exception than a rule for me to encounter education professionals who don't know their way around standardized test reports, school attendance/behavior data, staff/student/parent surveys, and the like. If the Accountability Era has accomplished anything, it has at least made us all much more proficient with data analysis.

Still, it's worth repeating: to succeed at school improvement, you have to start with performance data. It's the year-in-year-out proof of who is proficient and who isn't, who's growing and who's not, who's attending and who's truant, who's missing class time due to discipline referrals, and on and on. All subsequent planning should be driven by data—not our own idiosyncratic notions of 'how kids learn best' or 'what really matters' or 'the right thing to do'. Schools serve *kids and communities*, not their own ideals.

In short, study the data about your school thoroughly, know those data sets well, and use them to set priorities at every opportunity. Again, remember the improvements built under Dr. Bob at Osseo Senior to understand that setting priorities means saying no to a lot of worthy ideas. In none of our efforts did we try to improve everything at once. We established our pillars of improvement, then used our data to select specific actions for each one. Our goal was to install and refine a few practices a year, every year. For what seems like the millionth time: When everything is a priority, *nothing is a priority*. Or, more popularly, don't let the perfect be the enemy of the good. (Or just revisit the epigraph above.)

With that all said, my first recommendation isn't about how or why to study your data per se, but rather about the genuine value of data review continuous school improvement. And that's this: when you plot the trends over time, your school's deepest flaws will become readily apparent. And when everyone can see that the line we want to go up is going down, it's much easier to be honest with ourselves about which improvement initiatives to keep and, importantly, which ones to pull the plug on altogether.

To illustrate: in a K-8 school I was helping with continuous school improvement, scores on the state's standardized reading test were historically very low—with less than 10% of students proficient across all grades—and trending lower over time. The situation was dire.

As we dug deeper into the reading data, though, looking more closely at student retention (the school kept a majority of students from kindergarten through 8th grade), year-to-year performance of cohort groups, and more granular information from benchmark assessments, we saw a clear need to program the early grades differently. By the time kids reached third grade (the first year they were required to take the state test), so many of them were so far behind on the basics of reading (i.e decoding and comprehending the simplest texts) that making major changes to the core instruction was the most appropriate action. This was not a trend the school could reverse with more *intervention*, in other words.

Transforming the core instruction would take some astute politicking (this school needed to explain why it needed to diverge from the district's preferred literacy strategies), and the school would need additional funds for materials and staff training, so a lot of work had to be done. At the very least, however, an honest assessment of the relevant data clearly identified where to start.

And, crucially, the data showed what to *pull the plug on*. For years, this school had arranged for community-based partners (which cost money, remember) to provide reading interventions for struggling students. Obviously, this strategy was not worth continuing. In an ideal situation, after all, intensive interventions should only happen for a small percentage of students, not the majority. And in this particular school, 90% or more of all kids were below grade-level in reading. Just 'adding interventions' or 'seeking the right interventions' was never going to be enough. It was time to go back to the drawing board.

Subsequently, the budget dollars previously allocated to these unsuccessful interventions could be applied to more full-time staff and/ or materials. At the same time, this reduced the school-managerial burden caused by a herd of part-time literacy coaches roaming the building, pulling kids out of core instruction.

This moment of clarity was vital. It opened the eyes of school leaders after years of assuming that they had to follow the district's lead without question and throw lots of intervention at it when it didn't work.

The bottom line: know your school data thoroughly, because it will help you build a strong case for district superiors when wholesale, fundamental change—not incremental steps or technical tweaks—is what your school needs to improve.

As some of these fundamental issues have very deep roots,[5] it may take a tremendous amount of work to dig them out. Just as Dr. Bob did when he first approached his district-level superiors about starting the shared-leadership forum that ultimately became the CSI, make sure your requests to end certain initiatives and replace them with new ones are backed with a sturdy understanding of your school's recent *and* historic results.

2. Learn to be good learners: Build research into improvement processes

In the introduction, I acknowledged that—knowing what I know now—I'd definitely do some things differently at Osseo Senior if I could. In the introduction to the previous chapter, I said that while education has been increasingly fascinated with improvement science, this fascination won't produce any worthwhile results until we place more emphasis on evidence.

This recommendation sits at the intersection of those two assertions. Namely, I'm recommending that education leaders commit to building a vigorous research and learning component into any school improvement initiative. Frankly, we didn't give research much attention at Osseo Senior, and that's one of my biggest regrets.

To be clear, it wasn't like we didn't *want* to focus on research. It's just that doing thorough research and using the findings to guide school improvement weren't on our radar. Based on my experience, this is fairly typical in U.S. schools across the board. For the most part, working educators tend to accept vendors' claims that their solutions are 'research-based' at face value. It's hard to fault them for this, because the day-to-day of education is just *hard*. Nobody wants to take on a research project every time a vendor comes calling.

Over time, however, we became more attuned to research insights and built them into our collective and individual practices. Like when

Dr. Bob researched and implemented an early-action plan to stanch dropouts more effectively than the previous 'emergency' approaches,[6] and when the Academy team became more deliberate message-framers to shift students' motivation,[7] and when the CSI engineered a schoolwide increase in reading through the READvisory initiative.[8] Each of these examples helped us design a course of action that produced the outcomes we wanted.

In all, it makes me wish we would have applied research more consistently and purposefully in our improvement planning. We might've saved a lot of the trial and error, along with the aimlessness we occasionally endured.

Of course, I'd like to see teachers *everywhere* develop sound research habits and build what they learn into daily practices. In my view (and in others'), this is the only way we'll become a 'mature profession'.[9] It's precisely why I spend so much time attending, speaking at, and organizing ResearchED conferences,[10] as well as blogging and writing for a variety of education outlets. All of these tasks force me to stay immersed in the latest research.

Research is *especially* crucial for continuous school improvement. Making decisions based on all the available evidence—*not* just the inspiring words of education gurus or vendors—will prevent schools from spending all kinds of vital resources on solutions that are poorly conceived or simply the wrong fit for their most pressing issues.

Recall the Osseo Area School District's 'transformational system change'. None of these initiatives were well-supported by evidence of effectiveness, much less by evidence of general suitability for learning/preparation. Some, in fact, had what amounted to 'Buyer Beware' signs on them, in that they had produced little more than frustration elsewhere. If decision-makers had looked at the evidence (or, rather, the *lack* of it) up front, perhaps they would have thought twice and avoided a great deal of angst, wasted money, and meager results.

Last reminder: This is not a critique of the Osseo district's leadership alone. This dynamic is *very common*, in all kinds of schools, all across the country. The leaders in Osseo are, simply, one example of how continuous improvement can go from bad to worse if sound research is not part of the decision-making process. To wit, you may recall that the *entire state of Maine* thought standards-based grading was cool enough to mandate it in all schools, and then yank it back out after it failed miserably (Chapter 13, note 13).

I urge all leaders to take these examples to heart. Assess your school's needs carefully and accurately (see recommendation #1, above), then become what assessment expert Dylan Wiliam calls a 'critical consumer of educational research'.[11] That means learning about the available solutions/actions thoroughly and prioritizing those that have been shown to work, *not* ones that 'feel' right after, say, an inspiring TED Talk. (And, with all due respect, if you're basing school-improvement decisions on TED Talks, it is *especially* important that you heed this recommendation. Fascinating as they may be, those short clips aren't always particularly *rich* in evidence. Sir Ken Robinson's 'Do Schools Kill Creativity?' is the most-watched TED Talk of all time, for example, but its entire argument rests on very weak—inaccurate, even—evidence.[12])

As you become a critical consumer of research, be sure to involve as many fellow staff as you can. The idea should always be to strengthen *everyone's* research-literacy, not just your own. This idea is to develop a large team of evidence-driven people with a variety of perspectives and insights, not just one or two designated 'evidence gatekeepers.' (For starter resources, see the end of this recommendation.)

After your research helps identify a few promising options, begin the work of figuring out how your school can put them into practice (and then, of course, assessing them and continually improving upon them; more on this in recommendation #4).

If your research leads you to a *product or program* you believe fits your data-backed needs, be sure to subject it to the terrific step-by-step process recommended by cognitive scientist Dan Willingham in his vital *When Can You Trust the Experts?: How to Tell Good Science from Bad in Education*, which I've paraphrased here:[13]

1. **Strip claims down to their essentials** (i.e. remove emotion, analogies) and evaluate for scientific credibility.

2. **Flip promised outcomes.** Always consider the other side of the equation, which often goes unmentioned in promotional literature. If a new program promises a 70% pass rate, for example, the flip side is a 30% failure rate. If this sounds fine to you, continue on to the steps below. On the other hand, if the flip side doesn't justify all the time/dollars/angst you'll spend to enact the program, it's time to pause.

3. **Trace claims to the original source to verify them.** Don't assume that 'experts' or journalists or reviewers or any other third party is giving you a full, accurate appraisal of the product or program. Remember, they are selling you something.

4. **Analyze claims based on available evidence**, and ask sellers to provide that evidence if it's missing. You should care most about whether and how students improved because of the program under consideration. It's also ideal if the students who improved are similar to your own in terms of demographics.

5. **Ask 'Should I Do It?'** as in, 'Does this product or program make sense *for my situation, right now*?' It's an important question, because very few offerings are good for every student and teacher everywhere. If a program/product has made it past Willingham's first four filters here and you still think it's right for your school, be sure to align its proposed benefits with the data-verified needs of your school (from recommendation #1, above). Think again of Dylan Wiliam, who has very rightly said for years, 'Everything works somewhere, and nothing works everywhere'.

In the end, what's most important is being responsible with your kids' potential, your community's dollars, and your professionals' time and sanity. Yet again, Dylan Wiliam, from *Creating the Schools Our Children Need*, puts it best when he writes: '...there is now a great deal of well-organized evidence that shows that there are things that every school district could be doing, that have worked in a lot of school districts—rural, suburban, and urban—and that have worked with different state standards. Unfortunately, while these ideas are familiar, old hat even, they are not being implemented consistently in our schools. We need to stop looking for the next big thing and instead focus on doing the last big thing properly. The evidence about what we should be doing is actually pretty clear. We know what we should be doing. We're just not doing it.'[14]

With all that in mind, however, I realize that you and your team may have some catching up to do, especially regarding how people learn and Wiliam's 'great deal of well-organized evidence'. I also realize that this can be intimidating—bordering on paralyzing—because, seriously, who has time for all that research? And who in their right mind wants to read articles in academic journals? (Sorry, researchers.)

Lucky for you, right now is a great time to find research curators—people who've read the research *so you don't have to*. These curators are usually academics who are writing for popular audiences, and so they know how to package findings and translate key points into language that everyone from parents to classroom practitioners can understand, replete with references to the original sources if you want to take your research a step further.

I've provided a short list of 'starter' resources on the adjacent page that all educators will find valuable as they become more research-literate. I hope they provide a solid foundation and inspire you to develop your own set of trusted sources.

Learn to be good learners: research literacy starter kit

While this list could be *much* longer, I'm keeping it to just a few titles. The idea isn't to pack the staff-lounge bookcase, but rather to get you started with a few essentials. As such, I use subject-specific materials and have instead stuck to crucial overviews and one indispensable history. It's good to know how we got here, after all.

Welcome to the rabbit hole.

When Can You Trust the Experts? How to Tell Good Science from Bad in Education by Daniel T. Willingham

Creating the Schools Our Children Need: Why What We're Doing Now Won't Help Much (And What We Can Do Instead) by Dylan Wiliam

What Does This Look Like in the Classroom? Bridging the Gap Between Research and Practice by Carl Hendrick and Robin Macpherson (editors)

The Science of Learning, resources by Deans For Impact (access it freely online at http://deansforimpact.org/resources/the-science-of-learning/)

Visible Learning: A Synthesis of Over 800 Meta-Analyses Relating to Achievement by John Hattie (Note: Meta-analysis in educational study definitely has a few issues,[15] so please use this title with care. I include it here less as a definitive ranking system, and more for its wealth of references and its highly digestible format. It's very similar to Wikipedia in this respect: useful for how it gathers information into 'pools', but insufficient for reaching definitive, final conclusions. To do that, you have to dive in and swim around.)

Left Back: A Century of Battles Over School Reform by Diane Ravitch

3. Rethink 'PD': Make it continual and collaborative, and make the time

Essentially, 'school improvement' means strengthening instructional/ managerial practices to generate better student outcomes. *Continuous* school improvement, then, is the steady and logical integration of preferred practices within a school's culture over several years, making these practices permanent parts of, to borrow from organizational development expert Edgar Schein, 'the way we do things around here.'[16]

Integrating any preferred, effective instructional/managerial practice starts with professional development (PD), where practitioners learn. Before practitioners can simply 'flip' to preferred practices, after all, they must learn about them as deeply as they can: where they come from, why they are necessary, what they look like in the classroom, what resources support them, and so on.

And when it comes to providing this base learning, schools generally do a decent job. They send staff to relevant professional-development workshops, they bring in experts to instruct staff during allotted professional-development time, they conduct book studies, and all the rest.

The problem, though, is that traditional well-executed professional development of this sort doesn't make much of a difference in improvement. (Almost *none*, actually.[17])

In other words, if a school's improvement plan calls for 'Raising reading proficiency scores by 5% for all students', then decides to reach this goal by having 'All staff attend three two-hour professional-development workshops by consultants from MakeReadingAwesomED, provided on early release days in each quarter', they will not meet their proficiency goal. The same would be true for any other goal. For example: 'lower suspensions by 20% across all student subgroups' by 'Training teachers in Third Leap SEL curriculum, and embedding lessons from Third Leap into Advisory classes'. (Note: Names of training resources are fictional but should sound familiar.)

Very plainly, 'providing training' and 'implementing programming' do not change practice. They are worlds away from changing practice. Yet changing practice is the foundation of all school improvement, and so it is precisely what we should always set out to accomplish. To change practice, schools have to rethink everything they know about 'PD'. They need to reconceptualize it at the most fundamental level: what it is, what it does, and how it works. Here are three ways to do that.

Step one: Break from previous PD mindsets and methods

First, I urge leaders to break from the typical PD sequence: name the problem, set a goal, arrange for training, collect sign-in sheet, cross your fingers and hope. At best, this is a low-return approach. At worst, it erodes the professional will of practitioners. The teachers I speak with are getting *very* tired—like, fully-tuned-out tired—of one-shot PD engagements. I can't say I blame them, either, in that these sessions are often short on practical advice, disconnected from school-level realities, or both.

Don't get me wrong. Providing teachers with new information and learning is very important. As the results clearly show, the answer is not always 'in the room'. (And yes, I've seen more roomfuls of teachers and leaders hear this from some facilitator than I can possibly count.) As a field we still have a *lot* to learn, both about the science of learning and the instructional practices and beliefs that align with that science. Indeed, as the late Jeanne Chall, one of the 20th century's foremost experts in literacy instruction, put it in 2000's *The Academic Achievement Challenge: What Really Works in the Classroom?*, our field often opts for practices that go 'in a direction opposite from the existing research evidence'.[18] This recommendation should not be read as a call, then, to stop introducing new learning, because we need it. Desperately.

Rather, I'm urging leaders to adopt a different frame of mind about how to create and spread preferred practices, which means abandoning the notion that providing the right series of training or workshops will generate preferred practices. The research shows this approach doesn't work, or at least it doesn't work very well on its own. This reality seems very unlikely to change.

Step two: Aspire to continual learning and collaborative practice-planning

After you break from the 'more training' mindset, replace it with one of *continual learning and collaborative practice-planning.*

For a model of what I mean, think of how Dr. Bob required the Sophomore Academy teachers to discuss individual students and our collective expectations, policies, and messages *every single week*. The four of us didn't attend a three-day training over the summer. Rather, we continually met and constantly pushed each other to find the best solutions according to our shared improvement mission. In these meetings, we decided which practices to adjust and why, as well as what new practices would look like. We leaned on each other for support and advice when we hit a rough patch, and this proved absolutely vital to the longevity and flexibility of our work.

Step three: Make time through school systems

Invoking the Sophomore Academy brings me to the final piece of rethinking and redesigning PD, and that's *making the time.*

No problem, right?

I know, I know, it's by far the toughest part. As you may remember, though, Dr. Bob had to go to some extraordinary lengths to make sure the Academy teachers had a shared prep period for our weekly meetings. He had to secure agreements from various faculty leaders and rearrange huge chunks of the master schedule. For the CSI, Dr. Bob cut into district-provided professional development systems (the calendar days dedicated to professional learning, that is) to create the space the CSI needed to communicate with staff and harvest feedback. To do this, he had to find other opportunities to communicate the administrative details normally shared in those spaces, which was a hassle. But it was a trade-off he was willing to make. He made the CSI's work a priority, and he *made the time.*

It's tough stuff, sure. But it's instructive to note that he didn't send us to an isolated workshop, or require us to use a better self-analysis rubric, or whatever. He used *school systems* (like master scheduling and professional-collaboration structures) to make sure we had our continuing collaborative time. I'd urge school leaders to think about how to adjust systems to achieve the same. Though it may seem daunting, rethinking how professionals actually develop is definitely worth the trouble.

Rethink 'PD': Suggested reading and models

For more examples of education leaders working within school systems to make more time for their collaborative development and practice-creation, see the following books:

Schools that Succeed: How Educators Marshal the Power of Systems for Improvement by Karin Chenoweth

It's Being Done: Academic Success in Unexpected Schools, by Karin Chenoweth

How It's Being Done: Urgent Lessons from Unexpected Schools by Karin Chenoweth

Battle Hymn of the Tiger Teachers: The Michaela Way edited by Katharine Birbalsingh (particularly the 'CPD at Michaela: Question Everything' essay by Jo Facer)

Cage-Busting Leadership by Frederick M. Hess

4. Figure out if your improvements are working

No doubt, your school will be much better positioned for gainful continuous improvement if you can assess your school honestly, strengthening your research habits, and structure professional development more effectively. Unfortunately, that's the easy part. The next two recommendations are *big ones*.

First, it is absolutely essential to determine reliable, repeatable ways of knowing *if any of your efforts are working*. Just as with the formative assessment processes that are so beneficial to students' learning,[19] improvement actions must be systematically assessed so they can be supported.

And while that may sound simple enough, it's a step I see far too many education leaders trip on—or skip altogether. Some administrators get big operational changes rolling just fine but don't have a follow-up plan, which means these initiatives tend to bumble and stumble around a while before fading away. Other leaders have follow-up plans, but they focus too heavily on monitoring. They walk classrooms to make sure teachers are doing as expected, but they neglect to explain what success should look like, and they don't feed the assessment information they gather forward into improvement.

My point: monitoring and follow-up require just as much planning and forethought as any other step in your improvement initiative from the outset, because there are many ways it can go wrong. And if that happens, the resulting confusion, discontent, and apathy among frontline staff can derail even the best plans. To avoid this, here are a few critical points to consider when building the monitoring and follow-up loops improvement initiatives need to gain strength and stamina. Though I'll suggest examples of possible practices, I'll once again favor *principles over specific actions*.

With these principles in mind, you should get creative—and realistic—about the monitoring methods and routines you enact and how they will fit with your school's culture. (And, again, feel free to look at the models from Osseo Senior covered earlier. That's why they're here, after all.)

* * *

To begin, remember that there are two levels to consider when assessing the progress and effectiveness of any improvement action: adult behaviors and student results.

Monitoring adult behaviors lets you see whether a chosen, trained, and expected improvement action *is happening and at what level of quality.* Monitoring student results checks to see if the improvement action *is improving anything.*

The two levels are linked, but monitoring adult behaviors should come first. By observing those practices, leaders can learn where their practitioners need additional help, learning, or administrative encouragement. Frankly, it doesn't do much good to collect and analyze student outputs if the initiative you've planned isn't actually happening, or happening too inconsistently to count as an *initiative.* Put first things first.

Be sure it's happening, and to what quality (adult behaviors)

Monitoring whether or not an improvement action is being practiced from classroom to classroom is not complicated. If you're walking the building and observing, you've got it covered.

With Osseo Senior's READvisory initiative, for example, Dr. Bob and his admin team went from room to room during scheduled READvisory periods to see if teachers were indeed carrying out the practice. (And if they weren't, the admin team would engage teachers on the spot to see how they could help.) For the Sophomore Academy, too, Dr. Bob regularly dropped in on our team meetings to keep us focused. Again, it shouldn't be too difficult to see if what is supposed to be happening is actually happening.

Assessing the *quality* of adult behaviors is much trickier, however. I've seen principals take a number of approaches, from following the processes described in education-leadership books like Paul Bambrick-Santoyo's *Leverage Leadership*[20] to using classroom walkthrough apps and spreadsheets for cataloging observation data and beyond. I urge you to explore and find what works best for you. The important part is finding *something*.

Personally, I've found the *practice profile* to be a particularly effective tool for clearly describing preferred practices, assessing whether they're happening or not, and ascertaining a degree of quality from classroom to classroom. While it's difficult to trace the practice profile's origin in improvement science,[21] I first encountered it when working with federal School Improvement Grant (SIG) schools in Minnesota.

A practice profile is a brief document (1-2 pages) describing the features of a *single* preferred practice in categories of 'Expected/Proficient', 'Developing', and 'Needs Improvement'. Practice profiles also require leaders to provide a research-backed rationale for the practice's implementation. (Read: If a leader has to go on an endless, winding journey through the literature for a sound justification, they may want to rethink why they've chosen that action in the first place.)

In theory, practice profiles give leaders a common set of expectations to communicate to staff, a common set of 'look-fors' to guide classroom observations, and, over time, a growing set of clearly defined practices that formally describe school culture. To invoke organizational-leadership guru Edgar Schein once again, practice profiles serve as concrete representations of 'the way we do things around here'. As more and more of them accumulate and are refined over time, practice profiles can help leaders describe what they want to see in their schools clearly and definitely.

For the basic anatomy of a practice profile, see *Figures 11* and *12*. These are two actual profiles I helped build for a school in my continuous improvement work. While they are for two very different school operations (*Figure 11* describes a very granular and rudimentary practice related to positive school culture, while *Figure 12* describes a much more intricate administrative process[22]), these examples show how practice profiles work and what they include.

Practice Profile - SAMPLE		Greeting/Welcoming Practices, ALL STAFF		May 2016

Purpose/Rationale for using this instructional strategy or practice: The practice described here is a specific piece of an all-around more welcoming, caring school climate that can be readily observed.

Desired Outcome: The creation of a roundly welcoming, caring, and nurturing learning environment, and students' positive perceptions of the school's adults and of themselves.

Citation of Research used:
Birch, S.H. and G. Ladd. "The teacher-child relationship and children's early school adjustment." *Journal of School Psychology* 35.1 (1997): 61-79. Web. 13 May 2016.
Wentzel, K.R.. "Student motivation in middle school: The role of perceived pedagogical caring." *Journal of Educational Psychology* 89:3 (1997): 411-419. Web. 13 May. 2016.

Core Component or Critical Feature	Contribution to the Desired Outcome	Expected/Proficient	Developmental	Needs Improvement
SCHOOL STAFF MEMBERS VISIBLY & POSITIVELY ACKNOWLEDGE STUDENTS	*Greetings communicate to each student that he/she is a vital part of individual classroom learning communities and larger school learning community* *Greetings' tones contribute to a positive, optimistic classroom & school environment* *As student is greeted/welcomed by multiple school adults, senses of self-worth and connection to school community both grow*	• Every student in hallway is greeted, by name and in positive tones, by all SCHOOL staff • Every student entering classroom is greeted at or near the classroom door, by name and in positive tones, by their classroom teacher and/or classroom AE • All SCHOOL staff's greetings of students invite students' interaction through customary salutations in students' first language • Teacher consistently recognizes and responds productively to students who enter classroom needing additional regulation time/support	• Some students in hallway are greeted, by name and in positive tones, by SCHOOL staff • Some students entering classroom are greeted at or near the classroom door, by name and in positive tones, by their classroom teacher and/or classroom AE. • Some staff's greetings of students invite interaction • Teacher sometimes recognizes and responds productively to students who enter classroom needing additional regulation time/support	• Few to no students in hallway are greeted, by name and in positive tones, by SCHOOL staff • Few to no students entering classroom are greeted at or near the classroom door, by name and in positive tones, by their classroom teacher and/or classroom AE. • Few to no staff's greetings of students invite interaction • Teacher does not recognize and respond productively to students who enter classroom needing additional regulation time/support
SCHOOL STAFF MEMBERS PRESENT AND ENGAGED THROUGHOUT BUILDING TO GREET AND INTERACT WITH STUDENTS	*All school learning areas appear safe as overseen by caring adults* *Students become familiar with the school's adult staff, building additional comfort and trust* *Students and staff have additional opportunities to interact and thus strengthen connections*	• SCHOOL staff are consistently, reliably stationed at assigned checkpoints throughout school during common passing times (H5-5: day beginning, day end, buses; 6-8: day beginning, day end, buses, class-to-class transitions) • SCHOOL staff engage students throughout these common passing times in positive tones, encouraging students to follow expectations as necessary.	• Some SCHOOL staff are stationed at assigned checkpoints throughout school during common passing times (H5-5: day beginning, day end, buses; 6-8: day beginning, day end, buses, class-to-class transitions) • During common passing times, some staff engage students in positive tones and encourage students to follow expectations as necessary.	• Few to no SCHOOL staff are stationed at assigned checkpoints throughout school during common passing times (H5-5: day beginning, day end, buses; 6-8: day beginning, day end, buses, class-to-class transitions) • During common passing times, few to no staff engage students in positive tones and encourage students to follow expectations as necessary.

Figure 11 *Practice Profile Sample, Greeting/Welcoming Practices*

Practice Profile - SAMPLE   DATE

Purpose/Rationale: The practice described here is a strategic response to students who frequently leave their assigned learning environments, an issue that was determined a high-priority area for growth via the school's needs assessment work and subsequent staff/student experiences. The profile establishes common procedures, sequences, and expectations for all SCHOOL staff toward effectively and efficiently responding to this issue.

Desired Outcome: SCHOOL staff will appropriately and efficiently respond to students who frequently leave assigned learning environments, as progression of consequences gains consistency and ultimately full schoolwide incorporation, fewer students will choose to leave learning environments.

Citation of Research used:
Nelson, J.R., R. Martella, and B. Galand. "The Effects of Teaching School Expectations and Establishing a Consistent Consequence on Formal Office Disciplinary Actions." *Journal of Emotional and Behavioral Disorders* 6.3 (1998): 153-61. *Sage Publications*. Web. 25 Apr 2016.
Skiba, R.J., Peterson, R.L. "School Discipline at a Crossroads: From Zero Tolerance to Early Response." *Exceptional Children* 66.3 (2000): 335-46. *Sage Publications*. Web. 25 Apr 2016.

Core Component or Critical Feature	Contribution to the Desired Outcome	Expected/Proficient	Developmental	Needs Improvement
PHASE 1: STUDENT OUT OF ASSIGNED LEARNING ENVIRONMENT, 1st INCIDENCE	• Classroom staff notifies admin/behavior-support staff that a high-frequency out-of-class student has left the learning environment without permission • Student located by admin/behavior-support staff • Student coached back to assigned learning environment by admin/behavior-support staff • Student informed of status, expectations, and consequences for next incident by admin/behavior-support staff, possible consequences are In-School Service placement, Quiet Study placement, or Transport Home, and are assigned uniquely according to various student criteria • Admin/behavior-support staff and classroom staff achieve shared awareness & agreement on student status and create corresponding record	• Classroom staff reports student's choice to leave learning environment efficiently and accurately • Admin/behavior-support staff conducts respectful conference with student and successfully returns student to learning environment • Admin/behavior-support staff provide clear explanation of in-class expectations and next-incidence consequences to student prior to class re-entry • Admin/behavior-support staff and classroom staff confer briefly to reach agreement on student status and expectations • Admin/behavior-support staff and classroom staff create accurate record (using agreed-upon tracking tools) of student's status after first incidence	• Classroom staff reports student's choice to leave learning environment with some, but with incomplete detail and/or lacking timeliness • Admin/behavior-support staff returns student to learning environment • Admin/behavior-support staff provides some explanation of in-class expectations and next-incidence consequences to student prior to class re-entry • Admin/behavior-support staff and classroom staff confer regarding student returned to class, student status and expectations not mutually understood • Admin/behavior-support staff and classroom staff inconsistently create accurate record (using agreed-upon provided tracking tools) of student's status after first incidence	• Classroom staff does not report student's choice to leave learning environment • Admin/behavior-support staff does not respond to classroom staff's report, and student does not return to learning environment • Admin/behavior-support staff does not explain in-class expectations and next-incidence consequences to student prior to class re-entry • Admin/behavior-support staff and classroom staff do not confer to reach agreement on student status, expectations • Admin/behavior-support staff and classroom staff do not create accurate records of student's status after first incidence
PHASE 2: STUDENT OUT OF ASSIGNED LEARNING ENVIRONMENT, 2nd INCIDENCE	• Classroom staff notifies admin/behavior-support staff that student has left the learning environment without permission a second time • Student located by admin/behavior-support staff • Admin/behavior-support staff assign one of three possible consequences (In-School Service placement, Quiet Study placement, or Transport Home) communicated to student in Phase 1 conference • Admin/behavior-support staff contacts student's parent/guardian to inform of student's out-of-class incidence and assigned consequence • Admin/behavior-support staff coordinate chosen student consequence, arranging for transport off-campus—by parent/guardian, approved school staff, etc.—if necessary • Admin/behavior-support staff communicates chosen consequence to classroom staff, and each staffer creates corresponding record	• Classroom staff reports student's choice to leave learning environment efficiently and accurately • Admin/behavior-support staff conducts respectful conference with student to inform regarding consequences • Admin/behavior-support staff contact student's parent/guardian to respectfully explain chosen consequences and rationale • Admin/behavior-support staff efficiently coordinates next process steps in accord with chosen consequence • Admin/behavior-support staff and classroom staff create accurate record (using provided tracking tools) of student's status • Admin/behavior-support staff promptly and clearly communicate chosen consequence—and other relevant information—to classroom staff for future reference and action-planning • Admin/behavior-support staff reach effective agreements about student's classroom re-entry to learning environment, outlining necessary conditions for student's future success	• Classroom staff reports student's choice to leave learning environment with some, but with incomplete detail and/or lacking timeliness • Admin/behavior-support staff confers with student, consequences are unclear or not defined • Admin/behavior-support staff eventually contact student's parent/guardian to explain chosen consequences and rationale • Admin/behavior-support staff coordinates next process steps in accord with chosen consequence • Admin/behavior-support staff and classroom staff inconsistently create accurate record of student's status • Admin/behavior-support staff communicate chosen consequence—and other relevant information—to classroom staff for future reference and action-planning, but not in consistently timely fashion • Admin/behavior-support staff reach agreements about student's classroom re-entry to learning environment, but student's future expectations not consistently defined	• Classroom staff does not report student's choice to leave learning environment • Admin/behavior-support staff does not confer with some, consequences are never shared with student • Admin/behavior-support staff do not contact student's parent/guardian to explain chosen consequences and rationale • Admin/behavior-support staff do not coordinate next process steps in accord with chosen consequence, leaving steps and persons responsible uncertain • Either admin/behavior-support staff or classroom staff do not create accurate record of student's status • Admin/behavior-support staff do not communicate chosen consequence—and other relevant information—to classroom staff for future reference and action-planning • Admin/behavior-support staff do not collaborate to reach preliminary agreements about student's classroom re-entry to learning environment

Figure 12 *Practice Profile Sample, High Frequency Out-of-Class Student Procedures*

Once these profiles are built, either by administrators or (preferably) by cross-staff leadership teams, observation routines can be constructed accordingly. To avoid the impression that practice profiles are strictly an accountability exercise, though (which their 'rubric'-like format can inspire among staff), I recommend that building leaders task teacher-leadership teams with observations, communication of conclusions, and subsequent planning of supports and further learning. For instance, I always make sure to get school leadership teams on board for all practice profile operations. (It's exactly what Dr. Bob would have enlisted the CSI to help with.)

Remember, improvement is about creating the school everyone *wants to work in*, not just the school the admin team wants to see. Besides, when it comes to getting recalcitrant staff to shift their practices, no one's more effective in persuading teachers than *other teachers*.

Be sure it's improving something

As with monitoring adult behaviors, leaders can get as simple or as complex as they like when checking student outputs for evidence of change or improvement.

In the short term, start simple. Remember, you're playing the long game. The idea is that new practices, implemented reliably and at a high level, will ultimately improve your school's product in the big-picture sense, not just the short term. And as any disappointed education reformer will tell you, dramatic turnarounds in student results almost never show up in the short term, especially in complexly contingent achievement categories like reading proficiency and numbers of discipline referrals.[23]

With that in mind, I suggest collecting concurrent student outputs that help you know if your initiative is *on track* to achieve the bigger goal, not *definitively fulfilling* it. In other words, is the line moving in the right direction? I prefer assessing these immediate-term outputs because, just as in an effective formative-assessment feedback loop, you can actively respond if the desired effects aren't registering. This can look different for every objective, of course, so get creative with it, always being mindful that you're maintaining alignment with the improvement action.

To illustrate how this works, recall how the Sophomore Academy teachers checked on the consistency of our students' academic effort. We required students to complete frequent progress reports, we pored over those reports in team meetings to see if our expectations and messages were changing work behaviors, and we adjusted our actions accordingly. Similarly, the CSI monitored the effectiveness of the 'no hall pass' policy by simply having students demonstrate their preparation by holding up their writing utensils and notebooks, counting and logging the results, and tracking the data over time. We collected data about the change in students we aimed to see, in other words, and nothing else. What we believed, however, was that this simple action was tied inextricably to the larger goals of keeping kids in class and maximizing class time. If we could get the behavior to change, the school's performance would soon follow. (And, by and large, it did.)

To put this another way: if you're hoping to improve an element of school culture as opposed to academics, you may want to monitor discipline referrals over a certain amount of time, interview a few strategically selected students about how school *feels* to them lately, or distribute a quick student survey about culture-related matters. It's up to you to decide, however, what best represents the progress you want to see, and how that information—that *pulse*—can be measured.

In Dr. Bob's school-improvement culture, we took real-time data from kids to see if their habits were changing in the ways we imagined they would. This informed what, if any, changes we made immediately—additional learning for staff, tweaks to expectations or messaging, and so on. To see whether these habits would affect bigger-picture outcomes like student achievement, behavior, and attendance, we knew we would have to wait a little longer.

Note: Some improvement actions, like the high-frequency out-of-class students procedures shared in *Figure 12*, must be enacted and monitored more rapidly. As they are constructed in response to urgent school needs, they demand definite results in shorter time spans. In these instances, I recommend that practice-profiled adult behaviors and student outputs be monitored more vigorously. In case you're curious, the answer is yes: within a few weeks of instituting the procedures in *Figure 12*, the school saw its high-frequency out-of-class students marching themselves back to class—and keeping themselves together once there—at significantly higher rates.

Get active with results, and stick to it

To close out this recommendation, I suggest you *get active* with the results gathered from observations. Share your findings actively with staff, both in day-to-day interactions and in large-staff sessions. Figure out novel ways for staff to get their arms around the information, through full-staff learning experiences or by distributing guiding questions for PLCs to discuss. It's *your* school and *your* staff. When you get active, it gets teachers talking about the results of your monitoring. These efforts will also assure teachers that you're after more than just accountability.

To illustrate, here's an example from some schools I worked with in New York state as they sought to build more effective classroom-management practices. I created a 'film study' protocol based on how athletes improve their own practice by watching game film. In these sessions, PLC teams viewed videos of teachers' lessons so they could learn together. I provided some 'coaching', of course, but this approach made it easy for teachers to give feedback to one another, learn about promising techniques from one another, see how to work with kids they had in common, and decide on practices they wanted to build across the entire team.

My final note is more cheerleading than anything else, and that's *stick to it*. When you're working to change adult behaviors that will in turn change student habits, outlooks, and mindsets—and consequently achievement—progress will not happen quickly or easily. Throw the idea of 'quick wins' out the window and replace it with 'good teams find ways to win'. Trust that the actions you've chosen are right (because you did your research in recommendations #1 and #2, right?), continually work to understand how those actions can be improved through monitoring, follow up with the necessary (and novel, if possible) learning, and steadily build consistency across the staff.

It's going to take some time, but stick with it. Good teams find ways to win.

5. Let teachers lead (no, *really*: let teachers lead)

In recent years, the idea of making teachers true leaders in educational practice and policy has really taken off. Advocacy groups (like Teach to Lead, which launched in 2014 and 'envisions a world where teachers are valued as experts in instruction'[24]) host national summits where teacher-leaders think about how to increase their impacts, both in their own districts and in the national education-policy discussion. Many districts now allow sharp, experienced teachers to share their capacity for instruction beyond the classrooms through new job classifications. Positions like 'instructional coach', 'instructional specialist', and 'teacher on special assignment' have become commonplace, allowing licensed teachers to improve others' practices in ways they never could have—without becoming an administrator, that is—even a decade ago. It's been fun to watch, because good and important work can be accomplished through these new positions and leadership opportunities.

On the other hand, the 'teacher-leader' designation can have drawbacks. In some cases, being an 'instructional specialist' really means serving as muscle for district-imposed initiatives: holding struggling teachers accountable to the details of mandated professional growth plans, observing loads of teachers to keep teacher-evaluation systems humming, and overseeing PLC meetings. Taking a teacher-leader position, in other words, doesn't always guarantee that a talented teacher-leader will be able to help other teachers improve their practice, or even bring much of their wisdom to the table. And really, when teacher-leaders are perceived as enforcers of district policy, it alienates them from their colleagues—precisely the opposite of what should happen.

In short: though opportunities for teachers to become leaders of instructional improvement have increased, some opportunities—especially the formally conferred ones—are not always as rewarding as they first appear.

With all this in mind, teacher-leadership does not need to be formally conferred or validated. School administrators can empower aspiring teacher-leaders—and, indeed, build momentum for continuous improvement—if they bring teachers aboard as leaders of various practical improvements. Nobody needs a new job title to do this.

Informed by my own experiences, I actively engineer this kind of authentic teacher-leadership whenever I work with schools on continuous improvement. Whether I'm working with a school to build a new curriculum, write a new mission statement, integrate developmental psychology research into teachers' practices, design a new observation and coaching system, or *whatever*, one of my first steps is always to assemble a project team at least half of whom are licensed teaching staff. And I don't limit the scope to teachers who already believe in the cause; I actively invite teachers who have reputations as 'nay-sayers'. It's important to do so.

I call this team the leadership *nucleus*. Atomic nuclei exert a great deal of force, and, just like in the atom, this nucleus will become the center of the improvement enterprise. But that's just my personal favorite metaphor. If you build your own leadership group (and I highly recommend you do), you can call it whatever you like.

This central group of authentic teacher leaders is vital to site-based improvement design. At Osseo Senior, I saw first-hand how creative and realistic teachers are when solving problems (which is crucial for determining practices and monitoring), how closely teachers listen to each other (which is crucial for successful rollout and the ever-elusive 'buy-in'), and how hard teachers work when they know they are helping kids and their fellow teachers (which is crucial for the servant-leadership needed to keep initiatives running). I'd have to be a fool to leave all that capacity and passion untapped.

When I recreate this team in other school settings, I'm often impressed with the results. It takes some structure and facilitation, of course (in the Sophomore Academy and CSI, you may remember, we had very little), but the leaders do a great job of processing their site's data, producing novel and feasible solutions, and getting the attention of peers when they communicate.

Plus, I know first-hand that a lot of teachers out there would like to do more for their school (and for their career) than they can from their classroom alone, because I was one of these teachers. Through the Sophomore Academy and the CSI, Dr. Bob changed my life. (You may remember, too, how many of the teachers in Dr. Bob's collaborative-leadership culture later moved into educational leadership.) Not every teacher can assume an 'instructional leader' position, because there are only so many of them available. Every principal, however, can make any teacher into an instructional leader.

Very simply, involving teachers as leaders is critical for creating genuinely bottom-up improvement. While it takes some engineering, the immediate- and long-term benefits of letting teachers lead—*really* lead—are well worth the investment.

Let teachers lead: Quick suggestions

Keep these points in mind as you form your own initiative-leadership team.

1. Be inclusive: When assembling your nucleus, invite widely instead of leaning on the same few willing people. This will cut down on 'chosen one' side effects. Also, when you get pushback from your most reluctant teachers, it's helpful to be able to remind them that they were invited to help shape the initiative.

2. Involve the team in all phases: To make sure this group is as versed as possible in all parts of an initiative, from its rationale to the reasons it was selected to its monitoring methods, be sure to involve them thoroughly. Later, when a teacher-leader can tell their peers exactly why the group made a certain decision, this comprehensive exposure will come in very handy.

3. Be systematic (but not too systematic): To make sure ideas flow freely, don't over-structure this team with agendas and outcomes that are too strict or confining. Sketch out a series of meetings over several months and what each one should accomplish, but don't turn it into an overly formal affair. Doing so quickly makes this work feel more like an empty accountability exercise. Trust your leaders, and see how they do. Add more structure as needed, but err on the side of freedom and flexibility to start.

4. Don't inadvertently dis-incentivize: Whether or not you plan to provide a stipend for this type of leadership, don't dis-incentivize participation by making it too much extra work.

Teachers already have all their other duties to attend to. Work your systems (again) to make sure teams can meet during the school day, for instance, not after or before school. It matters. I also suggest you figure out how to provide some sort of benefit; Dr. Bob, for example, made sure CSI members were paid the hourly teacher rate for any work outside of school.

5. Share leadership, don't cede it: Through all the decision-making and action-designing, never forget your role. Respectfully push leaders away from paths you know they shouldn't follow, encourage paths you see as having promise, and teach the team about 'the big picture' they may not yet see. Always remember that this shouldn't be about 'handing the school over' to the practitioners, but sincerely asking for their help and growing their abilities as leaders.

Endnotes

1. My short list of these questions would include the following: 'How can we more rationally—not purely intuitively—select improvement strategies?', 'How can we train, create, and strengthen shared practice changes?', 'How can we get professional-learning systems and resources to actually work?', 'How can all schools design and implement improvement strategically and sensibly?', and 'How can we energize teachers in truly site-based, classroom-up practice reform?'

2. In the current moment, for example, educational leaders seem more worried about improving via innovative practices (e.g. 'flipping' classrooms, personalizing learning, building 'restorative' behavior approaches, and so on) and/or tighter accountabilities (e.g. better observation checklists, more defined protocols for teacher teaming) than on the more fundamental schooling issues I emphasize most strongly.

3. Kalenze, E. (2014) *Education Is Upside down: Reframing Reform to Focus on the Right Problems*. Lanham, MD: Rowman & Littlefield, pp. 119–132.

4. Yes, planning is a good thing—even if, as I offered in the intro to Chapter 15, schools' selection of strategies is too often flawed. I'll take that on a bit a few points down from this one, however.

5. Some of the community-based partners who were adding no value in this illustration, for example, had connections running back to the district offices, not the school, which made excavating them somewhat tricky. Similarly, questioning the preferred literacy philosophy (Balanced Literacy/Readers Workshop models, that is) of longtime leaders in the district's teaching and learning offices definitely ruffled some feathers. To suggest that we should go a different direction with our early-grades reading instruction, you would better believe that we had to have our case—and our proof—in full order.

6. Slate, J., R., and Jones, C., H. (2005). 'Effects of school size: A review of the literature with recommendations', in *Essays in Education*, 13, pp. 1-22.

7. Lakoff, G. (2004) *Don't Think of an Elephant!: Know Your Values and Frame the Debate*. White River Junction, VT: Chelsea Green.

8. See: Cunningham, A. and Stanovich, K. (1998) 'What Reading Does for the Mind' in *American Educator*, 22 (1/2), pp. 8-15. See also: Wiener, J. (24 February 2006) 'Cultivating a Culture of Literacy'. Sacramento, CA: Sacramento Bee.

9. Carnine, D. (2000) 'Why Education Experts Resist Effective Practices (And What It Would Take to Make Education More Like Medicine)'. Thomas B. Fordham Foundation. Available at: https://www.wrightslaw.com/info/teach.profession.carnine.pdf

10. ResearchED is an internationally reaching grassroots movement to improve educators' research literacy. Begun by a group of UK teachers seeking higher-quality professional development in 2013, ResearchED conferences have spread to countries like Sweden, the Netherlands, South Africa, Australia, Canada, and elsewhere, reaching thousands of teachers per year. As of this time of writing, I've spoken at ResearchED conferences in several countries and served as ResearchED's U.S. ambassador (and organizing conferences in Washington, D.C., New York City, and Philadelphia) for three years. For more information on the ResearchED organization, see https://researched.org.uk/. For a Q&A I did with Rick Hess at his 'Education Week' blog, see Hess, R. (7 September 2017) 'Straight Up Conversation: US Organizer Eric Kalenze Explains ResearchED'. Rick Hess Straight Up for Education Week. Available at: blogs.edweek.org/edweek/rick_hess_straight_up/2017/09/straight_up_conversation_us_organizer_eric_kalenze_explains_researched.html

11. Wiliam, D. (2018) *Creating the Schools Our Children Need: Why What We're Doing Now Won't Help Much (And What We Can Do Instead)*. West Palm Beach, FL: Learning Sciences International, p. 118.

12. Kirby, J. (12 October 2013) 'What Sir Ken Got Wrong'. Pragmatic Reform Blog. Available at: pragmaticreform.wordpress.com/2013/10/12/what-sir-ken-got-wrong/

13. Willingham, D. (2012) *When Can You Trust the Experts?: How to Tell Good Science from Bad in Education*. San Francisco, CA: Jossey-Bass, pp. 135-222.

14. Wiliam, D. (2018) *Creating the Schools Our Children Need: Why What We're Doing Now Won't Help Much (And What We Can Do Instead)*. West Palm Beach, FL: Learning Sciences International, p. 118.

15. Slavin, R. (21 June 2018) 'John Hattie Is Wrong'. Robert Slavin's Blog. Available at: robertslavinsblog.wordpress.com/2018/06/21/john-hattie-is-wrong/

16. Schein E., H. (1996) *Organizational culture and leadership*. 2nd ed. Toronto, ON: John Wiley & Sons Ltd.

17. To stay on track here I'll forego a lengthy discussion, either of my own experiences with, or all the research on, this assertion. Here's the short version, however: There are lots of reasons for it (including, of course, ordering up the wrong professional development for the accurately determined school issue—see 'school arts programming for low early reading scores' example from Chapter 15), but several studies of professional development in education have produced very meager effects on teacher practices. These effects are tragically meager, really, when considered in light of the amounts of money spent on teacher professional development each year. If interested in learning more, TNTP's 2015 report, *The Mirage: Confronting the Hard Truth About Our Quest for Teacher Development*, would be a good place to start (available online at https://tntp.org/assets/documents/TNTP-Mirage_2015.pdf).

18. Chall, J., S. (2002) *The Academic Achievement Challenge: What Really Works in the Classroom?* New York, NY: Guilford Press, p. 180.

19. As I'm assuming anyone reading this section will already know what formative assessment is, I won't elaborate fully on the concept. In short, though, it's is the process of regularly harvesting sound, accurate information about what students know and are able to do in order to provide each student the feedback they need to keep growing and learning. If my assessment of my audience at this point of the book is completely off, and they want to know more about the concept of formative assessment, a good place to start would be this seminal work by Paul Black and Dylan Wiliam: Black, P and Wiliam, D. (1998) 'Inside the Black Box: Raising Standards through Classroom Assessment', in *Phi Delta Kappa*, pp. 1–13. Available at: https://www.rdc.udel.edu/wp-content/uploads/2015/04/InsideBlackBox.pdf

20. Bambrick-Santoyo, P. (2012) *Leverage Leadership: a Practical Guide to Building Exceptional Schools*. San Francisco, CA: Jossey-Bass.

21. Though the practice profiles I ultimately built working with SIG schools differ from this format a bit, a pretty good description of practice profiles' objectives and operations can be found here: The Active Implementation Hub. (26 August 2014) 'Practice Profile Planning Tool'. National Implementation Research Network. Available at: implementation. fpg.unc.edu/sites/implementation.fpg.unc.edu/files/NIRN-Education-PracticeProfilePlanningTool.pdf

22. The practice profile in *Figure 11*, which describes something so simple as a school's preferred greeting/welcoming practices, actually has a fairly involved backstory. It began with the principal and assistant principal saying they wanted to do a practice profile on 'school culture', which led to me closing the office door and making them describe for me ten things they would be able to see each day in the culture they were envisioning. After the list got up to a dozen or so, I asked them to pick just one of those qualities so we could break it fully out into a practice profile. They chose to focus on how students were greeted/welcomed each day, and it's what I worked into the profile shared here. The practice profile in 16.2 is a decidedly more complex venture, prepared in accord with an issue that got out of hand in a particular school: In short, the students leaving classes without permission were, on top of not getting any learning done, wreaking such havoc around the school that they'd become a safety issue. After teachers and administrators collaborated on a process to deal with these High-Frequency Out-of-Class students (or, as we rather affectionately came to know them, H-FOOCs), this practice profile was prepared to monitor whether or not all necessary school personnel were carrying out their assigned roles.

23. And no, 'number of discipline referrals dropping because teachers are discouraged to give discipline referrals' is not necessarily a win at the student-outputs level. It is at the adult-behaviors level, perhaps, but shouldn't be recorded as progress at the student-output level until kids' actual achievement, habits, and/or outlooks can definitively show positive change. This detail is often left out, by the way, of districts' reports of their own positive strides to various media.

24. Teach to Lead. (2019) 'About Teach to Lead'. Teach to Lead. Available at: teachtolead.org/about/

Chapter 17

What the Academy
Taught Us

Well, we've covered a lot of ground between the big fight that opened this book and the five recommendations for effective continuous school improvement.

We've seen a cluster of Minnesota suburbs adjust to changing populations, schools in those communities work hard to improve the educational product for all students, and a school leader discover a better way to keep his school improving, all punctuated by recollections and insights from former students, teachers, and education commentators. We've been inside quite a few classrooms and meeting rooms, dived into the personal and professional lives of everyone involved, examined a variety of educational evidence, and visited over quite a few beers in Dr. Bob's and my favorite pizza joint.[1]

I hope it wasn't too overwhelming or all-over-the-place.

More than that, I hope the individual parts worked together to show you everything the Sophomore Academy taught us: what truly effective instruction looks like; why it's so important to challenge your assumptions and change your mind; why you have to get students *stable* before moving them to *able*; the value of strong relationships with students and colleagues; the critical role of research and evidence in improving professional practice; how to collaborate with fellow educators joyfully and productively; and the costs, yields, and trade-offs inherent to 'transformational' solutions across diverse systems. Again, I hope what I've shared about all of these learning experiences has been helpful for you.

Most of all, though, I hope this book's sequence, anecdotes, research, and recommendations spurred an interest in building effective school improvements *yourself*. In fact, out of everything the Academy taught us, the one I most want readers to take away is this: *you can make effective continuous school improvement happen on your own.* You can start right now.

I'm not saying it's *easy*. Embarking on an independent improvement effort will likely mean that your school will have to get creative with its systems of scheduling, training, and teaming, and that will in turn require hard work—and some smoothing of ruffled feathers—to keep everything moving ahead. Your school may even have to research and build a case for district-office superiors—evidence that your actions are worth the required resources and time, especially if you want to move in a different direction than the one they prefer.

The key, as the Academy taught us, is for you and your team to *work smart, stick to it, and hold each other up.* It's not particularly flashy or futuristic advice, but that's what it takes. And if you can do so faithfully, you too can build and constantly refine context-appropriate, continuous, and successful improvements in your school. In fact, you can come up with improvements that are an order of magnitude better than the mass-initiatives coming your way. And you can do it all without pre-packaged (but not quite ready for education) structures inspired by improvement science or a guiding visionary's unique blend of vacuous innovations and inane platitudes.

Again, if you can work smart, stick to it, and hold each other up, *you* can do this.

In our discussions about his principalship at Osseo Senior, Dr. Bob stressed over and over how he wasn't some kind of superhero of leadership. I've worked with enough administrators to know he doesn't give himself enough credit, but on the whole he was right. He wasn't a superhero. But he was always *adamant*. To the end, he maintained that he was a principal who could focus on what needed to change and who could remove the obstacles to those changes, but that it was *the people he gathered around him* who figured out what the changes should look like and how they should be continuously improved.

If you don't believe me, go back and look at his original improvement principles from Chapter 3. You'll see that they square with his self-assessment. Whenever Dr. Bob set out to create any kind of improvement, he didn't follow a specific playbook. He let the following principles guide him:

- Identify problems accurately.
- Match the right people to each improvement initiative.
- Give those people active roles in the initiative's design and communication.
- Respectfully build and maintain school-wide harmony.

These principles gave us all the structure we needed to build, operate, and continuously improve on targeted efforts like the Sophomore Academy as well as school-wide improvement actions through the CSI. They also brought individuals to Dr. Bob's office, pitching their own improvement ideas, all without a single SWOT analysis, PDSA cycle, standardized behavior protocol, or quality school review conducted by an impartial outside agency. And they're almost all you need to initiate your own improvements, along with the five successes and five recommendations from Chapters 15 and 16, respectively.

First, let's review the successes. Looking back on the Academy, the CSI, and all of the other improvements of Dr. Bob's tenure, this is what we got right. (After, of course, stumbling a bit and learning from our mistakes. There was a lot of 'sticking to it' and 'holding each other up' involved, believe me.) I hope they provide some valuable guidance for your own school-improvement aspirations.

Five successes of Osseo Senior High's continuous improvement

1. Set limited number of priority 'pillars', designed specific action for each.
2. Committed to *molding* consensus, not *holding out* for consensus.
3. Focused improvements on schooling's 'blocking and tackling'.
4. Fundamentally believed in students, set expectations accordingly.
5. Got genuinely personal.

Finally, the recommendations. The Academy taught *me* that I really wanted to work with other schools on their own improvement, an insight that led me to a career of improvement-driven research and advisory. I've been lucky to be in a lot of the right places at the right times, witnessing a wide range of school improvement requirements, obstacles, challenges, and victories. This field experience informed these recommendations, which are designed to work alongside the five successes.

Five continuous school improvement recommendations

1. Reflect thoroughly and assess your school honestly.
2. Learn to be good learners: Build research into improvement processes.
3. Rethink 'PD': Make it continual and collaborative, and make the time.
4. Figure out if your improvements are working.
5. Let teachers lead (no, *really*: let teachers lead).

That's all you need, really: 14 bullet points. You could probably squeeze all of them onto a single PowerPoint slide. Again, if this seems insufficiently flashy or forward-thinking or innovative or disruptive, that is entirely the point. There is no secret code to unlock the mysteries of continuous improvement. You do not need an app, or a piece of technology, or an acronym-based philosophy. The magic happens when committed teachers and leaders put these relatively straightforward ideas to work, starting from the classroom up. I sincerely hope your school can use them to start building effective improvements—immediately, of course, but also continuously. If you work smart, stick to it, and hold each other up, you will be able to create the school you want to work in, one that can help all your students move from stable to able, and find success in their schooling and beyond.

Endnotes

1. Broadway Pizza, that is. The one in Brooklyn Park. I recommend their thin-crust Classic Deluxe.

Acknowledgements

There are many people I wish to thank.

My family. Taxing as a project like this can be for me, I know it puts you all through a lot as well. I appreciate every last bit of your support, patience, and understanding.

Alex Sharratt at John Catt, who thought a book about school improvement, told in this way, would be worth bringing into the world. Without that initial belief (and all the encouragement and flexibility that followed), this book never would have happened. Relatedly, huge thanks to Meena Ameen and the design team at John Catt for bringing all the parts together. Your skill (and patience with me) is most appreciated.

I look to a wide range of education thinkers for inspiration, but a particular few were so important to this work that I must thank them here: The Education Trust's Karin Chenoweth and the teachers at Michaela Community School in London, led by Katharine Birbalsingh. Brilliant books by these two sources (Karin's It's Being Done series and Schools That Succeed, and the Michaela staff's Battle Hymn of the Tiger Teachers) reminded me how important it is to look at education from the classroom up.

The several people who looked at (often quite shabby) sections of this book as it was coming together. Namely, thanks to Jill Kellar, Sara Jane Lentz, Dr. Bob Perdaems, Kelly Skare-Klecker, Jackie Trzynka, and Gerry Zelenak for all the suggestions and cheerleading. You helped keep the story true, and my head on straight.

Lars Ostrom, my editor, who is both tremendously good at what he does and a better friend than I could possibly describe. I can't thank you enough, Lars, for all you give me. Again, count on me to pick up drinks and dinners indefinitely. (And let's have a lot of them, OK?)

All my former Osseo Senior High colleagues and Sophomore Academy students for sharing their stories with me over the past year and a half. When we worked together over a decade ago, you filled my personal and professional lives to levels that have never been reached since. Whether it was in person, by phone call, over email, or through survey responses, connecting with you again was for me this project's brightest highlight. Thanks for all your time, energy, and honesty. And, remember, my door's always open.

Finally—with some repeats from above, as they also helped with looking over the text; simply, their wonders never cease—I must give huge appreciation to Dr. Bob Perdaems and my one-time teammates in the Sophmore Academy: Eric Ruska, Kelly Skare-Klecker, Jackie Trzynka and Gerry Zelenak. The years I spent working with you all made me a better educator and a better person. Revisiting those times with you over recent months helped me remember what's possible, and I really needed that.